DATE DUE

DEMCO 38-296

The Last Word

WCW

· · · · · · · · · · · · · · · · · ·

MN

University of Iowa Press Ψ Iowa City

The Last Word

LETTERS BETWEEN

Marcia Nardi

AND

William Carlos Williams

Edited by Elizabeth Murrie O'Neil

University of Iowa Press,

Iowa City 52242

Copyright © 1994 by

Printed on acid-free paper

Library of Congress Cataloging-in-Publication Data
Nardi, Marcia.
     The last word: letters between Marcia Nardi and
  William Carlos Williams / edited by Elizabeth Murrie
  O'Neil.
       p.   cm.
  Includes bibliographical references and index.
  ISBN 0-87745-445-0, ISBN 0-87745-461-2 (pbk.)
     1. Nardi, Marcia—Correspondence.   2. Williams,
  William Carlos, 1883–1963—Correspondence.   3. Poets,
  American—20th century—Correspondence.   I. Williams,
  William Carlos, 1883–1963.   II. O'Neil, Elizabeth
  Murrie, 1936–   .   III. Title.
  PS3527.A5Z468   1994
  811'.52—dc20
  [B]   93-20999
                                                   CIP

98   97   96   95   94   C   5   4   3   2   1
98   97   96   95   94   P   5   4   3   2   1

TO THE MEMORY OF ROBERT O'NEIL

Contents

Introduction

. . . .

"Use *all* her letters. *She* has the last word": William Carlos
Williams wrote these words in a note[1] to himself on an early
draft of his long poem *Paterson*.[2] "She" was Marcia Nardi, a
little-known woman poet whose letters to Williams were, in
part, what prompted him to return to the composition of *Paterson*, the poem he had worked on sporadically for nearly twenty
years.[3] Williams's note referred to the many letters he had received from Nardi during their early correspondence (1942–
1943), letters he intended to use throughout his poem. In the
end, he did not use all the letters but excerpts from just three of
them, and only in Books I and II of *Paterson* (published by New
Directions in 1946 and 1948, respectively). But one of Nardi's
letters (written after Williams had attempted to put an end to
their correspondence) was used almost in its entirety; the long,
angry letter comprises 20 percent of Book II and, in fact, provides the dramatic conclusion to that book.[4] Williams added the
signature "La vôtre C." to the letter in an allusion to Chaucer's
Criseyde (who signed her letter to Troilus in this manner) and as
a means of protecting Nardi's identity; thus Nardi's letters in
Paterson became known as the "Cress" letters.[5] In them, a poet
("C.") addresses her thoughts to "Dr. P." (a Williams persona
in the poem) but never receives a reply, leaving the nature and
extent of their relationship open to conjecture. A reading of
the complete (surviving) Marcia Nardi/William Carlos Williams
correspondence, therefore, provides a new context for their literary counterparts at the same time that it brings to life the
actual relationship between the two poets.

Lillian Massell, ca. 1907.

Their correspondence began shortly after Williams and Nardi met in March 1942[6] at a time that both of them considered to be critical in their personal and professional lives. Williams, then fifty-nine, had not yet secured the awards and critical acclaim for his work that came to him a few years later.[7] He had become frustrated by his lack of progress in making sense of the large amount of raw material he had accumulated over the years for use in *Paterson*: fragments of prose accounts of the history of the area, newspaper accounts of bizarre happenings, letters from friends and acquaintances, together with older poems and some new lyrics. He was blocked; just days before he met Nardi, he had written to his friend Harvey Breit: "I'm not writing any poetry now. I can't. I hope I shall be able to surmount present difficulties."[8] As for Nardi, she was at an impasse: eager to return to the writing of poetry after the interruption of her promising early career, but without any contacts in the literary world. A Boston native, she had dropped out of Wellesley College twenty years earlier, borrowed one hundred dollars from an uncle, and moved to Greenwich Village. Once there, she renamed herself—Lillian Massell became Marcia Nardi—to avoid being found by her family and, more important, to gain the anonymity she needed to "reinvent" herself. For a few years, she managed to support herself as a free-lance writer and book reviewer and even had several poems published.[9] During those years, she met many people in the literary circles of Greenwich Village (even living in the same rooming house as Allen Tate and Hart Crane for a brief period) and thus had little trouble finding part-time work congenial to her interests. But the birth of a son in 1926 (according to Nardi, the child's father had abandoned her during pregnancy) and the responsibility of caring for him alone changed her life radically. She had no steady income and no husband and she was alienated from her family. The Depression years soon followed, and Nardi was forced to take any available job to support herself and her son. Her poetry, while not completely abandoned, was neglected for lack of time and energy.[10]

A problem concerning her then teen-aged son precipitated Nardi's first meeting with Williams. Oddly, it was Harvey Breit who (Nardi said) suggested that she ask Williams for advice regarding the problem. Breit (then working for the *New York Times* as a writer and editor) was Nardi's neighbor in Greenwich Village; the two had met the year before and had a brief affair. Although the affair had recently ended, Nardi turned to

Breit for help when the problem with her son became more than she could handle. Breit suggested that Nardi ask his friend Williams if (as a physician) he could help unsnarl what had become a bureaucratic nightmare at Bellevue Hospital, where Nardi's son had been hospitalized.[11] After calling ahead to Rutherford to be sure of her welcome, she traveled in a rainstorm from Greenwich Village to New Jersey—first on a Hudson River ferry, then by train, then by walking the short distance to the Williams home on Ridge Road—to ask for his advice. Seven years later, Williams described her arrival: "She was literally blown into my office one night, soaked to the skin by a heavy rain and in frightened need, in desperate need."[12] According to Nardi, they talked for a couple of hours in his office; before she left, she showed him some of the poems she had with her and left them for him to read.[13]

Ten days later, Williams received Nardi's first letter. She wrote to tell him that the situation with her son had been resolved and to ask that he return her poems. She assumed, since she had not heard from him, that he did not like her work. Somewhat defensively, she pointed out that she had been prevented by the problems of living from developing her poetic talent and from working in what (she quoted Poe), "under happier circumstances, would have been the field of my choice."[14] Williams's response was immediate: He wanted to see more of her work, which he liked but found to be of mixed quality and in need of development. The two exchanged a few more letters, then met for a second time on 16 June 1942, when Williams invited her to dinner at a restaurant in New York City, directly across from the new Bryant Park. At this meeting, Williams told Nardi he wanted to make use of her first letter to him in what he was then calling the "Introduction"—and which eventually became Book I of *Paterson*—and received her verbal permission.[15] Whether Williams explained to her (if he knew then) how he intended to use her letter is unclear, and Nardi may have assumed he intended to quote from her letter in a prose introduction to *Paterson*. What is clear is that, very early in their correspondence, Williams found in Nardi's letters what he needed for the poem

Lillian Massell, 1921.

that he himself could not provide: a woman's voice. Her voice
served to articulate in the poem what Nardi called "woman's
wretched position in society" and the difficulties faced by
the unconventional woman—particularly the woman poet—in
contemporary society. There is no question that Nardi needed
something from Williams also. She badly needed the friendship

of another poet to whom she could show her poems and with whom she could discuss them; and she hoped that, with his help, her work would be published and her literary career reborn. Furthermore, she needed Williams to act as a sounding board for the issues she raised in her letters—and her confidence that he would play that role was fostered by his continued interest in her. He had little reason to refuse the role when the issues in her letters so perfectly echoed the themes of his poem: the failure of love, the failure of communication, the alienation of the poet.

There is evidence that at one point during his composition of *Paterson* Williams considered sharing authorship of the poem with Marcia Nardi and with another correspondent of his: David Lyle, an engineer from Paterson, New Jersey, who had been writing to him since 1938. Among Williams's notes for *Paterson* at Yale is a handwritten title page reading "PATERSON or Any/Every Place. By W.C.W. D.J.L. M.N."[16] As Mike Weaver points out, Williams was intrigued by Lyle's unique method of correlating the writings of persons in widely divergent fields in his effort to find a common language. Lyle expected to thus "open the way to a sense of common purpose in the world," and Williams thought this method could be applied also to the material he had amassed for *Paterson*.[17] Later he reconsidered the way he would credit Nardi's and Lyle's help and crossed out the heading on the title page. Above it he wrote: "William Carlos Williams" and underneath "with the assistance of D.J.L. and M.N." In the end, of course, *Paterson* was published under his name alone; but the importance Williams attached to the influence of both Lyle and Nardi on the poem is further evidenced by another note found in an early draft for *Paterson*: "Lyle: is he" and under that "Nardi: is she."[18] In a letter written a few years after the publication of Book II, Williams remarked on the significance of the long letter, calling it the "woman's reply" to the hero of his poem and saying that the writer (he did not refer to Nardi by name) could conceivably be called "Mrs. Paterson."[19]

But however important the early Nardi letters were to

the concept of *Paterson*, Williams eventually grew weary of receiving them. He would later tire of Lyle's letters also; Mike Weaver describes Williams casting them aside unopened once they had fulfilled their purpose.[20] He had done his best to provide Nardi with what he thought she needed most—technical help with her poems and a sympathetic ear for her personal problems. He had successfully urged James Laughlin, his publisher, to include some of her poems in the 1942 *New Directions Number Seven* anthology. And he had tried to help her find work. Yet there seemed to be no way that he could change the difficult circumstances of her life, and finally, in February 1943, he wrote to say that as far as he was concerned their correspondence was finished. Nardi's reply (her "last word") and the two letters that followed it are among the most forceful letters Williams ever received from her, but he did not answer them personally.[21] His only response was to incorporate the letters into his poem, thereby accomplishing two ends: he used her words to further the themes of his poem and, at the same time, he gave her ideas a forum they would not otherwise have had.

Very little is known about Nardi's activities in the years after the early correspondence with Williams came to a halt, except that she met a man named John Charles ("Chuk") Lang, a writer and painter, and lived with him as his wife, first in New York City, then in Woodstock, New York. In 1945, when Book I of *Paterson* was about to be published, Williams tried unsuccessfully to locate Nardi to obtain the necessary written permission to use her letter. In the end, he left the short excerpts in that book unsigned.[22] Again, in 1947, when Book II was about to be published, the same was true: Nardi was nowhere to be found. But now the situation was different, for the letters he intended to incorporate in Book II (39 and 40) had not been written by Nardi until after Williams had broken off his side of their correspondence—long after he had received her verbal permission to use her first letter. This time he chose to leave some of the excerpts unsigned and gave the long letter at the end the signature "C."[23] Williams was thus able to keep "Cress's"

Marcia and Paul Nardi, ca. 1932. Courtesy of Paul Nardi.

real identity confidential for more than twenty years—and Nardi was not identified publicly as the author of the "Cress" letters until 1971, eight years after Williams died.[24]

Some of the early commentators on *Paterson* II barely mentioned the "Cress" letters or cursorily dismissed them. One reviewer referred to them simply as the "long pages from the letters of a frustrated poetess."[25] Leslie Fiedler complained that Williams was guilty of "blatant" self-indulgence by the "injection into the work's progress of some old letter given at needless length."[26] Others were not aware that the letters had been written by someone other than Williams; they thought that "Cress" was a Williams persona. One of them, Joseph Bennett, accused Williams of being "intensely self-preoccupied, entranced with the image of his own ego," and said that the long letter (from the presumed Williams persona) was "an unusually cantankerous display of priggishness, of moral superiority." Bennett asserted that this was in keeping with what he saw as Williams's theme: "the poet as a sacrificial victim of society."[27] Richard Eberhart also mistakenly attributed the letter to Williams but nevertheless believed it to be an authentic portrayal of "a woman not content with woman's position in the world."[28] One critic, Ruth Lechlitner, never doubted that the letters had been written by an actual woman; she saw that the letters were "too painfully real to have been wholly 'invented' by Dr. Williams himself."[29]

Most critics of *Paterson* II were aware that the letters were from a real woman (Robert Lowell called them "the letters of a lacerated and lacerating poetess"), but there were wide differences of opinion about Williams's use of them in his poem.[30] Louis Martz claimed that the letters were an important part of Williams's complex analogy—"Paterson the city is to the park as man is to woman"—and that the prose letters described "the painful need of a woman for intimate friendship with a man (Dr. P.), who has seen her not as a human being but as material for literature."[31] Edwin Honig thought that "the trouble with Williams lay in his way of communicating: he could write about the people who inhabited his world, but not to them." But Honig concluded nevertheless that the use of the long letter (even with its "depressive weight") was justified, in that it echoed the "divorce" theme running through Book II.[32] Vivienne Koch saw the Cress letters serving the poem in a "curious double agency," and she considered them an important part of the total design in *Paterson*. She contended that the historical "prose-threads" documented the text "objectively, at the level of public life or society," while the "acute yet distraught" letters of the woman poet documented the poem subjectively, "at the level of private life, in her case a losing revolt against society."[33] But

Elizabeth Bishop (in a personal letter to Robert Lowell, written after she read his review of *Paterson* II) reacted negatively to Williams's use of the letters:

> when I read it all [Book II] I still felt he shouldn't have used the letters from that woman—to me it seems mean, and they're much too overpowering emotionally for the rest of it so that the whole poem suffers. . . . And then maybe I've felt a little too much the way the woman did at certain more hysterical moments—people who haven't experienced absolute loneliness for long stretches of time can never sympathise with it at all.[34]

A few years later, Ralph Nash earned praise from Williams for his assessment of the importance of the prose passages (especially the Cress letter) in *Paterson*. "No one to the present moment has so looked within me," Williams wrote to him in January 1954. Nash called the letters a "remarkable corroboration of Williams's exploration of his age" and claimed that Williams's use of prose in the poem was an example of " 'invention' in the classical sense—the discovery of material appropriate to the meaning and the decorum of the poem."[35] Randall Jarrell, however, questioned Williams's judgment in using the "Cress" letter at all. Writing in 1951, he asked:

> Should so much of this book [*Paterson* II] consist of what are—the reader is forced to conclude—real letters from a real woman? One reads these letters with involved, embarrassed pity, quite as if she had walked into the room and handed them to one. What has been done to make it possible for us to respond to them as art, not as raw reality? to make them part of the poem *Paterson*? I can think of no answer except: "They have been copied out on the typewriter."[36]

Williams himself (in letters to Horace Gregory, James Laughlin, and Srinivas Rayaprol)[37] has explained his appropriation of Nardi's words, saying variously that her long letter served some of his thematic purposes in *Paterson*; that the subject matter was germane to the poem; that it represented the "woman's

William Carlos Williams. Undated photograph by Elliott Erwitt. HRHRC Photography Collection.

reply" to the man; and that it demonstrated that "writing" (or prose) can co-exist with poetry. To another correspondent, he offered one more reason for using the letter—that to "hide" it would be cowardly:

> I did not compose it. It is, as you see, an attack, a personal attack upon me by a woman. It seemed a legitimate one. It had besides a certain literary quality which was authentic, that made it a thing in itself worth recording . . .
>
> . . . In the first place it was a reply from the female side to many of my male pretensions. It was a strong reply, a reply which sought to destroy me. It was just that it should have its opportunity to destroy. If I hid the reply it would be a confession of weakness on my part.[38]

Nardi's own reaction to the use of her letters in *Paterson* was somewhat delayed. On March 30, 1949, a year after the appearance of Book II, she wrote Williams to say that, while browsing in a bookstore in Woodstock, she had come across a

At Woodstock, ca. 1952.

copy of the poem and had discovered her letters in it. She asked
him to send copies of Books I and II to her.[39] Williams replied
the next day, telling her of his unsuccessful efforts to find her—
and their correspondence resumed. This time, their letters took
on a cordial and less formal tone: he addressed her as "Marcia"
and she called him "Bill." But, strangely, neither of them ever
mentioned his use of her letters in *Paterson* to each other again.
Williams did not explain to her (nor did she ask) why he had
chosen to use the signature "La vôtre C." on her long letter, and
Nardi was not aware of the allusion to Chaucer's Criseyde until
many years later.[40]

During the time she had been out of contact with Williams,
the difficult circumstances of Nardi's life had not improved. For

most of the previous six years, she and Chuk Lang had been residents of the Maverick—an artist's colony in Woodstock—where they lived a life of little more than what Nardi called "shared economic problems." She was still poor, and she was still lonely—and now her problems were complicated by her fragile health and by her unhappy relationship with Lang. In a 1950 letter to Williams, she wrote that her "economic problems, serious as they continue to be,—fade away and become nothing alongside my loneliness." He replied sympathetically:

> . . . by this time you must realize that I have always been convinced of your distinction as a poet and that I have done what I could as a friend to assist you.
>
> As artists we do our best work when we are most moved, not when we are unhappiest, tho' it comes sometimes to that. We need close friends, surely, to whom to "confess" at times with a sure feeling that we shall be given unfailing sympathy and unquestioning support in our emotional agonies. I am that sort of friend to you. But the battle itself we must undergo entirely alone.[41]

The later Nardi/Williams correspondence began, as it had before, in a period of their lives that was critical to both of them. Williams's health had begun to deteriorate after his first heart attack in 1948, forcing him to cut back his practice. A stroke in March 1951 was followed by another in August 1952; and, briefly, in the winter of 1953, he was hospitalized with severe depression. However, he was beginning to earn the critical acclaim for his work that had eluded him until then. In 1948, he won the National Institute of Arts and Letters Russell Loines Award for Poetry, and he was invited to read his poetry and lecture at colleges across the country. The first book on his work (by Vivienne Koch) was published in 1950, the same year that he won the first annual Gold Medal for Poetry, given by the National Book Awards. But continued health problems and other concerns forced him to turn down another honor—a Consultantship in Poetry for the Library of Congress (1949–1950).

As for Nardi, she again had reason to hope that her lifeless literary career might be revived, aided by Williams's renewed interest and encouragement. In the fall of 1949, because of his efforts, her work appeared in the *New Directions Number Eleven* anthology and in the prestigious international journal *Botteghe Oscure*. He urged Nardi to ready a book of poems for possible publication by New Directions, and, as a result of the letter he wrote to Norman Holmes Pearson (who directed the fund) praising Nardi's work, she was awarded $250 by the Bryher Fund.[42] But Williams kept himself aloof from her personally, and, although Nardi frequently asked to meet with him, the two met in person only one more time, in the late summer of 1949.[43] Nor did Williams make an effort to introduce her to other poets (Marianne Moore, for instance)[44] who might have provided what she most sorely lacked: someone with whom she could discuss her work face to face. Nardi lamented this lack of contact with other poets; among her papers is a quotation from Henry James she had copied from his book on Nathaniel Hawthorne:

> The best things come, as a general thing, from the talents that are members of a group; every man works better when he has companions working in the same line, and yielding to the stimulus of suggestion, comparison, emulation. Great things of course have been done by solitary workers; but they usually have been done with double the pains they would have cost if they had been produced in more genial circumstances. The solitary worker loses the profit of example and discussion; he is apt to make awkward experiments; he is in the nature of the case more or less of an empiric. The empiric may, as I say, be treated by the world as an expert; but the drawbacks and discomforts of empiricism remain to him, and are in fact increased by the suspicion that is mingled with his gratitude, of a want in the public taste of a sense of the proportion of things.[45]

Nardi was an empiric, and it was her knowledge—gained from personal experience as a woman and as a woman poet—

At Woodstock, ca. 1952.

that made her letters to Williams so important. It was her articulation of that experience—what he called the "lifting of an
environment to expression"—that Williams borrowed for his
poem. At the conclusion of Book II, "Cress" accuses Williams
of taking her thoughts seriously because they could be turned
into literature "as something disconnected from life." She as-
serts: "You've never had to live, Dr. P.—not in any of the by-
ways and dark underground passages where life so often has to
be tested." Nardi herself, however, came to a greater appreciation and understanding of Williams in later years. In one of her
last letters to him, she writes: "I think it's wonderful how your
poetry has gone from greater to greater development all the
time—always saying something new and fresh and never repeating. I tie this up with the moral and human side of your

work, and also with the spiritual side, because it is so rooted in love that transcends time as all major poetry has to be (at least for me and my evaluations of it)."[46]

But there was an underlying issue that complicated that understanding and appreciation and continued to puzzle Nardi: the issue of Williams having remained distant from her personally. In 1981 (when she was nearly eighty), Nardi reread her letters in *Paterson* for the first time in many years and speculated about the reasons for that aloofness in a letter to Theodora Graham:

they [her letters] depressed me terribly by forcing me to relive in memory all the wretched poverty and loneliness of those far-away days which resulted from my being an "unwed mother" . . . a situation which cast a blight over my entire life, though I don't think Williams was aware of this because he was aware of me *only* as a poet and not at all as a person, a human being—which is what the *Paterson* letters are all about, without his even realizing the nature of my "attack" on him.

. . . Williams is quoted there [in Mike Weaver's book] as saying that my attack "was a reply from the female side to many of my male pretensions." But those letters had nothing to do with his male "pretensions," of which I was not especially aware; for, as you must have noticed already and certainly will notice if you read my letters again, what I resented was his double-dealing in responding with sensitivity and understanding and admiration to the thoughts and ideas and awarenesses that I expressed in my poetry, but completely ignoring them where my private life was concerned and even abandoning me for my inability, *in living itself*, to cope with the very same experiences that inspired those poems of mine which he admired the most!

As I turn to those letters now . . . my eye falls on the following sentence: "But where my actual personal life crept in, stamped all over with the very same attitudes and sensibilities that you found quite admirable as *literature*—that was an entirely different matter, wasn't it?" And my eyes alight on an even more important sentence that goes: "I didn't need the *publication* of my poetry with your name attached to it, in order to go on writing poetry, half as much as I needed your friendship in other ways (the very ways you ignored) in order to write it."

And as I read these indignant comments of mine now, after all these years, I feel no less crushed and demolished than I did then at having been shoved aside *as a person* by Williams while being offered haloes and wreathes as a poet.

. . . I also feel (but just instinctively) that if I had been a *male* poet whose work attracted Williams and was admired greatly by him, he would have offered his friendship and even perhaps invited him to his home.

. . . Anyway, I met him at a very crucial time in my life, so that his rejection of me except in connection with my poetry had a particularly serious effect upon me, for I had had (long before I met him—at least ten years previously) a very strong foothold in the literary world *socially* and needed to regain it, as I might have done through him.[47]

A few weeks later, in another letter to Graham, Nardi continued:

But I'm glad I telephoned you, because it got me to thinking again about my "double" relationship with Williams (his admiring my poetry so much on the one hand; and on the other, keeping me at a distance as a woman).

And this no longer puzzles me! I can see the reason for it now, quite clearly; and am amazed that I did not do so before this, because it has been a subject of special interest to me (as it was, and is, to Simone de Beauvoir) for a long time.

What's involved is the fact (and it *is* a fact, according to my observations and experiences) that no matter how much a man admires a woman's work, or her intelligence (i.e. if she is a woman *without* a menage, such as yours) his interest in her as a friend (and I mean a *close* friend) depends very much on his feeling about her sexually. If she has no sex appeal for him, he tends to keep her at a distance socially, regardless of her achievements. And he might still keep her at a distance socially in a case where she does attract him sexually but makes him wary of an entanglement which might have *impractical* consequences.

This aspect of "woman's position in society" (which I mentioned in the *Paterson* letters) has not been given enough attention by the Women's Lib movement and is why I have not joined any of its groups here in Boston.

... I dare say that other factors too entered the situation. ... the illegitimacy of my son, [for instance,] for Williams was definitely a very conventional man (with an *admitted* horror of "bohemia," with which he could have connected me). Also poverty itself affects one's social position (as indicated by the serious effect upon Baudelaire's life of his poverty); and everything that affects a man's social position in the world, affects a woman's even more—which brings me back to my strong feeling that if I had been a male poet whose work Williams admired as much as he did mine, I would have had a much more satisfactory personal relationship with him. Yes, of this I do feel certain! And also that I would now be a well[-known poet, but I admit also?] that no woman could have survived as a poet, what Baudelaire survived.[48]

Whatever his reasons for keeping Nardi at a distance, Williams was always sympathetic about her predicament. So were many of the other artists, writers, and musicians Nardi met (such as Thornton Wilder and Alec Waugh) during the 1950s and 1960s, when she was often a resident at Yaddo and the MacDowell Colony.[49] Most of them, like Williams, found themselves overwhelmed by her neediness and by the intractability of her problems. Randall Jarrell, in a letter commenting on some of her poems (which Nardi had sent to him under the name of "Irene Mannix"),[50] remarked on the inadequacy of words to convey his sympathy: "I do think you have a real talent for poetry. You've had to write it under the most difficult circumstances; I feel funny about saying anything

Sketch of Marcia Nardi by Rosemarie Beck, 1953.

sympathetic, it sounds so much like people on the shore sympa-
thizing with the sailors being shipwrecked—but I do sympa-
thize, and if I can do anything about a recommendation for the
grant or fellowship you mention, I'd be very glad to."[51] In a
1950 letter to Nardi, Williams (after writing of his respect for
her "extraordinary abilities") used the word "tragic" to describe
her situation: "[It is] tragic in that you cannot escape it."[52]
Later, Nardi used the same word in a letter to Jarrell; in the copy

Portrait of William Carlos Williams by Emanuel Romano, 1951.
Reproduced with the permission of Hugo Dreyfuss and the Romano
estate. HRHRC Photography Collection.

(or earlier draft) she retained of a 1965 letter to him, she discussed what she called the "tragic irony" of her relationship
with Williams:

> there was a tragic irony connected with my whole relation-
> ship with him. He represented (and still does) my only contact

with another poet (of any importance). And yet I got hardly any benefit from it. I mean psychologically or intellectually or spiritually (for I'm not talking about material benefits, as it goes without saying). Perhaps it was because he praised too highly (though I may be mistaken in this—I can't tell, being a poor judge of my own poems) the work of any poet who represented as much as mine did a considerable departure from the traditions which Eliot stood for (though Eliot was one of my own favorite poets). And perhaps it was also because he was extraordinarily innocent in regard to so much of the corruption and evil in the world and in human nature (that evil of which the Jameses—both William and Henry— understood so well, and which Baudelaire was so acutely aware of and from which I was too unprotected socially, and too poverty-stricken, to cope with); and equally naive (another extraordinary thing) regarding the obstacles placed in my path, as a poet, by my lack of any solid ground whatsoever beneath my feet.

I found this same kind of innocence and naivete in Thornton Wilder (another irony which I cannot help but tie up with my bad luck in every aspect of my miscarried literary career)—an example of this being the following episode: after his great enthusiasm for my poems (and a completely unsolicited one), it was quite natural for me to inquire of him, a few months later, if, with his considerable influence, he could put me in the way of any congenial source of an adequate income suitable for a poet. How amazed I was, therefore, at the reply I received from him! That not belonging to any literary circles nor any academic ones and having become so closely affiliated with the theatrical world and also living so much of the time in Europe, he had no connections apt to be of any help to me with jobs (for thus he explained it in his letter)— that did not surprise nor bother me. But the concluding sentence of his reply—"you talked about nothing but your financial problems, whereas about your poetry which is so much more important, you say nothing, so what about it [the poetry]?"—well, you can well imagine my reaction to such an

Painting of Marcia Nardi by Rosemarie Beck, ca. 1953.

amazing question on his part (especially since he is so terribly rich himself)—as if there were no connection between my being stuck at the ribbon counter in Woolworth's for eight hours a day at the minimum hourly wage, and my inability to function as a poet![53]

In general, the difficulties that Marcia Nardi faced are familiar to many poets—such as the poverty which results from having neither a private income nor another profession to pay the bills, and the loneliness and isolation from a society that places little value on poetry. And Nardi's articulation of those difficulties (in her letters to Williams) is in harmony with the themes of *Paterson*, for, as Benjamin Sankey suggests, the subject of *Paterson* is "in a sense . . . not the American past or the modern city, but simply the poet's attempt to do his own work." Furthermore, Sankey contends, *Paterson* "threatens at times to become a discourse on poetry, or on the psychology of the writer"[54]—

and certainly the "Cress" letters contribute to that discourse. But the letters introduce also a dissonant note that disturbs the harmony: a woman's voice—angry and indignant—telling the story no one wants to hear, of the heavy additional burdens placed on a woman poet who attempts to do her own work.

The hero of *Paterson* never answers the woman's letters, except indirectly, through the medium of the poem. The Williams letters in this collection, therefore, not only offer a fresh context for the relationship of "Dr. Paterson" and "Cress" but also reveal for the first time the role Williams himself played in his friendship with the real woman, Marcia Nardi. At the same time, the publication of the complete surviving correspondence serves another very important purpose: it allows Marcia Nardi to speak as herself and for herself. From the time that Nardi was identified publicly as the author of the "Cress" letters, the danger has existed that readers and critics of *Paterson* will confuse the character of "Cress" with that of Nardi herself. In that case, Nardi would be remembered in literary history only as the "double" of a fictional character created by someone else. From the beginning, Marcia Nardi had considered her personal identity and her poetic identity to be one and the same. She took her name and the title of poet at the same time, determined to establish an identity that was uniquely her own. Since that identity—as a woman and a poet—was earned at great personal cost, readers of *Paterson* and all readers who are interested in women who "write their own lives" need the fuller picture of Marcia Nardi that is provided by these letters.

NOTES

1. The note was made on a sheet (part of a draft for Book II of *Paterson*) cataloged as item E18b by Baldwin and Meyers in *The Manuscripts and Letters*, 217.

2. Williams, *Paterson*.

3. Mariani claims, in *William Carlos Williams: A New World Naked*, that Nardi was the "impetus" that made Williams go back to work on

Paterson (461), and Graham refers to Nardi as Williams's "extraordinary Muse" in her article "Her Heigh Compleynte," 164.

4. See letter 40 in this volume.

5. In a 1944 letter to Marianne Moore, Williams commented: "You remember how Chaucer had Cressida sign her letters to the man she left behind her in Troy? 'La vôtre C.' Marvellous!" Thirlwall, *The Selected Letters*, 233.

6. In a 1946 letter to his editor, James Laughlin, Williams wrote: "From what you say the book [*Paterson*, Book I] should appear sometime in early March—a good sign, since everything of most significance happens to me in March, has been so all my life." Letter from William Carlos Williams to James Laughlin, 18 January 1946, Beinecke Rare Book and Manuscript Library, Yale University (Za Williams/295).

7. For more information about Williams during these years, see Mariani, *William Carlos Williams: A New World Naked*, Chap. 9, "Clearing the Field: 1938–1942."

8. Thirlwall, *The Selected Letters*, 194.

9. See chronology for Nardi's published works.

10. For more biographical information on Nardi, see Elizabeth M. O'Neil, "Marcia Nardi: Woman of Letters," in *Rossetti to Sexton: Six Women Poets at Texas* (Austin, Tex.: Harry Ransom Humanities Research Center, 1992), 73–111. This article also appeared in a special issue of the *Library Chronicle of The University of Texas at Austin* 22, nos. 1–2.

11. See letter 1, note 2.

12. Letter from William Carlos Williams to Norman Holmes Pearson, 31 August 1949, Norman Holmes Pearson Papers, Yale Collection of American Literature, Beinecke Rare Book and Manuscript Library, Yale University (see letter 61).

13. Letter from Marcia Nardi to Theodora R. Graham, 22 August 1981, private collection.

14. See letter 1.

15. As of 16 June 1942, Williams had received just five letters from Nardi. One of them was sufficiently personal that he apparently did not keep it, thus it does not survive in "sent" form. However, Nardi had retained her draft of the letter and it has been included in this volume as letter 5. Nardi often kept the handwritten drafts of letters she wrote in longhand, in addition to carbon copies of her typed letters.

16. Miscellaneous notes for *Paterson* in the Williams Collection at the Beinecke Library, Yale University (catalog designation Za Williams/185).

17. Mike Weaver, *William Carlos Williams: The American Background* (Cambridge: Cambridge University Press, 1971), 122.

18. Draft of *Paterson*, Williams Collection, Poetry/Rare Books Collection of the State University of New York at Buffalo.

19. See letter 72, William Carlos Williams to Srinivas Rayaprol.

20. Weaver, *William Carlos Williams*, 123.

21. See letters 37, 39, and 40.

22. Williams, *Paterson*.

23. In two letters from WCW to his editor James Laughlin (dated 10 December 1945 and 13 June 1947), he discusses his unsuccessful attempts to locate Nardi. The letters are in the Williams collection at the Beinecke Rare Book and Manuscript Library, Yale University (cataloged Za Williams/295).

24. Mike Weaver was the first to identify Nardi in print as the author of the Cress letters (127). In giving Nardi the name of "Cress," Williams (in addition to his thematic purposes) may have been influenced by the memory of the time he had been sued for failing to change the names of actual people in a short story he wrote (based on a real event) and by his wife, Flossie's, subsequent insistence that he change the names of any real people in all of his work (Mariani, *William Carlos Williams: A New World Naked*, 254–255). He also changed the names (or initials) of other correspondents whose letters he used in *Paterson* I and II: Edward Dahlberg became "E.D." or "Edward"; Alva Turner became simply "T." (Williams at one time had intended to use the signature "Le vôtre T" on his letter.) For more information, see MacGowan's notes for *Paterson*, 260–263.

25. William Van O'Connor, the *Saturday Review*, 25 September 1948.

26. Leslie Fiedler, "Some Uses and Failures of Feeling," *Partisan Review* (August 1948): 924, 927–931. Reprinted in *William Carlos Williams: The Critical Heritage*, ed. Charles Doyle (London: Routledge and Kegan Paul, 1980), 191–195.

27. Joseph Bennett, "The Lyre and the Sledgehammer," *Hudson Review* 5 (Summer 1952): 295–307.

28. Richard Eberhart, *New York Times*, 20 June 1948, 4.

29. Ruth Lechlitner, "Lyric Satire, Stark Revelation" (review of William Carlos Williams's *Paterson* Book II), *New York Herald Tribune Weekly Book Review*, 27 June 1948, 4.

30. Robert Lowell, "*Paterson* II," *The Nation*, 19 June 1948, 692–694. Reprinted in Robert Lowell, *Collected Prose* (New York: Farrar, Straus and Giroux, 1987).

31. Louis Martz, "Anticipating Williams' Conclusion that 'The Virtue Is All in the Effort,'" *Yale Review* (Autumn 1948): 147–150.

32. Edwin Honig, *Poetry* (April 1949). Reprinted in Mariani, *William Carlos Williams: The Poet and His Critics*, 87.

33. Vivienne Koch, *William Carlos Williams* (Norfolk, Conn.: New Directions, 1950), 143.

34. Letter from Elizabeth Bishop to Robert Lowell, 30 June [1948], Houghton Library, Harvard University.

35. Ralph Nash, "The Use of Prose in *Paterson*," *Perspective* 6 (1953): 191–199; reprinted in *Studies in Paterson*, comp. John Engels (Columbus, Ohio: Charles E. Merrill, 1971), 21. Williams's letter to Nash is mentioned by Paul Mariani in *William Carlos Williams: The Poet and His Critics*, 101.

36. Randall Jarrell, "A View of Three Poets," *Partisan Review* 18 (1951): 691–700; reprinted in *Profiles of William Carlos Williams*, comp. Jerome Mazzaro (Columbus, Ohio: Charles E. Merrill, 1971), 68–69.

37. See letters 41, 44, and 72 in this volume.

38. Letter from WCW to Robert D. Pepper, 21 August 1951, quoted by Weaver, *William Carlos Williams*, 209. Sandra Gilbert has suggested that by using Nardi's angry letters accusing him of separating life from literature, Williams was adopting the strategy of Minister D in Poe's *The Purloined Letters*, "concealing the threat implied by the dangerous letters . . . by placing them so frankly in the open that no one would ever suspect their power." See Sandra M. Gilbert, "Purloined Letters: William Carlos Williams and 'Cress,' " *William Carlos Williams Review* 11, no. 2 (1985): 5–15.

39. See letter 42.

40. In a 1981 letter to Theodora Graham, Nardi wrote: "About your questions in regard to the signature 'La Votre C.' No, I never referred to myself as being like 'Criseyde.' I couldn't have, because I have never read Chaucer's 'Troilus and Criseyde' or hardly anything else by Chaucer because he is not a poet I care much for. But I'm glad that you explained how Williams came to choose that signature, for I was puzzled by it. I also thought that the 'vôtre' (being French) was awfully affected and silly (not being familiar with its source until now when you have explained it)."

41. See letters 75 and 76.

42. See letter 61.

43. See letter 64 for a reference to their third meeting.

44. However, Christopher MacGowan, in his notes to *Paterson*, mentions that Williams had asked Moore to make job inquiries on Nardi's behalf in 1942 (277).

45. Henry James, *Hawthorne: A Critical Essay on the Man and His Times* (New York: Collier Books, 1966 [1879]).

46. See letter 94.

47. Letter from Marcia Nardi to Theodora R. Graham, 5 August 1981, private collection. In an earlier letter (18 May 1981) to Graham, Nardi

had written that what Williams lacked for her was what she called "intelligence of the heart."

48. Letter from Marcia Nardi to Theodora R. Graham, 22 August 1981, private collection.

49. Letters from Thornton Wilder and Alec Waugh to Nardi are among Nardi's papers at the Beinecke Library at Yale University (uncataloged Za Nardi).

50. A draft of her letter, signed "Irene Mannix" and dated 6 March 1956, is part of Nardi's archive. At the end, she offers an explanation of her use of a false name:

The surname I sign here (that of an ex-husband) is not the one under which my few published poems have appeared nor that by which I am known to people in general, since only under the cloak of anonymity, would I have the courage to thrust this letter and the enclosed poems upon you. I feel too that in this way I can perhaps be more certain of your telling me outright—without any kindly euphemisms—that these poems are nothing much, if that should be your opinion of them.

Sincerely yours, Irene Mannix

P.S. If you *should* think that the writer of these poems has more than just a modicum of talent, I would perhaps in that case ask permission to refer to your opinion in applying for the financial help I so urgently need—and also in trying to get into Yaddo and the MacDowell Colony for the entire spring and summer—because I am literally penniless, and have on hand not only many unfinished poems but also a prose work which has been growing in my mind for some time now and parts of which I have already written.

51. Randall Jarrell's letter to Nardi (addressed to "Dear Miss Mannix") is at the Beinecke Library at Yale University (uncataloged Za Nardi).

52. See letter 76.

53. Copy (or draft) of letter from Marcia Nardi to Randall Jarrell, 16 July 1965, MN archive.

54. Benjamin Sankey, *A Companion to William Carlos Williams's Paterson* (Berkeley: University of California Press, 1971), 224.

Chronology

The Life and Works of Marcia Nardi

. . . .

1901

6 August. Born Lillian Massell in Boston, Massachusetts. First-generation American, oldest child of Joseph and Pauline (Chaloff) Massell.

1914–1919

Attends Girl's Latin School in Boston and Horblick's Preparatory School in Roxbury.

1919–1921

Attends Wellesley College, leaves in junior year and does not graduate. Her poem "Resurrection" published in the *Wellesley College Magazine.*

1922–1923?

Moves to Greenwich Village in New York City and changes her name to Marcia Nardi. Lives at one time in the same rooming house as Allen Tate and Hart Crane.

1924

Moves for a short time to Baltimore, works there for the *Modern Quarterly,* a radical magazine edited by V. F. Calverton.

The *Modern Quarterly* publishes "Villanelle" (Spring, vol. 1, no. 4), and "Epitaph" and "Spring Song" (Summer, vol. 2, no. 1).

September. Three sonnets (two called "Sonnet," another entitled "Skeptic") are published in the *Measure* (no. 43).

9 November. Her "Sonnets I and II" appear in the *New York Herald Tribune Book Review* (p. 5).

1925

28 January. Her review of H.D.'s *Heliodora* is published in the *New Republic* (p. 266).

29 March. Poems "They Thought, Of Course" and "Most Certainly" are published in the *New York Herald Tribune Book Review* (p. 4).

14 June. Reviews *41 Poems* by e. e. cummings for the *New York Herald Tribune Book Review* (pp. 4–5).

30 December. The *New Republic* publishes her review of Babette Deutsch's *Honey Out of the Rock* (p. 170).

1926

January. *Bookman* publishes her poem "To a Psychoanalyst" (p. 550). Reprinted in the *Literary Digest* (30 January, p. 32).

1926

25 July. Her poem "Reverie" appears in the *New York Herald Tribune Book Review* (p. 5).

1926

23 October. Her son, Paul Nardi, is born at New York Nursery and Child's Hospital. She never divulges name of son's father and claims that her married lover deserted her when she was six months pregnant.

1927

18 February. Poem "A Request" published in the *New York Times* (p. 20).

30 March. Poem "When Women Talk" published in *The Nation* (p. 345).

16 July. Poem "I Only Ask" published in the *New York Times* (p. 10).

1928

15 August. She writes a review "Five Women Poets" for the *New Republic* (pp. 180–181).

1929–1941

Takes any available work—newspaper reporting, writing publicity for a social service agency, editing, department store clerking, waitressing—during the Depression to support herself and her child.

1941

Meets Harvey Breit, her neighbor in Greenwich Village.

1942

29 March. Meets William Carlos Williams at his home office in Rutherford, New Jersey.

16 June. Williams and Nardi meet for dinner in New York City; he informs her he wants to use her letters in *Paterson*.

November. Seventeen of her poems appear in the *New Directions Number Seven* anthology.

[1943–1944]

Marries Charles (Chuk) John Lang, a writer and painter, who is thirteen years her junior.

1947

Moves with husband to Woodstock, New York.

1949

30 March. She writes to Williams saying she has read her letters in *Paterson*. Their correspondence resumes.

October. Wins the Bryher Award.

November. Four of her poems appear in the *New Directions Number Eleven* anthology.

Fall. Her long poem *In the Asylum* appears in *Botteghe Oscure* (no. 4) and receives special notice in a review of that periodical in the *Times Literary Supplement* (17 February, p. 110).

1950

March. Poem "They Said It Is All Clear Now" is published in *Poetry* magazine (p. 331).

Fall. *Botteghe Oscure* (no. 6) publishes "And I Knew the Body a Sea."

Fall. Leaves husband, goes to New York City with composer William Ames, a neighbor at the Maverick Colony.

1951

Spring. Ames abandons her in New York.

1953

March. "How the Rich Move Softly" is published in *Commentary* (vol. 15, no. 3) under the name of Marcia Nardi. The same month, the *Ladies Home Journal* publishes her poem "More North and South" under the name of Marie Lang.

May. Spends one month at Yaddo in Saratoga Springs, New York.

August. Makes the first of many visits over a period of twelve years to the MacDowell Colony, where she meets and becomes friends with Thornton Wilder and Alec Waugh, both of whom greatly admire her poetry.

September. *Ladies Home Journal* publishes her poem "Tune" under the name of Marie Lang.

1954

July. Her poem "Was It the Honey-Hearted Vowel?" appears in *Poetry* (pp. 212–213).

1955

Summer. "News from Our Town" is published in the *American Scholar* (vol. 24, no. 3).

1956

April. Her poem "I Can Believe" is published in the *Ladies Home Journal*, again under the name of Marie Lang.

April. Begins two-month stay at Yaddo.

Spring. Two of her poems, "Ah, But the Unloved Have Had Power" and "Love I Make It Because I Write It," appear in *Botteghe Oscure* (no. 17).

September. Her book *Poems* is published by Alan Swallow as part of the New Poetry Series.

1956

October. The *Ladies Home Journal* publishes her poem "Meeting You on the Street Today" under the name of Marcia Nardi.

1957

Spring. Wins Guggenheim Fellowship.

1960

March. The opera *Beatrice* (written by Lee Hoiby with libretto by Marcia Nardi) is produced by the Louisville Opera.

1964

October. Poem "Femelle de l'homme" appears in *Atlantic* magazine.

1968

Meets and begins corresponding with Robert Lowell, who tries to find a publisher for her work and offers to write a book jacket blurb for her next book of poems.

1969

6 May. Wins an Ingram Merrill Foundation grant.

1970

13 April. "Senior Citizen" is published in *The Nation*.

1971

16 October. Her poem "Beautiful Women" appears in the *New Yorker*.

1990

13 March. Dies in Watertown, Massachusetts.

Notes on the Text

. . . .

The originals of the letters in this volume are located primarily
in the special collections libraries of three universities: Yale (at
the Beinecke Rare Book and Manuscript Library, hereafter referred to as the Beinecke), the University of Texas at Austin (at
the Harry Ransom Humanities Research Center, referred to as
the HRHRC), and the State University of New York at Buffalo
(in the Poetry/Rare Books Collection, referred to as Buffalo).

Most of the extant letters from Marcia Nardi to William
Carlos Williams (thirty letters and two postcards) are at the
Beinecke Library (catalog designation Za Williams, W.C./Corre-
spondence, uncat.). In addition, there are eight letters and one
postcard from Nardi to Williams at Buffalo. One of the letters
(28, dated 8 December 1942) was omitted from the Baldwin/
Meyers catalog describing the Williams collection at Buffalo;
the rest are cataloged as items F437–F444. One letter from
Nardi to Williams (42) is in the New Directions archives, along
with one from Williams to Laughlin (43) asking Laughlin to
keep both letters in his possession.

Williams's surviving letters to Nardi (also thirty letters and
two postcards) are preserved at the HRHRC, filed under
Williams, W.C., Letters. Along with these, the HRHRC ac-
quired from Nardi two handwritten drafts of letters from her to
Williams (cataloged under Williams, W.C. Recipient), the origi-
nals of which have not been located. One of these is a draft
dated 22 February 1943, included here as letter 37. The other is
Nardi's draft of the long letter used by Williams at the end of
Book II of *Paterson*, which exists also in typescript form (item
E5b in the Baldwin/Meyers catalog) among Williams's notes for

Paterson at Buffalo. I have chosen to use this typescript (as letter 40) because it bears the signs of being a transcription and is, therefore, probably closest to the original letter. The Nardi letter from which Williams used excerpts earlier in Book II of *Paterson* exists only in the form of a typescript (item E5a in the Baldwin/Meyers catalog); it is included here as letter 39. Christopher MacGowan discusses these typescripts and another (E19) in his notes for Book II in the 1992 edition of *Paterson*.

A few of the other letters included in this volume have not been found as "sent" letters. One letter from Nardi to Williams that cannot be found (75) is the long intimate letter which he sent to his lawyer, James Murray, "for safekeeping," according to Paul Mariani. I have transcribed it from a photocopy of the "sent" letter, which I found among Nardi's papers; the original letter (once in the possession of the Williams family) has been misplaced. The incomplete draft of another letter (5) found among Nardi's papers is included here because Williams's next extant letter (6) seems to refer to the information in it and because it may represent the kind of letter from Nardi that Williams chose not to retain. Letter 97 (from James Laughlin to Nardi) was transcribed from a carbon copy of the original, which Nardi did not retain.

Some of the letters included here (7, 11, 15, 18, 48, 50, and 96) have been published previously in Hugh Witemeyer's *William Carlos Williams and James Laughlin*.

Additional letters from Williams to correspondents other than Nardi and Laughlin have been added to this volume in order to clarify or enlarge upon some of the issues raised in the Nardi-Williams exchange. For instance, in a letter to Horace Gregory (41, from Williams's *Selected Letters*), Williams explains some of his reasons for including Nardi's letter at the end of Book II of *Paterson*, as he did again several years later in a letter to Srinivas Rayaprol (72). The previously unpublished letter to Rayaprol is in the Williams collection at the HRHRC, as is a letter from Florence Williams to Nardi (93). Material from *Selected Letters of William Carlos Williams* (copyright © 1957 by William Carlos Williams) is used with the permission of New Directions Publishing Corporation.

Wherever possible, I have inserted copies of the Nardi poems discussed in the letters. In a few cases (following letters 1, 33, and 65) I have reproduced the manuscripts of the poems Nardi sent to Williams. The original of "Life among the Poets" (1.1) is part of Nardi's archive and contains marginal comments by Williams, as does the original of "Alone with a Poem" (65.1), which is with Nardi's letters to Williams at the Beinecke. Nardi's poem "In a Frame . . . " (33.1), with her explanatory note on it, is in the Williams collection at Buffalo (item G131d in the Baldwin/Meyers catalog).

All the Williams and Nardi letters have been reproduced in their entirety, without editorial changes; some of the other letters have been edited to eliminate irrelevant material. Where certain words could not be deciphered (as in the case of some of Nardi's handwritten letters) or when part of a page was missing from the original letter, I have chosen to use my best guess and to paraphrase the missing words (followed by a question mark) within brackets. Each letter is preceded by a headnote, giving its number in the present volume, its form, and the number of its pages, followed in parentheses by a letter indicating the library or collection where the letter is held. I have used the following abbreviations to designate the information in the headnotes:

ALS   autograph letter signed
APCI   autograph postcard initialed
APCS   autograph postcard signed
T   typescript
TD   typed draft
TLS   typed letter signed
TPCS   typed postcard signed

B   Buffalo
MN   Marcia Nardi archive
ND   New Directions archives
SL   Thirlwall, *The Selected Letters*

T   Texas

Y   Yale

All Williams's letters were sent from his home in Rutherford, New Jersey; therefore, the letterhead (or the inside address) on his letters has not been reproduced. Many of Nardi's letters had no date at all or did not give the year; they have been dated by internal evidence, and where the year is missing it has been added in editorial brackets. The positions of the dates, salutations, and closings have been regularized, and typed signatures which follow autograph signatures have been omitted. Errors in punctuation and spelling have been silently corrected except, as in the case of some of Williams's letters, where the misspellings seemed intentional. Both Nardi and Williams were inconsistent in using accent marks on French words; marks have been added where missing for the sake of uniformity.

A footnote in an article (on the "Cress" letters in *Paterson*) by Theodora R. Graham—telling of her interview with Marcia Nardi in Cambridge, Massachusetts, in 1981—helped me to locate Nardi in Boston in September 1987. Dr. Graham generously provided me with copies of Nardi's letters to her (written in 1981 and 1982), in which Nardi writes about her relationship with Williams and his use of her letters in *Paterson*. Portions of these letters to Graham are quoted in the introduction. My own interviews with Marcia Nardi, her friends, her son, and other family members provided important biographical information for this volume; some of this information also appeared in Elizabeth M. O'Neil, "Marcia Nardi: Woman of Letters," *Rossetti to Sexton: Six Woman Poets at Texas* (Austin: Harry Ransom Humanities Research Center at the University of Texas at Austin, 1992), 77–111.

William Eric Williams and Paul H. Williams graciously gave permission to publish the letters of their father (some of them previously unpublished) and one letter from Florence Williams to Nardi. Previously unpublished material by William Carlos Williams and Florence Williams (copyright © 1994 by William Eric Williams and Paul H. Williams) is used with the permission of New Directions Publishing Corporation, agents. James Laughlin kindly searched the New Directions archives to locate two very important letters (42 and 44) and provided me with copies of them; his previously unpublished letters to Marcia Nardi and William Carlos Williams (copyright © 1994 by James Laughlin) are used with his permission.

I want to gratefully acknowledge the cooperation of the following university libraries: the Yale Collection of American Literature, Beinecke Rare Book and Manuscript Library, Yale University, for permission to publish the letters of Marcia Nardi to William Carlos Williams, of William Carlos Williams to James Laughlin (1942, 1949, and 1956) and to Norman Holmes Pearson, and of James Laughlin to William Carlos Williams (1949 and 1956) and the manuscript of Nardi's "Alone with a Poem"; the Poetry/Rare Books Collection, University Libraries, State University of New York at Buffalo, for permission to reprint Nardi's letters to Williams and her poem "In a Frame . . . " and two typescripts from Williams's notes for *Paterson*; and the Harry Ransom Humanities Research Center, the University of Texas at Austin, for permission to publish Williams's letters to Nardi and Srinivas Rayaprol, letters from James Laughlin to Nardi, and a letter from Florence Williams to Nardi.

I have benefited also from the help of the following librarians: Patricia Willis, Daria Ague, and Steven Jones at the Beinecke Library, Cathy Henderson and Cynthia Farar at the Harry Ransom Humanities Research Center, and Robert Bertholf at the Poetry/Rare Books Collection at Buffalo.

Many other people were instrumental in helping me bring these letters together into readable form. The advice, information, and material assistance of Christopher MacGowan (who helped in dating the letters, with annotation suggestions, and by reading the manuscript in its many incarnations) were invaluable to me. I was fortunate also to have the steady encouragement of Dennis Barone, Richard McDougall, and Marjorie Main, all of whom read the manuscript and offered essential comments. I am indebted to Rosemarie Beck for the use of her drawing and oil painting of Marcia Nardi and to Alice Galanka, who brought diligence and enthusiasm to the demanding task of transcribing the letters. I am particularly grateful to Paul Nardi for sharing his memories and insights into his mother's life with me. And finally, I thank John and Matthew O'Neil for their patience and their conviction that the job would get done.

Early Correspondence

1942

· · · · · · · · · · · · · · · · · ·

1943

242 West 12th Street, N.Y.C.

April 9th [1942]

Dear Dr. Williams,

I should now believe that audacious telephone call and visit[1] of mine a week ago last Sunday to have no more reality than a particularly vivid nightmare, if upon moving to a new address and collecting all my personal belongings, I were not faced with the irrefutable circumstantial evidence of my having left those poems with you—which gives my return to the normal every-day problems of living the aspect of something utterly fantastic: as if, for example, upon waking from a dream in which I had lost my shoes, I jumped out of bed and began dressing only to find that my shoes had strangely vanished.

It is with the consternation of a person in such a preposterous fix, that I am communicating with you.

But I was, believe me, in a most desperate situation[2] that Sunday. I didn't know a soul except H.B.[3] (at least no respectable person) outside the world where only standardized conceptions of parenthood prevail; and there I was faced with an investigation of my decidedly irregular private life which would have amounted, for me, to the most ghastly kind of inquisition—especially since my son, by the way, is illegitimate.

Fortunately I was able to stave all that off. I won't burden you with the details (quite a long story). But that boy of mine is now out of that God forsaken psychopathic ward and up in the mountains with a nice simple wholesome family; and my own doors are bolted forever (I hope forever) against all public welfare workers, professional do-gooders, and the like. But thank you more than I can express for having let me come. I otherwise might have been completely robbed of my wits, and thus have been unable to straighten out the situation.

In regard to the poems[4] I left with you: will you be so kind as to return them to me at my new 12th Street address? And without bothering to comment upon them if you should find that embarrassing—for it was the human situation and not the literary one that motivated my phone call and visit. Besides I know myself to be more the woman than the poet; and to concern myself less with the problems of poetry than with those of living; and to have always been prevented by the latter from doing any really concentrated and thoughtful work "in what, under happier circumstances, would have been the field of my choice". And also I think that with rare exceptions (such as Emily Dickinson and Marianne Moore) even a talented woman writer depends, much more than a man, upon her social environment and her personal relationships, to gain definition for her personality and to develop her own minor creative potentialities. André Gide[5] makes this true of most of his women; and the great disillusionment of the male characters in his books is when they find that those qualities of mind and soul which they love in some particular woman have been little more than a couch on which she could lay her thoughts next to theirs. That Gide's male characters are homosexual enables them of course to understand this easily about women, since they thus escape being hoodwinked by desire.

I agree with Gide about all that. I have always sensed it in the work of *most* women poets, and I feel it to be true of myself, so that even if—with more leisure and more reading and fewer educational lacks and more companionship with people in the world of art and literature—I'd been able to write better verse than I've done, it might have been just a better imitation of good poetry rather than good poetry in its own right. It seems that way very much to me just now when I am far more unhappy about my broken friendship with Harvey than I could possibly be about the most unfavorable criticism of my verses.

But my feeling so, at least relieves you of any embarrassment at having those poems on your hands, and not quite knowing what to do about them if you find them pretty bad. It *should*, anyway. I'd like them back, however, since I have no copies of most of them; and want to thank you again for having let me turn to you as a "reference" in case I needed it. I cannot thank you enough for your kindness in that.

Sincerely yours,
Marcia Nardi

1. Nardi had visited Williams at his office in his home at 9 Ridge Road, Rutherford, New Jersey, on Palm Sunday, 29 March 1942.

2. Nardi's fifteen-year-old son had been taken to Bellevue Hospital for a psychiatric evaluation as a result of an almost comical train of events. When neighbors called the police, alarmed by a shouting match between Nardi and her son, she told them that the boy was a chronic truant and that school officials had threatened to have him evaluated by a psychiatrist if the truancy did not stop. After her son was taken to Bellevue, Nardi regretted her action and tried unsuccessfully to have him released. It was at this time that she approached Williams and asked for his help; however, the boy was released after the required period of observation without the need of further action on Nardi's (or Williams's) part.

3. Harvey Breit (1909–1968), a neighbor of Nardi and friend of Williams; author, columnist, and assistant editor (from 1948 to 1957) of the *New York Times Book Review*.

4. The following are photocopies of the originals of two of the poems: (1.1) "Life among the Poets," with marginal notations by WCW, and (1.2) "To Bernard in *The Counterfeiters*." Neither poem was ever published (MN archive).

5. André Gide (1869–1951), French author and winner of the 1947 Nobel prize for literature.

LIFE AMONG THE POETS

I

Closing your eyes from something
Known once in dream
And lost,
Scornful of pity
Fostering hate
Yet fearful of loneliness —
At fame you snatched
To make desirable and rare
(Beneath a great man's touch)
What otherwise one pityingly might
You turned to (only) in despair.

Certain women gain thereby
Whose hair,
Unmixed with yours, had been
Not bright enough
For myth or history;
But you —
Safe now from pity,
Free now to open
Your eyes again.

TO BERNARD IN THE COUNTERFEITERS

"...if anyone were to ask me today what
virtue I consider finest, I should answer
without hesitation honesty. Oh Laura, I should
like all my life long at the very smallest shock
tp ring true with a pure authentic sound."

But honesty is what one knows

And what one sees

And to confirm or to dispute

The beauty of an invisible rose

Bright in another's garden

Can hardly be more false

Than a false humility

Before apparent blindness, *suspicious*

And to what avail

Denial?

The most you can achieve

Is a futile self-honesty, *others*

With the hope that people's paintings

Of the unwronged face one bravely faces

In that private looking-glass

Will differ no more greatly

From both the original and each other

Than a Greco from a Renoir,

And the courage of a madman

To keep the mirror dusted

And the ceiling lights still on

(continued)

If one's so luckless as to meet

~~Only those persons bent on a~~
Only those persons who bent on a ~~c~~raftsman's accuracy

Put tracing paper' on the glass

And thus obliterate your image.

In love, Bernard,

Two with unseeing eyes can see

And with seeing eyes n~~o~~t see

The same phantom or reality,

In darkness or in light

Jointly creating a world and a truth ,

Which is no meeting of two naked souls

But a sweet unlonely partnership in flight

From the terror of sincerity .

April 10, 1942

My dear Marcia Nardi:

Curiously enough, since you ask nothing of me concerning them, these poems have in them definitely some of the best writing by a woman (or by anyone else) I have seen in years. They also have plenty of bad writing in them, unfinished, awkward writing. I do not want to give them up but since you demand them I am returning them. I have not had time to go over them as I should like to but I am not letting go of them completely. There's something here that is not going to be lost if sufficient attention is given to develop and refine it.

What I'd like to see you do is to copy them all out clean and let me have a copy of *all* of them. Don't make a selection but add any new poems if you want to. Just let me keep the poems and work on them from time to time. I'll do precisely what I please with them and return them to you. If you care to accept my criticisms that will be your responsibility. A valuable book may come of them in the end.

I'm glad you've been able to solve your personal problems. It has been a privilege to know you.

Sincerely yours
W. C. Williams

. . . .

3. ALS-3 (Y)

242 West 12th St., N.Y.C.
Sunday [April 1942]

Dear Dr. Williams,

Your kind offer in regard to the criticism—yes, I welcome it and most eagerly.

You know how it is sometimes with that sort of encouragement—how it unshackles all one's deadlocked self-confidence; and so ever since I received your note, all my neglected unfinished poems of the past few months have suddenly come to life for me again—so much so that I can hardly wait to get at them, with the feeling that they are much better than any of my others, and yet spoiled no doubt by that same awkward writing which is the result of my having no technical mastery at the fingertips of my untrained sense of poetry.

But I am not well at the moment, and therefore lack the physical energy to add a lot else I'd like to say about the great value your criticism will have for me. It's nothing for medicine to cure. Just one of those unfortunate temperaments which cause any and every emotional upset to take itself out most horribly on one's body.

I have just been glancing at a copy of Poetry magazine and trying to read a poem by Saint John Perse[1] in it; and although I couldn't, being too tired, I noticed some lines: "Dit l'Etranger parmi les sables, 'toute chose au monde m'est nouvelle'. Et la naissance de son chant ne lui est pas moins 'étrangère'." And the source of mine—Heaven knows what it is, because my family is the worst kind of white trash—you have no idea—some of its members almost imbecilic (and perhaps one of the reasons for my having been born with a sick nervous system); and most of the people I've had to associate with during my adult life have been either on the mental level of grocery clerks or else of the gutter. Which is probably one of the reasons why I became so drawn toward Tristan Corbière three years ago, and had to teach myself French in order to read him—because he was not of the "cenacles" and "pas de métier".[2]

I am going to type all my poems during the next week or so (I have a routine job and not much time to myself) and will send them to you. And in the meantime please know how much I appreciate your doing that for me.

Most sincerely,
Marcia Nardi

Since I told you a little about all that with Harvey, I ought to mention that I received a post-card from him. Nothing at all intimate. But at least friendly, and he's to come to see me when he "feels right" and "has the leisure". That may not be for a long time—especially since his economic problems as well as his emotional ones are so difficult. But something that belongs to all really civilized human relationships has been saved by that card—which is well, H. being too fine a person for anything else.

<hr />

1. St. John Perse, "Exil," *Poetry* (March 1942): 295: "Says the Stranger on the sands, 'the whole world is new to me,' And the birth of his song is no less alien to him."

2. "Not of the 'cenacles'": not part of the "in" literary circles; "'pas de métier'": had no professional background.

. . . .

4. TLS-3 with ALS-2 (Y)

242 West 12th Street,
New York City
Sunday, April 26th [1942]

Dear Dr. Williams,

I have had all kinds of interruptions in getting even these poems to you (under separate cover—and not *all* included). Continued poor health, some economic difficulties, and much worse than those problems and aggravating them, an inability to throw off the crushing effect upon me of my broken friendship, such as it was, with Harvey. Many things have happened there in regard to him during the past ten days (not outwardly, but within myself) which have just about broken me to bits, so that I have been quite unable to do any work at all on all those unfinished poems which I am so anxious to complete.

But I have done one new poem (the one that begins "how difficult the erection of even")[1] which I am including with the copies of those you already had. I have kept out two which do not really represent at all the kind of thing I'd like to do with poetry, but added a few others which I did not give you the first time, and shall send all those incompleted ones later as soon as I'm in a state of mind to work out the few missing and concluding lines which is about all most of them require.

I told you that I wrote a great [deal] of poetry when I was very young—from the time I was 16 to shortly after my son was born,[2] and then a long period of no writing at all except the vilest kind of hack stuff, until recently. I mention that again because I notice something very interesting in comparing that early work (most of it completely discarded) with these poems which are mostly (except two) of the past couple of years. It's this: I had just started to develop in the very last poems I did then long ago, almost the same way of writing which I now feel to be particularly my own. And yet when I first went back to poetry again (that is, about three years ago) I had to spend almost a year evolving all over again the very fashion of writing with which I'd left off, so that during the first year of my recent return to poetry, my work was almost as bad as that I'd written at 17 and 18, and had to undergo the very same processes of experimentation and development all over again before eventually growing into a continuity with the point where I'd previously stopped.

None of this was conscious. I have only lately realized it—which makes me regret so much all those wasted years, especially since my hours of physical well-being and really fresh energies become increasingly few.

I have sent you back the very same copy (without retyping it) of "life among the poets," because I don't know if your suggested changes are complete and so that you can see those you already made.[3] Those changes which you pencilled in there make so much difference. They indeed make that poem so much better! But one thing disturbs me, or, rather, raises a problem. Is it quite legitimate and fair of me to let stand as entirely my own those poems which your criticism improves as much as it has already done in the case of that one poem? It's right enough for the sake of the poems themselves. But is it otherwise, and will you please tell me if it is?

And now I wish to ask you something of a more practical nature. Do you think it's possible for me to get any of these poems into Poetry Magazine and other literary publications? If so—I could indeed use whatever few dollars I might get that way. I have to pay ten dollars a week for my son's board, and while my salary from my job is supposed to be $20 a week, I actually earn much less than that (some weeks only about $15) because I don't get paid on legal holidays and if ever I am out ill (which happens not infrequently) that also is deducted from my salary. And apart from that I should like now, for the first time, to get some of my poems published for the sake of that in itself. When Harvey made that offer in regard to Poetry in the summer, I was utterly indifferent to it for reasons that I can't go into here except to say that the outward seeming mattered very little to me then and never has meant much to me in any aspect of my life. But I feel now that it's important (the way of the world makes it so) when the inner props fail, to have the outward ones to hold on to no matter how false they may be. I say that, I'm afraid, with some bitterness which is a feeling I do [not] at all approve of. But you know how all that is. And there is so much that I have really wanted to do— secretly—with that dead-locked kind of self-confidence I mentioned before, but didn't and couldn't not so much because of my educational lacks nor my continued money problems (whatever the seriousness of those obstacles) but mostly because it's so hard (the psychological difficulty, I mean) to make words hold their own against all those utilitarian occupations of the world unless one's guilty feeling at being [a] slacker there (as with a man not in uniform during wartime) is mitigated somewhat by knowing other people whose own values condone one's own.

Even in prose, if I should attempt anything there (and I have considered it during the past few months, with definite ideas in mind) I would have to concern myself almost entirely with ideas—and not even with current ideas that lend themselves so easily to journalistic writing, because even in regard to world affairs, I have little interest in politics and economics in themselves, but only in their relationship to much that goes beyond them. And Harvey is the only person I've ever known in any personal way whose own attitudes and sensibilities did not leave me with that awfully crazy feeling of talking to myself which I tried to express in that poem about "honesty".[4]

I do hope it isn't too presumptuous of me to burden you with all this about my personal life just because of your great kindness in offering to criticize the poems. But it's so hard to separate any one phase of one's life from all the others.

Thank you again for what you have offered about the poems. And will you let me know when you can about those two matters of possibly getting some into the magazines, and of whether it's completely honest for me to represent as mine whatever poems are improved by those changes and suggestions which you make?

Sincerely,
Marcia Nardi

. . . .

Sunday—April 27th [1942]   later
Dear Dr. Williams—

In that new poem I sent with the others ("how difficult the erection of even") I made a mistake in copying a much erased and revised pencil first draft.

The first word of the line containing "bird-circuit" should be "simple," not "tricky". Will you please change it, because "simple" is most necessary to go with the whole idea of ignorance in that first part of the poem, and "tricky" therefore doesn't do except for the short "i" sound which I wanted there.

Maybe I'm making a lot of fuss about a bad poem. But if so, then I have no critical sense in regard to my own work, and for me to know *that* (should it be true) has its own importance.

Sincerely,
Marcia Nardi

1. See 4.1. Published as "Poem" in *New Directions Number Seven*, 417–418; revised and retitled "But Here in One's Self" by Marcia Nardi for inclusion in her collected poems.

2. Paul Nardi was born on 23 October 1926.

3. See 1.1. Nardi later retitled this poem "Portrait" for inclusion in her unpublished collected poems; she retained just two of Williams's suggested changes.

4. "To Bernard in *The Counterfeiters*" (see 1.2).

POEM

How difficult the erection of even
That fence of a hair's breadth
Between
Body and soul of another,
Whose presence crams
Ten worlds:
Like trying to keep entirely to the right
Or to the left, jostled,
On a city pavement;
Or on a country lane,
When letting a car pass,
Having
One foot upon grass
And another on gravel.
How easy the innocent saunter there
From adjoining room to room,
The simple bird-circuit
Of star and tree,
The sure amphibian stride
From the eye's deep to the causeway
Of coffee offered and sipped—
With the highroad
Of what's unoffered or unwanted
Still a component.

But here within self—
Ah the terror of that leap
From where the estranged and disemboweled
    ache
Of the disciplined heart
Draws neatly as a magnet
The wrist-bone's secret pulse
And the blood's knee-reflex,

To where—
Across the derangement of a sea-wide lake—
The verbal journey's wind-up trains,
And the trained seal's handshake
Of life going on as usual,
Are marooned.

. . . .

5. TD-4 (MN Archive)

[May ? 1942]

Dear Dr. Williams,[1]

My communications regarding those poems have all contained so many uninvited references to my private life that you
may well regret your kind offer about the criticism. After all, it's
one thing to take an objective interest in a stranger's literary efforts and quite another to have that person burden one's consciousness with all her personal woes.

I'm aware of all that as I start this letter. But my problems
with poetry have been so intermingled with my personal problems (the latter having so often taken me away from the former)
and I have spent the past month so unable to cope with the isolation that surrounds my life in its intellectual and spiritual aspects, that I feel at the moment as if I'll go mad unless I did [sic]
some talking about it to someone who would at least understand it, however helpless in altering the situation.

Do you mind? And how I hope you don't, because I've continued to suffer horribly over my broken friendship with Harvey.

After I received that post-card in which he said that sooner or
later he'd be around to see me, I thought and hoped that I might
run into him on the street, and that that accidental meeting
would re-establish for me perhaps some sort of personal relationship with him, people's physical presences being more effec-
tive there than written words. It seemed not unlikely, since we
live in the same neighborhood within a few blocks of each other,
and so you can well imagine my feelings when I did run into him
one warm sunny morning only to have him deliberately avoid

noticing me and then cross over to the other side of the street to evade an actual meeting. It's barely possible of course that he really didn't see me. And yet all the indications were that he did, and my heart-sick feeling at having it seem that way so strongly became mingled with indignation as the day wore on. So I wrote him a long angry letter—not at all nice and frightfully indelicate, I'm afraid, in its outrightness about many things that people don't come out with generally. And yet everything I said and pointed out was true, if the appearances of much that had happened weren't deceptive; and if they concealed certain matters I wasn't aware of, then Harvey certainly might have set me right in my blindness—especially about that episode on the street. But he didn't. He ignored the letter—which amounted either to confirming what I suspected, or else (and even worse) of not thinking that it mattered what I thought or felt.

If at that time and in that wretched state of mind, I'd had money enough for any wholesome distractions it wouldn't have been so bad—though even with money I mightn't have had the will for them. Anyway here I was locked up in my room with no place to go and no one to see, and quite unable to do any writing because Harvey's attitude toward me began to have an undermining effect upon that phase of my life too—for it seemed to me that if he had had any respect for the genuineness of my literary interests, all his former friendliness would have survived, in spite of everything else. So just about perishing from ennui and with [the] confines of my small room unbearable, I succumbed almost inevitably to the invitation of two very ordinary men whom I know to go out drinking with them, at several bars about town. And all that drinking, not for just one night but for several, demoralized me frightfully, and made me feel like some God forsaken tramp, so that in my disgust with myself and with my drinking companions, I was seized with the unconquerable desire to see Harvey—thinking and knowing that if I did, and if only for the fewest minutes, all the vanished punctuation marks gone out of my disorganized life would spring back into place.

Anyway I wrote to him then again. Quite a nice letter, saying just how things were with me, and how I was sure that everything so messy and disordered would straighten itself out for me if I could see him for a short while.

And that letter too he ignored. And I don't know what to think. Except that the wrong must be in *me*. Though I don't know where.

After all, I possess few of the heart's illusions. I can rarely survey the tragic drama of frustrated emotions—even my own—without a strong sense of irony and satire, as my poems indicate; and I have found myself very much exasperated at times by Rilke's idealization of women and of woman's love, as if there really were such a thing as "A woman's love" in any absolute kind of way, and as if the potential bitch and slut in every woman biologically weren't just as strong as the stallion in most men. And yet that over-romantic champion of my sex got at the very core of so much that's narrow in even the broadest humanity when he said that there can be no really mature and civilized relationship between men and women until man learns to love and desire not only as a male and an opposite but also as a friend and neighbor.

I feel the truth of that so strongly just now and so unhappily. Certainly I loved Harvey and very much—which ordinarily might have made for an awkward situation. But there is love and love and love, and the inner pattern for every person who lives by the intangibles is so unique, that there can't be any general rules for what one needs and wants and demands even in those emotions for which our vocabulary has only one word, though they differ so greatly in their meaning for each individual. In my own case, it happens that I am quite indifferent to the actual form of my relationship with anyone I care for a great deal. The more I like a person the less I need or want from that person, and my feelings about Harvey were such that all I cared about really was to see him occasionally and in any fashion that he himself determined. And that presented no great complications or obstacles for him. His own life is a difficult one, and he probably has his own private inner sicknesses as much of a torment to him as my own are to me. And yet living so very close by and having already started a sort of friendship with me and knowing so well how I know not another soul with whom I have any common interests, surely during those two months which have now elapsed since the night of that ill-fated intimacy, he could have found time to drop in here for some few occasional hours or half hours. And had he done so what a great difference it would have made to me! I can't find words for that great difference, for in not doing so, he thrust a million daggers into the basic human being in me—which is something a lot worse than merely hurting my emotional self as a woman.

I did not even want Harvey's love. I should not have wished it could I have had it. The things that go with love, its particular offerings, and especially its blind sympathies and unsound understandings—these were just what I wanted least, needed least, and had and have no place for in my own life of which the greatest needs were and are on the side of friendship. And not only that. But that bridge between the senses and the affections which exists for most people has been pretty much broken down for me, so that one of my greatest problems is the terrifying gap that so often exists for me between my animal and spiritual selves. And also I feel my life to be pretty much over and done with, and much too broken and sick both physically and otherwise to shackle itself to any other person's healthier existence, so that if I had any large sum of money, there's nothing I'd like better than to go off to the country somewhere and spend a year or two working on poetry, and then call it a day.

And Harvey was aware of all that. I did not make it out to be otherwise, and so there can be only one reason for the great difference in his attitude toward me "before and afterwards"—the reason that even for the nicest and finest men, a woman has very little existence beyond her purely biological identity, except perhaps in theory and objectively and at a distance, all of which means very little when it comes to flesh and blood living.

I cannot tell you how heart-sick I am at having had to learn that all over again from a person like Harvey, and to just what extent that sort of thing, even more than the obstacles of my money problems and of my difficult motherhood, have interfered with my getting anywhere with writing. No one is quite so self-sufficient as to escape becoming to some extent what one is believed to be, or as to be able to become completely what one is given no credit for, so that the innocent man accused of murder and believed guilty by the whole world, might just as well be guilty. Even if he should succeed in making a get-a-way, the knowledge of his own innocence would in no way save him from developing the same psychoses (in his relationship to the world) as an actually guilty man under the same circumstances. And thus it is (the psychological processes being much the same in both instances) that woman does not develop fully as a complete human being (and it's why her creative work has so little scope) because only one phase of her nature is given soil in which to grow or die.

I'm talking only about private living in what I have just said, and not about literary relationships which people do not live by in the deepest sense of what living means. And my concern with the former so greatly overshadows my interest in the latter that not infrequently in lonely jaunts about New York, when talking to some stranger on a park bench or at a bar, I have put myself forth as a housemaid or a Woolworth salesgirl or something of that sort, in order to safeguard my contacts with what was most basic between people.

Something much less simple and much more complex in what's basic was involved in my feelings about Harvey of course. And yet that particular level of consciousness on which he existed for me most fully was indeed not the natural habitat of those particular emotions or emotional demands in fear of which he allegedly stopped seeing me; and even fled from seeing me that day on the street.

Am I all wrong in everything I say here, Dr. Williams? It is to ask you that, to have your point of view, as much as for the talking, that I write you all this. Everyone almost inevitably recreates the external situation to some extent and I cannot have escaped doing so—no not entirely, I know—in regard to all that with Harvey, and his own story colored by his own private inner world could most likely be very different from mine. But it's not for nothing that I have managed to survive, however unhappily, the worst kind of hardships during this past year, whereas ever since I received that note from Harvey at the time of all that difficulty with my son, the whole structure of my life in all its aspects—and fatally so in practical ways—has caved in. In a way, my failure with him has become for me a symbol of my failure with that whole distant world in which he moves and in regard to which I have always been so much of an outsider and interloper. And I am pretty much of a barbarian there, I know. At least according to the standards for women which prevail among cultured and cultivated people. And yet I cannot find any foothold for myself in any other world either, and the desolating sense of belonging nowhere, neither to the literary circles, nor to the menage, nor to the women's clubs, nor to the brothel, sweeps all solid ground from under my feet as I write this. It is only the purely abstract world of ideas, that ever seems to really reconcile me to myself, only when I [am] writing or reading that my activities seem to proceed from my whole personality. Occasionally (though rarely) my responses to another person similarly put an end to that destructive sense [of] duality from which I find it so hard to escape in any outward way. Harvey was for me such a person, and that alone was enough to leave me indifferent to [the] nature of my relationship with him so long as I could see him occasionally. I had spent many months waiting for the circumstances of his life to make that possible. Directly after I met him (and he liked me then on those three first occasions when I saw him) he went to Yaddo,[2] so that it was not possible in the summer. When he returned (at least so he wrote me) he was completely submerged in all kinds of difficulties, with Clara,[3] and . . . [Letter ends here, final page or pages missing.]

1. This incomplete letter draft was found among Nardi's papers. No corresponding "sent" letter has been found. Nardi's note at the top of this letter reads "Part of the letter to W.C.W. (re-written afterwards) March (?) 1942." The actual date probably was early May (see reference in letter 7 to a letter written to WCW in early May).

2. Yaddo is an artists' colony in Saratoga Springs, New York.

3. Clara was Harvey Breit's first wife.

May 13, 1942

My dear Marcia Nardi:

Please forgive my slowness in answering your last letter, I could not even get to read it until this morning, one pressing duty dovetailed into another all day yesterday—and in the end I lost a baby I was most anxious to save.

Your letters show you to have one of the best minds I have ever encountered—I say nothing of its reach which I have had no opportunity to measure but its truth and strength. Your words as I read them have a vigor and a cleanliness to them which constitute for me real beauty. I sincerely and deeply admire you.

Writing should be your outlet. This may be impossible at the moment, I don't know. It should nevertheless be your constant aim. It is probably the one thing that will give you confidence and relief. Whether or not you can ever bring over into writing the truth that is in your letters and in your thoughts is purely a matter of the technical side. You have the mind.

In the technical side of writing I may be of some assistance to you and you may believe me I'll always be ready to be of assistance if I can. Your feelings relative to the present object of your misery I find to be altogether correct, more than that, I find them to be distinguished and altogether amazing for one—for anyone.

Believe me,
Your friend
W. C. Williams

. . . .

June 9, 1942

Dear Jim:[1]

Just got your letter—speaking of tips, while this one is hot— and don't think I'm specializing in women—for the past month or two I've been pondering over some poems by a woman that have got under my guard. I think they are as close to honest work as I've seen in a decade and that's not all.

This ain't no ingenue and she ain't dumb. But she's open and mind and body have formed something distinguished and low (and high). I wish I could do something for her, an unknown and unwanted. She has enough for one of your Poet of the Month series. I ain't foolin', she'd make a hit. Her name's Marcia Nardi. Don't write to her as I have all her stuff here going over it carefully.

She's pint size, bedraggled to the point of a Salvation Army reject but she's got the guts of a Kelly. I'm afraid the damned thing will die if we don't pick her up. Take my word for it she's a piece of good steel.

More on other subjects later but I wanted to keep this single.

Bill

1. James Laughlin (1914–), founder of New Directions, Williams's publisher.

. . . .

8. ALS-2 (Y)

242 West 12th St. NYC.
Friday, June 12th [1942]

Dear Dr. Williams,

I was in the very midst of trying to write to you[1] when your special delivery letter[2] came. I had begun three different letters, but each time couldn't complete even the first sentence, because that unhappy experience which I wrote you about early in May, ended up by completely paralyzing me inwardly. These spiritual and intellectual comas which sometimes follow acute mental anguish—and all the waste of them!—It is through one of those living deaths that I have lived during this past month; and I am faced now with the difficult task of trying to collect and piece together all the fragments of my scattered personal identity.

I therefore cannot discuss the matter of my poems at the moment—at least, not with pen and paper. But perhaps I could if I saw you.

All that time in May, the one thing I wished especially much (and I think it might have saved me from a great deal that has happened since) was to see you again. But I dared not ask it.

I ask it now, because I feel that it would enable me to throw off that deadly inertia of mind and soul—to which I am particularly susceptible and invariably succumb when things go wrong with me in the way of personal relationships.

With only two mail deliveries on Saturday and the last at noon, I don't know whether this will reach you tomorrow or Monday.

But I hope to hear from you by Tuesday or Wednesday about my possibly seeing you—whether I may, and where and when and how soon.

Sincerely

Marcia Nardi

1. Williams at one time considered using this letter in *Paterson*. An early draft of the poem includes a sheet with the word "SHE:" followed by a transcription of this letter (without an address or salutation). The sheet is identified as item E17(u) in Baldwin and Meyers, *The Manuscripts and Letters*.

2. The letter MN refers to here is missing.

. . . .

9. TLS-1 (T)

June 14, 1942

Dear Marcia Nardi:

Won't you have supper with me Tuesday at 6:30 in the city? I'll meet you at the corner of 40th St. and 6th Ave., there's a good restaurant there on the second floor, if I remember rightly though I cannot remember its name. I'll hang around until 7 o'clock and then go up and take a table. Come when you can—or if you prefer, drop me a card on receipt of this telling me what you can do. I realize your hours may make it impossible for you to get away at the time mentioned.

Sincerely yours

W. C. Williams

June 17, 1942

Dear Marcia Nardi:

The enclosed have been marked up as I told you, if you care to accept my suggestions for changes make copies and return me the poems. I have sent the others to Laughlin telling him at the same time that you have a few others to show him—which I will forward later.

Don't, please, accept my changes unless you believe they clarify the sense or aid the pattern in one way or another. You may not at all agree with me, for instance, that the beginning of the poem "How difficult the erection   etc." shd [*sic*] be changed at all. If so you are probably right. This is one of the best of the poems.[1]

Try to make the sense of the one beginning "Like formless shore-robbed waters etc" crystal clear: just the first stanza needs touching, the rest, I believe, should remain as it stands.[2]

It was a pleasure to talk with you last evening. I'll report progress or the lack of it later.

> Sincerely
>
> W. C. Williams

1. Nardi did not retain the copy of this poem (see 4.1) with Williams's comments on it.

2. This poem has not been found.

. . . .

June 17, 1942

Dear Jim:

She ain't Auden or Eliot, hasn't any of the smell of such swine—don't forget I live near Secaucus and know what I'm talking about—but don't reject her hastily, especially for that reason. She has something else. May I add that it would give me the greatest pleasure if you could find room for a good selection of the enclosed verses in the next *New Directions*. I am sending what I take to be a fair sample of her work, there is more of it but not much more.

She asked me not to plead for her, wants the verses to speak for themselves. I told her she needed a push, that her work did not appeal at first glance since its virtue was not on the surface of it—no matter how good a critic might pick it up. The form is nil but there are lines and passages that are worth all the facile metrical arrangements ever invented and these do actually give the verse a form of its own.

She speaks the language, speaks it to a purpose and says more than enough that is worth hearing. The effect is poetry.

That's as strong as I can put it. I wish you'd take my word for it that this is authentic stuff besides which it is a seed that needs planting. Her work would greatly benefit from publication now. Please let me know what you can and will do, at an early opportunity. I'm not personally involved, don't make that mistake. But if the publication of such work as this woman offers isn't the primary purpose of an annual such as *New Directions* then I don't know what it's [*sic*] purpose can be.

I'm having a hell of a time with the Anaïs Nin thing.[1] I've rewritten it four times and am going into the fifth. It requires as much discretion as insight. At first I was inclined to overpraise. Now I'm at the point where criticism must be somewhat reined in. I hope to hit the proper level of sane judgement somewhere between these two positions shortly. . . .

[Williams writes of other matters unconnected with Marcia Nardi, then adds this postscript:]

6/17/42

I've just read these over again, there are some swell line[s]—which (with your pardon) I've marked. I'm so worried that you may not agree with me as to the excellence of these poems. One is an Emily Dickinson and skip that. All I ask is that you read them *all*.

W.

If you're going to turn her down please address *me*. If you want her she is: Marcia Nardi, 242 West 12th St., New York, N.Y.

1. "Men . . . Have no Tenderness," WCW's review of Anaïs Nin's *Winter of Artifice, New Directions Number Seven*, 429–436.

. . . .

12. ALS-2 (B)

Saturday, June 20th [1942]

Dear Dr. Williams,

Although the poems with your note arrived on Thursday, I did not get them until late yesterday, because I had been away from my room on 12th Street for a couple of days and overnight.

That you have sent all the others to Laughlin alarms me somewhat, because a few of those (at least it seems so to me) are not so good, whereas four of the ones which I have back with your suggested changes are, I feel, more representative of my writing at its best; and I'm so afraid that if Laughlin sees any of my work at its worst, he might have his mind closed against whatever you forward to him later. I'm therefore most anxious for you to get these others to him as soon as possible (before he completely makes up his mind)—and with the addition of three more poems which I'm finally able to complete now, stimulated by the prospect of appearing in New Directions. But it will take me this entire week-end (since I have other matters that also require my attention) to carefully consider your suggested changes, and to add the other three poems.

This means I can't send them to you until tomorrow night, so that you won't receive them until Monday; and I do hope that that is soon enough and that Laughlin won't in the meantime have said no. And if that unfortunate thing should happen, will you send him what you receive from me on Monday and ask him to re-consider my work on the basis of those?

It is very kind of you to say that you enjoyed talking with me on Tuesday. But I'm afraid that actually my end of the talk amounted to little more than a rambling inconsequential chatter. This is because conversation brings me up on the surface of my consciousness, whereas it's only from way down in its depths (accessible more easily when one is alone and silent) that I can strike off words most effectively. Moreover, that amazing balance which exists between your private life and your life as a writer, and the calm, sane, well-adjusted and wholesome person that you are, made me particularly self-conscious in regard to my own neurotic, maladjusted, and altogether sickly soul.

But this is chiefly about the poems—and primarily to say that I'll have them back to you on Monday together with three others which you have not seen.

Sincerely,
Marcia Nardi

P.S. For the next 10 days, my address will be 74 Charles Street, (care of Bauer). The apartment belongs to a man now in the army; but the rent is paid until July, and it's pleasanter than my room. Mail sent to 12th Street will still reach me; but I'll get it more promptly at 74 Charles.

. . . .

13. TLS-2 (Y)

74 Charles Street
(care of Bauer)
New York City
[late June 1942]

The typewriter ribbon isn't working properly—so please overlook this messy letter.

Dear Dr. Williams,

I couldn't send these before today because my personal problems continue to break in on all my other plans.

In the poem "Florence" [1] I liked your suggestion that I change the position of one line, and made that revision.

I am sending back only one of the two poems under the title formerly "Life Among the Poets" (and no title at all now) [2] because I don't like the second one [3] much. And in this one, "closing your eyes . . ." I welcomed the changes you pencilled in except that I felt the need to keep the final thought in the form of a question.

The poem beginning "here now your life" has been changed a bit too—mostly as you marked it, with one other revision of my own.[4]

But I'm not sending back either "Relief Bureau" (the one in which the "flown" seemed without meaning to you)[5] or the one about "honesty" under the quotation from the Counterfeiters, because I need to spend more time than I have right now with the thoughts and ideas they express before improving the poems technically.

Concerning that poem which begins "how difficult the erection of even . . .", I have left it almost exactly as it was. In the first part I made two slight changes which you suggested and which make that part much better, and also added two lines there not previously in the poem. But I felt that the second and third parts were right (I mean for me, in what I wished to express) as they were. I couldn't tell whether you suggested changing "knee reflex" to "knee jerk" for reasons of meter or meaning, and I wish so much in regard to this particular poem that I'd had it with me the night we had dinner together so as to discuss it with you personally. The idea of it has to do with the conflict between what we seem and what we are, and with how other people (even a person we love) belongs pretty much to the external world of appearances which is always at such variance with the world of our private inner realities.

I finished two of the other three poems I wanted to include, but the endings please me so little that I can't let them stand as they are. So I have added instead some other verses, which (though I didn't send them to you previously) were written a couple of years ago. I'm not sure about them—whether they are any good or not. So will you use your judgment about whether or not to send these to New Directions?

My continued problems with my son are of such a nature that I don't know at the moment what my address will be after July 1st. If he stays in town for the summer I will need two rooms, whereas one small one will do of course if he goes to the country. But in the meantime it's 74 Charles, with my mail sent to

12th [Street] still being called for—and I'll let you know of a change as soon as I myself know what that will be.

Sincerely,

Marcia Nardi

1. See 13.1.

2. See "Life among the Poets" (1.1). Later, Nardi retitled this poem "Portrait."

3. See photocopy of original (13.2). This poem, entitled "Life among the Poets—2," has a marginal note reading "For Allen Tate," which Nardi subsequently crossed out.

4. Retitled "Near Every Bed Where Two Selves Meet," in Marcia Nardi, *Poems* (Denver: Allan Swallow, 1956), 39.

5. This poem cannot be found under this title.

. . . .

13.1. MN Poem (MN Archive)

FLORENCE

Oh always huddled in a bun
Since Donnie cooled—
Her golden hair—
And slinking under a scarf or hat
That flung once laughing down her back
Happy as children coasting,
Since Edgar said:
The fool! And planning how
I'd father the brat!

But what will become of the kid?
Was all the neighbors said,
While the welfare workers echoed
It's the child we must think of, of course—
With no one asking,
What will become of her golden hair?
Ah, no one asking—not even one—
What will become of that?

II

Quite disillusioned as to certain qualities
 The books beneath her arm
Deceived him into thinking
Were also in her head,   (mind)

His pride
(Because he took her to a resturant
 where people went who knew him
 who on the following day
 would ask
 who was she ?)
Suffered ~~immensely.~~   immeasurable
 ?

And so perhaps to justify
Their being seen together
He seduced her.

At any rate,
More skilled in just such matters
He never would have had to say
I love you;
Nor when she clung
To fabricate "another woman",
And conscience-stricken hasten home
To finish ~~[for that new Revue~~
~~[All politics the Nation-]~~)
An over-due translation
Of something from ~~Villon,~~ Rimbaud
His recent essay, by the way,
On whom
Had long since cast upon his private life
Sufficient implication
To make as bird-song on Broadway
Her eager indignation.

40 Perry Street, New York City
July 10th, 1942

Dear Dr. Williams,

I received that card from Laughlin[1] which you sent to my former 12th Street address. Ordinarily I might be greatly distressed at his thinking so little of my work, and possibly would not want him to publish any of it when he feels that way about the poems. But I am so much at the mercy of my great need to get into print and to assert myself publicly as a poet of whatever merit, that under the circumstances I am very much relieved and glad to know that at least six of the poems will appear in New Directions. And maybe other people will have a better opinion of them than the editor himself.

But will he—how do those things go?—let me know which ones he is using. I naturally am curious as to which he liked best (or least), and also I may try to get the others published elsewhere (maybe send them to Poetry).

I have taken it for granted that you received those poems which I sent back to you a couple of weeks ago, but because I had hoped and thought the New Directions editor would like three of those particular ones much better than his card indicates, I am wondering if they did reach you.

That I was able to fix up only those which required hardly any work and had to let those two longer and more difficult ones go, and that I have done no new writing in such a long time, may seem to indicate that your interest in my work, your encouraging letters, and all your help and kindness, have been lost on me—that I have not been cooperative enough and sufficiently responsive. But no, it is not that (in case it should seem so). Not at all that.

It's merely that what I wrote you in my very first letter (about being too much distracted by the problems of living to have much time for those of poetry) continues to be true. And also I have been unable to throw off, even though so much time has elapsed, that sense of failure and defeat in my personal life which took hold of me as a result of that experience with Harvey. Then too this is the first time in weeks (I've been here at this address only a few days) that I had a room of my own and any chance to be entirely with my own thoughts. When my son came back to town, I let him have my room on 12th Street through lack of money for larger living quarters, so that I myself had to stay with friends who, as active Trotskyists and Party workers, and with all the revolutionary worker's scorn for the intellectual (with even more scorn for the intellectual sympathizer than for anyone else) continually attacked me and just about made my life miserable. In a friendly, well meaning way, of course, but nevertheless charging the whole atmosphere of the apartment with so much antagonism between their point of view and my own which is not an approved party attitude and never could be, that I wouldn't have been able to do much reading or writing, even if I hadn't had so many other problems to distract me.

Now my son is again in the country, with the same people he'd been with, but this time (since school is closed) doing a little work in return for his room and board, and I have just gotten a job which pays the grand salary of $12 a week. But I can get by on that, at least manage rent and meals on it, and so perhaps I'll start doing something with poetry again in my spare time. And yet having so little equipment as a craftsman, and therefore being so completely dependent on what I have to say and my need to say it, I invariably suffer from the feeling that I shall never again be able to write another poem, during periods of inward bankruptcy—such as this very long and seemingly interminable one which has persisted for about three months now.

One of the advantages of having a reputation as a poet or of moving in [a] circle of people with common interests is, I suppose, that it forces one into writing or trying to, even when one has nothing to say, or is lacking in the will to say it. And that purely mechanical kind of work is good in its own way—helping one to perfect one's self technically. And the discipline is good too—better certainly than letting one's mind get awfully slothful and sloppy, as I do whenever my heart and soul become arid.

But what I asked about my poems—if you received those I sent back and also whether Laughlin will be letting me know which ones he plans to use: may I hear from you about that? My address, even now, is not definite beyond the day. Though I do have that job with the subsistence wage which I mentioned, I'm not to start it until Monday morning, and then of course have to wait a week before getting paid, and if my new landlady won't wait that long for the rent almost due again, I may once more have to go off and stay in someone else's place. But I shall in that case put in a forwarding address at the post office—so that mail will be forwarded to me from both 40 Perry and my former 12th Street address.

I'm afraid that this is a frightfully rambling letter. If so, it's because much that is most on my mind, I hesitate to express here—having bothered you too much already, I think, with all those purely personal problems of mine apart from poetry. But thank you for everything, and if I *should* do any more writing, I shall send it to you if I may. And in the meantime I hope to hear from you in regard to the two things I asked about.

Sincerely,

Marcia Nardi

P.S. If Laughlin has no particular preference for any six special poems, would he possibly consider my own in deciding which ones he will use? And also does he pay for material used in New Directions before or after publication—a matter which interests me at the moment when I have been living on hamburgers and coffee for about a week, and had to sell some back numbers of Transition and Horizon and Partisan Review in order to have enough carfare money while looking for a job.

1. MN did not keep this postcard.

. . . .

15. TLS-1 (Y)

July 13, 1942

Dear Jim:

Working like hell on *Paterson*, it's coming too. I'm limiting myself to an "introduction", a summary of the whole poem which will in all probability not come to an end for another twenty years if I live that long. The Introduction serves all my purposes and will make a book in itself. I'm getting really excited about it. Thrilling material I'm digging up every day you might say. It's a theme for everything I've got and more. Wish I had more. I'm trying my best to have in shape for this fall, hope you'll be able to handle it. You'll see. It'll be a book.

Yesterday I went to Paterson for a contact I've long delayed making, a man I've written to but never seen, David Lyle.[1] A strange character, fits marvellously into my material both personally and symbolically (tho I hate that word, it robs all actuality from the meaning). He's a New Englander, Gloucester was his home, has a grand head filled with God knows what—but very stirring. I've never known anyone with such a background of reading in the fields he affects, with names, page numbers right there tic tic tic right on the button. Quite a thrill to find anything like that around these parts. And he's NOT writing a book, just living and moving among people, organizing groups, etc. etc. A wonderful guy, good to look at, six foot three etc. etc. Blond [sic]. Has read everything on God's earth, including poetry, Whitehead and so many others I was dizzy. But I gotta throw him, somehow. I know how those British generals in Lybia [sic] must have felt facing Rommel.

He sez he wrote to New Directions for a copy of my Collected Poems and was told the book is out of print. How come? No need to answer only don't make it too long a wait. I told him to get in touch with Gotham Book Mart.

Would you mind dropping that Nardi woman a note that you have accepted the six or more of her poems you're using? She has some others you might want to see. Do it, please. Her new address is, Marcia Nardi, 40 Perry St., N.Y.C. AND if you can manage it, will you not send her something in advance? She can use it. I seldom ask, gimme a break this time.

Always glad to hear from you if there is any news. A good bit in the current *Poetry* on writing verse for the stage by one Alan S. Downer. Have you seen the first issue of VVV. Look it up.

Bill

1. See introduction, note 10. For further information about David Lyle, see Mike Weaver, *William Carlos Williams: The American Background* (Cambridge: Cambridge University Press, 1971), 122–127.

. . . .

16. TLS-1 (T)

July 13, 1942

Dear Marcia Nardi:

The second lot of poems were received and promptly forwarded to Laughlin. He has them together with the first. I don't know which he has selected.

I have written him asking him to get in touch with you direct at 40 Perry St. If he writes I'd drop him a brief note saying you'd like him to see a few additional poems of which I had thoroughly approved and send them forthwith. I think you'll hear from him shortly, at least I hope you'll hear. If not please write me again after a reasonable wait.

My long "Introduction" of which I spoke to you is moving along slowly, the material is so abundant I am having to go slow with its organization. It is in this material I am incorporating your letters.[1] I'll see that you are properly informed of what I'm doing before printing anything.

Sincerely yours

W. C. Williams

1. *Paterson* Book I (1946) included three paragraphs of Nardi's first letter to Williams; in 1948, he incorporated two of her letters in Book II.

. . . .

17. TPCS (T)

[postmarked July 16, 1942]

This will confirm Dr. Williams' report that we will be using a small group of your poems in New Directions 42. Payment will be at the rate of 1.25 per ND page. Kindly forward to this office some biographical information about yourself, together with a list of persons interested in your work, or who might be interested in New Directions books in general.

Thanking you,
J. Laughlin

. . . .

18. TLS-1 (Y)

July 21, 1942

Dear Jim:

The difficulty encountered in trying to make a small selection from these poems is twofold. First there are two classes of poems, the early fairly regular partially rhymed ones and the later freer ones. The separation is sharp. You shouldn't mix them. Either the selection should be made from one group or the other. I chose the second, the later group. But that isn't quite fair. The second difficulty is that the poems are chiefly valuable for the excellence of a few lines here and there, a limited selection doesn't bring in enough of the total material to give the sense of the whole which I want.

If your verdict is inexorable, it must be six poems, we'll have to do the best we can but I wanted to print all the poems in this lot or, as I first said, to give her a small paper book. I think she's good enough for that. The trouble is, you see, that if you don't do the right thing by this writer you're going to lose everything. She has a rare spirit, a very rare spirit in a woman and she is a woman in a very special and, I think, valuable sense. I think she's got a very small percentage of metal in her ore but it is a valuable metal.

You see, as you say, it's very difficult to get the good out of her work. Very few people will stop to refine, in the judgments, so poor an ore. That has been her life and it is palpable in everything she does. The rare is so very diluted but when it comes out it surpasses in excellence the bales of facile work one sees everywhere. Besides nobody is going to stop in a busy life to bother with her. They won't. That's why it is important for N[ew] D[irections] to give her a break.

I think the woman is wrapping up in the shoddy of her miserable existence a flash of real merit. If we turn her down then she is lost. Even that isn't what I mean because I'm not sentimental in these things. I mean that if we let her go by the board the very thing we purport to live for, excellence as a writer, is junked. Can't do it, Jim. Give her more space. I've done my best to make a selection of six poems but a few more came over than I intended. Do what you can for the woman. Perhaps something can be extracted from this letter to serve as a note otherwise I'll scribble out a few words later. If you want biographical material she'd have to give that herself.

Best, Bill

. . . .

19. TLS-2 and ALS-2 (Y)

21 Grove Street,
New York City
[mid-August 1942]

Dear Dr. Williams,

This is a reply to the note I received from you yesterday.[1]

What you say in the post-script (your willingness to assist me by a small loan if that will enable me to hold a job should I find one) means a great deal to me of course, and I cannot help but appreciate deeply that kind offer which, had it been available to me from some other more usual source long before this, would have gone a long way to circumvent the critical situation I'm now in.

But (I say this in reply to the first part of your letter) there is a world of difference to me—a vast world there—between your offering me that practical assistance with doubts and suspicions as to my worth and integrity, and your offering it to me with some actual faith in me not only as a poet but as a human being aspiring to high moral qualities, even when not able to achieve them always.

I'm afraid that much of my long letter to you (and perhaps also the one yesterday about my painful relationship with my family) must have sounded frightfully self-indulgent, maybe disgustingly mawkish with self-pity, and overbearing and supercilious in my attitude toward "ordinary" people.[2] But if so, that note which crept in was a false one, and due to the fact that in a letter of that sort, the balance between *all* one's evaluations both of one's self and of others is bound to be lost, and the stress accidentally placed where it might not actually lie.

Believe me, I have suffered hellishly—really in inexpressible misery and at times to the point of agony—both from that particular loneliness to do with lack over many years of any intellectual companionship, and also from that simple ordinary physical loneliness of the ordinary unattached woman—the one of course deepening the other; and this has been at the root of everything else. And please believe too that my desire to go on with writing and to lead the kind of life that will enable me to do so with a little comfort and peace and security, is not the socially irresponsible "ivory tower" one which seeks to exempt the poet from the ordinary problems of existence—that being so little true of me that years ago when the stage was all set for me to have become then without much effort another Dorothy Parker or Edna Millay, I fled, as for my very life, from the little literary circles that existed in the Village at that time, because I couldn't bear the falseness and the artificiality and the narrowness of attitudes toward life which were held by the particular literary people I knew then at a time before world affairs began to make almost everyone a lot more serious-minded. As a matter of fact "pure art" which has no moral purpose and no social usefulness exists for me much less than for most people, and I have rarely been able to completely isolate any personal problem of my own from its relationship to those larger problems of society as a whole, and I remember saying to Harvey (though he did not agree with me) that Yeats as a man failed to achieve any real greatness (despite his marvelous development as a poet) because—judging from his personal correspondence—he had failed to attain in his old age the kind of outlook that takes one out of time.

I tell you all this because I could never have turned to you in my desperation, if only for your practical assistance, and not for your understanding also. In whatever creative work I do, I am not inclined to be romantic—all my attitudes there leaning toward the realistic and sometimes toward the ironic. But there are moments when in one's personal life, and however "hard-boiled" one may be in one's general philosophy and point of view, one's need for understanding and sympathy (despite the assault of that need on one's pride and dignity) is stronger almost than any other. And it was in such a moment that I wrote to you on Friday, and again on Sunday, and that I do so again now.

The 70 hour working week connected with that country job honestly would [have] been too much for me physically in my present condition. Had it been a 45 hour week or even 50, I'd have dashed up there eagerly in a mood of positive exultation at the prospect of having any kind of opportunity to lead a normal healthy regular life out in the country. But the drain of 70 hours weekly of entirely physical work, upon my limited physical energies, would have completely cancelled whatever good I might ordinarily derive from a job in the country with normal working hours. (By the way, you know of course, that the existing Labor laws and union rulings make it impossible for city restaurants and hotels to permit women to work so many hours without even one day off, even if the women themselves should be willing to.)

But now I'm pretty sure that I can get some sort of job paying enough for me to live on in ordinary comfort, with a small loan from you available. But would you let me have it now, so that I can immediately get a pair of shoes, pay a small dry-cleaning bill, give the landlord $4.50 for this past week's rent, and have a few dollars left for carfares and food over a period of 10 or 11 days—that is until a week from this coming Friday or Saturday. I think, yes, I'm almost certain, that if I look hard for a job, all day long, following up all the newspaper ads (there are a lot of such ads for women these days) for the rest [of] this week (one can look on Saturdays too in regard to certain jobs) and also (should I get nothing this week) next Monday and if necessary Tuesday, that at least by next Wednesday (and very likely sooner) I'll have [some] sort of employment paying at least $20 a week, and certainly no less than $18 which is normal pay on the most ordinary jobs in department stores, restaurants, et cetera, so that by a week from this Saturday I'll [have] some sort of pay coming in, even if my first pay envelope is only for half a week.

That plan which I have, and which seems pretty sound (and the only one I can think of) makes it necessary for me to suggest my borrowing $25 from you—half of that amount for food and carfares over a period of ten or eleven days, and half of it [for] those items I mentioned, (the shoes, back week's rent, dry-cleaning expenses et cetera). This will not only put me in shape and keep me in shape while looking for and starting the job, but also (and that's so very important) it will save me from spending so much of the time that should go into job hunting, on the demoralizing business of running around here and there to get a quarter from this chance acquaintance, a meal from that one, and all that sort of thing which has such a destructive effect upon one's morale.

There's been no one over all these past wretched months from whom I could have borrowed as much as $25 in a lump sum—and borrowing a dollar from this person and fifty cents from another has not only been of no practical value to me in the long run, but also has done some pretty dreadful things to my self-respect.

But back of whether or not we know anyone to help us out when we are in financial difficulty—and *always* in back of it— is whether or not we know anyone who believes in us enough to help—the faith being just as important as the practical help and the lack of it being just as disastrous in its own way as the practical aspects of the situation. So in my writing to you about all these ghastly conditions surrounding my life for the past four years, it wasn't only for the practical help which of course I need so badly, but also for the other—the understanding.

About the factory jobs—Bendix or Wright—I don't think I'd have any difficulty in getting my birth certificate. I don't see why I should, having been born in this country, and having gone to the public grade schools in the town where I was born. But I'd rather have almost any other kind of job—work that involves a lot of activity (whether mental or physical) being more bearable to me than just sitting at a table and doing some purely mechanical task by which I am thrust into a state of suspended animation for hours at a stretch.

However, it's not being able to get a job on my own which has been my problem; but, as I said, not having the wherewithal to live decently while seeking and starting one. And so, if I may borrow $25 from you, as soon as possible, for the purposes already mentioned, I've no doubt that I'll be able to straighten things out right here in the city without Yaddo[3] or anything else of that sort; and I'll appreciate your aid to that extent more than I can tell you.

But the way you feel about me—your attitude toward those problems of mine—*that* counts a lot with me too; because to the full extent that anyone can be completely honest (and there's always some slight alloy of self-deception in everyone's honesty), I am, indeed,

Most sincerely,
Marcia Nardi

1. MN did not keep this letter from WCW.
2. This letter from MN has not been found, if indeed WCW kept it.
3. An artists' colony in Saratoga Springs, New York.

. . . .

20. ALS-4 (Y)

General Delivery, Norwich,
New York
[late August 1942]

Dear Dr. Williams—

The day I sent you that post-card, I had answered—in the afternoon—a newspaper advertisement asking for 500 bean pickers on an upstate New York farm; at the wage rate of from $6 to $8 a day, plus board, and free transportation. A large seemingly reliable produce firm at Washington Market inserted the ad, and conducted the interviews; and I seemed to have at my disposal a solution to my desperate situation that fitted in marvelously with all my needs—both economically and in regard to my health.

But it turned out to be a phony ad—one of the most *incredible* rackets I've ever come across. I can't go into the details (they make too long a story) except to say that the State troopers had to be called out because all of us (several hundred) found ourselves 200 miles out of N.Y. with no place to sleep, no money for food, and wages amounting to 15 cents an hour under working conditions which are like a chapter out of Tobacco Road.

Some of the people had a little money with them and families back home, so that they were able to leave the next morning. But others like myself were without any money, and had no families back in New York—so that I am stranded here, temporarily sleeping on an army cot at the home of some people in the nearest town (Norwich) who were kind enough to put me up, but who are very poor themselves with two babies to provide for.

I got one day's temporary work substituting for the regular dish-washer in a restaurant and earned $2 dollars [*sic*] for doing a man's dish-washing job for ten hours at a stretch; without having had much sleep the night before because we were transported up here at 5 A.M., and because I had to spend the previous hours that night washing clothes to take with me, and then leaving the house at 4 A.M.

I'm planning to do a newspaper feature article on this whole situation which (so I've learned) is nothing new. It's been going on for several years—many of the growers for miles around here getting cheap labor at share-cropper wages by running these false ads in out of town papers, with the idea that if people are stranded miles away from home, they will be more or less forced to work at 15 cents an hour and sleep in chicken coops. But that doesn't do me much good at the moment, when I'm in the same situation as when I first sent you that long desperate letter—and an even worse one now, when it's harder to get employment here than in New York City and with only farm clothes in my valise, and with my physical health undermined to an even greater extent by this awful experience.

'So what I asked in that 3rd letter, just before my post-card,— I'm forced to make the same request now. About your loaning me $25 which I'll definitely pay back just as soon as possible.

It will cost me $3.56 to get back to New York by bus (the train is even more); and the balance will be enough for me to pay for a cheap room and meals until I find a job.

Possibly I could get something in the neighboring cities and towns up here—Utica, Binghamton or Syracuse. They need people badly in those towns because so many have given up their regular jobs for defense work. But I have no money for getting around—most of my $2 from the day's work, having gone for food.

May I please hear from you, Dr. Williams? I had no reason to be suspicious of the "ad" nor to regard it as anything but "bona fide", because it was inserted by a large business concern which has been established for many years in Washington Market. The other "pickers" still up here and in the same position as myself, are very young and strong—17, 18 and 20 years of age; and most of them boys, so that they can stand it better than I can, even though they too are in a tough spot. I've just met a group of them in the village here—all of them having spent the past few days looking without success for jobs in this town, because they are without money to look elsewhere.

I don't know when this letter will reach you. I'm hoping that by air-mail it will get to you tomorrow, though maybe it won't arrive until the next day. But whenever it does get to you, if you could and would loan me some money immediately and send it up here without delay, I'll appreciate it so much. I had looked forward so eagerly to getting all straightened out by that farm job—and to have it turn out like this is just about the last straw.

Most sincerely,
Marcia Nardi

P.S. A letter sent to General Delivery, Norwich P.O., Norwich, N.Y. will reach me.

Woodstock, New York
September 29, 1942

Dear Dr. Williams—

It has been neither through carelessness nor lack of gratitude, that I have waited this long to thank you for that money order,[1] my receipt of which you doubtlessly were notified about by the post-office report on registered letters.

It's been, rather, that I haven't known how to interpret the blank piece of paper in which the money order was enclosed. It could have meant merely that in a rush to come to my aid, you had to dispense with any accompanying letter or note—not wanting to wait until you had time for one. Or it might have meant something a lot different—thus confirming my fears that it was somehow all wrong for me to have bothered you in the first place with those phases of my life connected with my inability to meet the practical problems of existence at all successfully.

That distressed concern of mine with your attitude toward my private life would not have interfered so much with my writing to you sooner than this, had it been as simple as it might seem for me to have straightened out, with that money you kindly sent me, the further tangles and complications caused for me by that hoax of a farm job. But it wasn't simple—was most difficult,—is still difficult; and, because one feels a definite *obligation* to get straightened out, toward a person who comes to one's aid with possible misgivings and doubts, I have felt at a loss and still do, in communicating with you under circumstances which have made it impossible for me to fulfill that obligation, so much of a psychological nature, but nevertheless a strongly felt one.

The time I wrote to you from New York in reply to your offer about the loan, I still had nearly two weeks to get a job and to have a salary coming in by the time I again would have to provide (I thought I would at the time) a home for my son (with me or elsewhere)—his summer with free room and board not coming to an end until after Labor Day. That was one of the reasons why I asked if you could extend it to me immediately—each day of delay in getting a job being a frightfully serious matter; and when a few days went by without my hearing from you, I snatched eagerly at that newspaper advertisement for farm help, with the idea (I mentioned that, I think in my letter from Norwich) of having my son come up to me there on the farm when his summer at the mountains was up, and with the idea too of his doing some work there also after school and on Saturdays, so that by the time the frost set in, we'd have saved, between the two of us, (not having room or board to pay for) at least a hundred dollars, possibly one hundred and fifty, and thus be able to get a good start in New York later upon our return.

But by the time I wrote to you from there and received the money order (I had tried first to get a job there in Norwich, but without success), Labor Day was already on hand; and just as I was about to ask those people with whom my son was staying, if he could possibly remain a while longer so that I'd have a chance to get back to New York and find employment with only my own personal expenses to meet while doing so, I received word (at the very same time I got your money order) that he was coming to me that very week of Labor Day. It was a letter from my son himself much delayed in reaching me, having been forwarded from one place to another (because I'd moved so much);—and so there I was faced with the situation (so I thought) of having to provide suitable living quarters for two people, and meals for two people (while looking for a job) out of what would remain of the $25 upon my getting to the city. An entirely different situation certainly from having only my own expenses to meet while looking for a job—and a very alarming one under circumstances where my relationship with my son was already such a strained one, that the prospect of having him with me in one furnished room (his unsatisfactory home environment having played a large part in my difficulties with him) was a pretty ghastly one.

I therefore sent a letter immediately to where he was, asking that he remain there for a few days until further word from me;—and tried to think of what would be the best and wisest plan of action under the circumstances.

Out of that money order, I had to give $1.50 to the people who put me up for a few nights to re-imburse them for a few meals they had given me (I offered it and they accepted it); and there was a taxi fare to the bus station (quite far away and my suitcases too heavy to carry); and meals to be bought on the trip back; and *no* way of reaching New York before quite late at night when it would be too late to find a room that same day so that I'd have to stay one night in a hotel. So there I'd be with no more than $18, and my son as well as myself to provide for then—and what was the best step to take?

I finally decided to come back across state and then down, via Kingston, thinking that if I could get a job in Kingston and could make some arrangements for commutation to and from Woodstock (it's only a 25 minute drive), I might be able to live very cheaply here with my son, and at the same time provide him with the kind of healthy wholesome country environment which would better enable me to reach his heart and mind; and incidentally provide myself with some freshening of experience, some interruption of what threatened to become a pattern in my life in New York (thus killing a lot of birds with one stone). Woodstock, in the winter, (as you may know) is an ordinary country village comprised of the *natives*, with all the summer pseudo-intellectuals gone back to town.

As my continued bad luck would have it, it rained heavily (one continual down-pour without any let-up) for two whole days after I set foot here and I had no raincoat or umbrella, so that I couldn't get around to investigate anything. But as soon as the rain stopped, I found that there were jobs available for women in Kingston—at somewhat lower salaries than in New York; but with living standards lower and also rents. I also found two Woodstock people with jobs in Kingston, either of whom would be willing to take me back and forth in their car for $1.00 a week—and I discovered too that boys were so badly needed for the apple crop (with all the young men in the army) that farmers were paying school boys forty cents an hour for picking apples, and that the school board here had extended a temporary leave of absence to boys doing such work—permitting them to return to school later than usual by three weeks. This meant that my son (who has spent much time on farms and who likes farm work of any kind) could earn $15 a week at least, for three weeks; and I found a small house (living-room, bed-room, and kitchen) for ten dollars a month; and a job for myself in a store for $14.50 a week.

All those factors, considered in total, made for a better situation, it seemed, than if I were living in some cheap New York furnished room with my son—again forced, by the urgency of getting immediate employment, into some make-shift job no better than the one in Kingston, with that boy of mine continually playing "hooky" from school, consorting with undesirable companions and staying on the streets until midnight, and getting into serious trouble.

So I started to work things out accordingly, on the basis of course of having my son with me, because unless one has a small private income and can remain pretty much at home, "roughing it" in the country is pretty hard for a woman alone—the cheaper houses here having no running water (only a pump outside), and no heating equipment except coal and wood stoves.

But, in an almost fantastic way, the same mischancing of things which hovered about that farm job, has surrounded all my plans here too.

I immediately dispatched messages of course to my son and the people he was staying with, in regard to my plans for him and requesting that he come here right away—and thinking how glad he would be to come because he so frequently had begged me to live in the country. Several days went by, and no sign of him, and no word. More letters from me (finally a telegram) and still no replies of any kind. I was frightfully worried; and in the way one does under such circumstances—I thought of all possible catastrophes in explanation of why he hadn't gotten here. Finally, after ten days, I received word that he *could* go on staying where he was for the winter, without cost, in return for light chores after school and on Saturdays, that he wished to do so, and that he had *previously* written me to that effect (cancelling the letter I got)—at the very time, it seems, that I was stranded up there on that farm, and where (as I learned later) much of my forwarded mail never reached me.

What a damnable situation—that I had been afraid to go back to New York without a job and so little money for two people, and had made other plans instead, as the lesser of two evils, when all the time I *could* have and *would* have had only my own expenses to meet while job-hunting! (even though I still would have wanted to have my son with me—at least on week-ends—and so, closer to the city, after I'd gotten a job).

But my plans were already made; and there was no changing them for the moment, since I couldn't very well go back to New York then without any money; (having used it for things here) and so I decided to have my son come here anyway (even though he *could* stay there), because I have a great need within myself to establish some happier relationship with him; and because I find whenever I am separated from him for any length of time, that my maternal feelings and emotions in regard to him are pretty deep, despite the fact that we have so little in the way of common interests. Also I know that many of his very serious behaviour problems were caused by his environment (poverty in the city being even worse for a boy who is not scholarly and whose interests are all outward, than for one who is wrapped up in his school work). The fact that he hadn't come when I first sent for him and when he could have earned $45 over three weeks by helping with the apple crop, would then have made things more difficult in practical ways; because it was my idea that we could use half of that money (and he could have the rest for a bike) to get in a supply of coal and wood—my own wages going for rent and food. But still, I figured out, Paul could get a Saturday job (most boys of his age have one if their families are poor) and with those extra couple of dollars we could swing things just the same—with the possibility of my getting a some-what better job, in the way of wages, before the real cold weather set in.

But again, something happened to spoil my plans! My full-time job in the store was reduced to a part-time one—not because my services were unsatisfactory (I'd have been fired altogether in that case of course) but because there wasn't enough business at certain hours of the day.

So here I am living in the country under conditions which are very difficult for a city-bred woman (and one who is no Amazon) *unless* she has a boy or a man with her; having come here because of that mix-up and misunderstanding in regard to my son's economic dependence upon me when I left Norwich; needing to have him come here for practical reasons if I am to stay here; wanting him to, for other emotional reasons also; not being able to send for him at present certainly when I'm earning not even enough for one person; and yet just as certainly not being able to give up the whole country idea and return to New York, because I haven't the funds for that now.

I suppose the only thing I can do is to stick it out here with or without my son, and with however little money—with the hope that by the time the cold weather comes (one doesn't need coal throughout October and not so very much wood) I'll either have gotten another full-time job in Kingston or else have found some way of getting back to New York. Yes that of course is what I have to do, and in the meantime it would mean so much to me to be conscious of still having your friendship, not so much in practical ways as in spirit and in your attitude toward all these ghastly economic troubles and disasters, from which I can't seem to escape.

I remember that you said (the night I had dinner with you) that some talents are *bound* to perish. I don't know whether you meant that they are bound to, only in our existing society which is still so far removed from the state of real civilization which it can and may some day attain; or whether you meant that they are bound to, by those same so-called natural laws which cause the waste of so many seeds in the plant and vegetable world.

If it was the latter you meant, then *no*, that kind of waste in the human world doesn't at all have to be, and *is* only because its inevitability is so rarely questioned; and because that "laissez faire" attitude so little tolerated in our time in matters of politics and economics, is pretty much the rule of the day when it comes to other issues of just as much importance in making for a civilized world.

I know that in my own personal life (and God how bitter I am about it) it's been a lot more than the workings of some blind fate, a lot more than mere accident, which has caused the terrible mis-chancing of all my dearest dreams and hopes and deepest interests (which are certainly not in sales clerking).

My relationship with Harvey Breit was typical of my relationship with any and every man I've ever been fond of. I am completely irrevocably exiled now from what is "normal" life for a woman, simply because instead of seeking primarily the lover or husband in those men I liked best, I sought primarily the friend, the brother, and the fellow creature, even in the face of my own intense physical desires and of my need for economic security. And no one is going to convince me that my bitter failures in what I sought most and above all else (bitter as gall to me now) had their root in the unalterable "sorry scheme" of things—in so-called unchangeable human nature; because if that is so any talk about the "equality of the sexes" is the most idiotic kind of gibberish; and the practice in old China of binding the feet of girl-infants, so that they'd remain tiny and doll-like, should, in that case, never have been discontinued. And no one is going to convince me either, with some "c'est la vie" remark, that a woman is *naturally* faced with a tough economic problem, if she can't measure up to those demands which the commercial world, no less than the social, makes upon women in the way of purely decorative qualities. I've been turned down for more jobs then I can count, (it's one of my greatest job difficulties) solely on the basis of not being what the advertisements specify as "attractive," and for having absolutely no talent for looking "chic" and "smart," even if I possessed a whole trunkful of Lord & Taylor clothes.

That I have suffered a great deal in my private emotional life from never having been a beautiful woman, is an entirely different matter. Yes, that *is* in the sorry scheme of things, that those who are the most beautiful physically should be loved the most. But when it comes to things like jobs, like friendships, to one's life outside of bed, I demand the right not to have to be beautiful, to be positively ugly even, and also to be any age at all, whether 16 or 60, and still be able to hold my own as an intelligent human being. And that right has always been denied me.

Nor am I to be convinced (my greatest bitterness is tied up with this) that it's entirely because the general public isn't interested in poetry, and because poetry therefore doesn't "sell" that poetry (except in the narrowest cultural circles) is the one bastard among all the arts—and the one outcast among them all. There's a kind of tradition, along with the other traditions which make for so many of our social evils, that the writing of poetry is the one and only activity which—for absolutely no sound and intelligent reason—is not to be considered as a full-time profession or vocation, holding its own with other full time professions and vocations (unless one has a private income). There's no such tradition in regard to any of the other arts. A painter, whether he's rich or poor, devotes his day to painting; and the same thing holds true for sculptors, actors, and musicians.

I happened to spend a short time the other night talking with Grace Greenwood[2] (you may know of her) who's a fairly well known mural painter. She was without any money at all—not even enough to get back to New York. But did it occur to her—or would anyone expect such a preposterous thing—that she could go out and earn a few dollars in a factory, or a store, or as a nursemaid, a scrub-woman, or a waitress? Of course not; painters aren't supposed to do those things, any more than musicians are or actors. Hook or crook, she'll get hold of enough money to go on existing, as she's always done, as a painter. And the general attitude (even among people who in their souls have no more feeling for painting than for poetry) gives her the right to do so, because it's "public opinion" that strongest of all forces, which creates not necessarily the practical and material background, but the all-important psychological one against which all other artists (except poets) are able to assert themselves as such in their daily full-time living—even when they don't possess private incomes, and even when the financial returns from their work are precarious and slight.

The government's WPA subsidization (before we entered the war) of all kinds of creative work, *except* the writing of poetry, is an excellent example of how public opinion and tradition, much more than anything else, makes it necessary for purely cultural writers to always earn their living in some other profession, or, if they lack one, by doing the most menial underpaid kind of labor.

The painters and sculptors on those easel projects weren't asked or expected to turn their talents to commercial art of any kind. They were paid for their own serious, purely cultural, creative work; and the same thing was true of all the people employed by the Federal Theatre and the Federal philharmonic orchestras. But the writers projects operated quite differently. Except for a handful of some 8 or 10 favored individuals in one tiny branch of the Guide Book, the writers on WPA were not permitted, as were other artists, to do their own serious creative work in return for their salaries. Even old-time vaudeville and circus performers were maintained as such. But the writers were put on all sorts of non-literary writing projects, in order to justify their existence on the WPA rolls. They were forced to waste reams of copy paper (thus squandering and misdirecting both their own energies and the government's money) on the kind of writing which did not have even the remotest connection with literature, and most of which was accumulated (great tons of it) mostly to satisfy the tax payers that no one on WPA was allowed to be idle, and not because the material in itself meant anything much to anyone.

And yet that state of affairs roused scarcely a murmur of protest—not even among literary people themselves; and in general it's the poets and intellectuals themselves who are utterly indifferent to the accepted tradition that poetry and other forms of non-commercial writing are something to be worked on, on Sundays only and in one's spare moments unless one possesses a private income. They in particular nod assent to it.

It is almost invariably true of course that it's the very people toward whom a wrong is directed who concern themselves with it least. But quite apart from the peculiar apathy which is always so much stronger in the victim of some evil than in the observer, there's a very interesting situation in modern literature which is a not unlikely explanation of why writers themselves don't seem to give a damn about the attitude of the general public toward the writing of poetry. If you should make a list of those poets who have been the greatest influence in contemporary literature, you will find that nearly all of them (there are some few exceptions, of course) are people with all the advantages of the moneyed middle-class, and who, even if they possess no actual private incomes have been able, by those advantages, to equip themselves for earning a fairly easy living in those professions for which both money and social position are necessary, at the very beginning, in order to obtain the right preparation for them. And if you should then make a list of the painters and sculptors who have been the greatest influence in the contemporary art world, you will find a much greater deviation from that situation which exists among the men and women of letters. There's no world comprised quite so completely of the elect, none quite so snobbish in its smug acceptance of the economic and social advantages which enables it to survive without any real hardship in our existing society, as the contemporary literary world. That so many members of that world have been—merely in their theories and in their writings—in the front ranks of the left-wing movement with its strong Marxist convictions and its scorn for a society dominated by middle-class bourgeois values—in itself means nothing. What's far more significant is that the majority of our present-day poets, at least those who wear the crowns and sit in the thrones, depend for their personal survival and in their private living upon their strong safe roots, socially and economically, in that very class, which theoretically and on paper only, so many of them disdain. After all it's the external problems or lack of them in one's personal life, and one's advantages or disadvantages there (far more than one's theories) which determine one's status in the world socially and economically; and since so many of our modern poets (we don't have so many born in stables and in mangers) manage to get a fair amount of leisure for doing their literary work with things as they are, and also a fair amount of material comforts with things as they are, why should they bestir themselves to any pioneer work in destroying that stupid tradition which causes the general public to regard the writing of poetry as an entirely different matter (even though it makes equally great demands upon time and energy) from work with paints or with clay?

The intellectual revolutionary has the erroneous idea that all the poet requires is the outward, economic set-up of a socialistic world, in order to suddenly come into his own, without depending for his survival upon those particular advantages which are so necessary for his survival under capitalism. Those same revolutionaries uphold certainly the Marxist concept of history, and understand perfectly well that the revolutionary movement, when it succeeds, serves as little more than mid-wife in the birth of what had already been destined for birth by historic processes in themselves. And yet they suppose so inconsistently that poets and poetry will gain their proper place in the world by the entirely different method of springing as suddenly into power as Minerva from the head of Jove—which of course is decidedly unlikely and unsound, because the existing tradition in regard to the writing of poetry must first undergo slow and gradual changes before poets, under any economic set-up, can derive their identity entirely from being poets without needing to *first* use some other respectable and esteemed profession as a spring-board.

And the very people who have the power to make those changes possible, do nothing about it. Places like Yaddo are pretty much in line with old age pensions and social security insurance for the old. What the "old" require is not some pittance to retire on, but a very different attitude toward old age which will make it possible for working men and women in their 50's and 60's to get jobs according to their intelligence and efficiency, and not according to how successfully they dye their hair. If there weren't another stupid tradition about time (it's another which needs very much to be exploded and shattered) old age pensions would be necessary only for those no-longer-young people who are physically handicapped—and not for the physically healthy ones. And it's the same way with places like Yaddo and the Guggenheim scholarships and the various poetry prizes. All that money would be more constructively spent in helping along a state of affairs where poets would be able to earn at least something from the publication of their work; and a tremendous lot *could* be done in that direction. Any suggestions from me along that line will sound frightfully naive, because after all I'm not a business woman. But I don't care if I do sound naive—preferring to naively concern myself with what I recognize as unfair and wrong, than to merely shrug my shoulders at it. Besides I do know that it's the literate, educated, cultured people (the very ones who are regular "subscribers" to the little literary magazines and to the semi-liberal journals such as The Nation and New Republic) who are always most generous in contributing to "Noble Causes"—when it's merely a matter of a few dollars and cents and involves no serious threat to the smug security of their private lives. And I dare say that those people wouldn't fly up in arms, if the cost of those periodicals were raised from 15 to 20 cents or from 25 to 35, provided that the owners and publishers very much publicized the fact that they were forced to raise the price *in order* to pay their reviewers a couple of pennies more per word and their poets a few more dollars per poem. All sorts of promotion ideas go into everything under the sun: from putting across some bit of merchandise to making people patriotic in war-time; and so I didn't think that a few promotion ideas for enabling purely cultural writers to get paid a little better than they ordinarily do, would be at all out of the way. And even without any promotion ideas, newspapers like the Herald-Tribune, for instance, which gives huge salaries to its news reporters and to its composing-room employees, could well afford, without going bankrupt, to pay 5 cents a word, instead of 1 or 2 cents, to the people who do the literary criticism for "Books" on Sundays. And those well-off cultured book publishers—people like Laughlin, for instance—probably wouldn't be up against starvation if they paid their writers something more than the prevailing rate of pay for non-commercial writing in order to set a kind of *precedent*—even if doing so meant a little personal sacrifice on their part.

It occurred to me, at the time Laughlin sent me a list of the poems he was using, that if one could get paid at least ten dollars a poem for a group of poems (which is comparatively little when you consider that a painter, if he sells his work at all, gets at least 50 dollars for some tiny canvas which may have taken just an afternoon to complete) then, upon receiving the huge sum of 60 or 80 dollars for 6 or 8 poems (it would be an awfully large lump of money to me) I could spend a month and a half (maybe two) only writing; and thus, in that time complete another group of poems and possibly an article (there are a number of literary articles I've been wanting very much to do) from which I again, from some other source, could get another few dollars for another month or two of just writing, and so on.

Of course one can't possibly *live* according to accepted living standards on ten or twelve dollars a week. But one can get along somehow, if one is willing to dispense with modern conveniences, to heat one's own place with coal and wood, to bring in one's own drinking water, and to make all the sacrifices of roughing it, in order to be free for the things one wants most to do. Naturally I find it a beastly, sickening business to earn a mere subsistence wage from work in which I have no interest whatever; and which is not only an abnegation of myself, but which is also of such a nature that I contribute nothing at all to society nor the welfare of mankind in that surrender of my welfare as an individual. But no living is really a subsistence one—not in the most significant sense of the term "living" if it's connected with labors (however little one may get from them financially) in the field of one's choice; and so, intolerable though I find it to receive only 30 cents an hour from being a sales clerk in a "dime to dollar" store, if I could possibly find some way to average a meagre ten or twelve dollars a week from activities in which I have my heart and soul, I'd consider myself among those whom God had blessed, whom fate had smiled most sweetly upon, and would be loathe to change places (even if the opportunity presented itself) with anyone earning a hundred a week, or even a thousand in the commercial world. And my "subsistence" income in that case, would not affect my relationship with my son, with my family, nor with the world in general—except for the better. The people whom I am thrown up against, and whom chance has made a part of my private life, have no respect for my interest in literature and in poetry particularly, and no sympathies with my frustration there, because, as typically average people, they have no respect for any activity or concern which has no value at all in dollars and cents, whereas they would consider a pre-occupation with non-commercial writing as important at least as they do sales clerking or waiting on tables, if I could earn any money at all from writing; and under those circumstances they would not cut me off so completely from that normal exchange of small favors and helps in purely practical matters which usually takes place among people intimately connected with each other, whether by choice or by accident.

It is true that what I want so much for myself—some tiny bit of money from writing—is available (even with poetry and non-commercial prose holding the sorry place they do) to some few persons. Harvey had no source of income whatsoever, during the nine or ten months of my contact with him, except what he got from poems and book-reviews and from sometimes being in a position (as when he lived at Yaddo or his former wife's apartment) where he had no expenses to meet in the way of rent. But those few people are generally individuals whose social lives are rooted pretty much within the narrow confines of the literary world. They are the people with the necessary "contacts"; and with also (just as important as the contacts for doing book-reviews *professionally*) that intimate relationship with the literary world which enables them to observe closely that subtle weather-vane of a particular editor's personal prejudices, personal ambitions and aspirations, and personal literary friendships which so often have as much to do with the intellectual atmosphere and weather of a particular magazine as absolute literary standards. Yes, even there in the matter of doing book-reviews, a person without a private income and with no vocation apart from writing, must stick close to the breast of the little literary world, in his social contacts, his private life, in order to derive the necessary nourishment for preserving his identity as a writer; and what's so important is that a poet should be able to hold his own as *such* in his relationship to society in general, and not to just some handful of people who are themselves poets or readers of it. I mean hold his own there socially (I'm not concerned in what I say here with his audience) in a way which has nothing to do with whether or not his next-door neighbors read and like poetry, any more than a clergyman's highly respected social position has anything to do with whether or not his next door neighbor goes to church or believes in God.

In all these pages (that is clear, I hope) I've not been wasting your time or my own in the mere re-iteration of all those taken-for-granted commonplaces about a poet's position in the world. The subject of this letter is that taken-for-grantedness in itself, because I can think of no other tradition (if you can, do tell me what it is) which has been accepted so resignedly and passively from one age to another as that which causes the writing of po-etry to be regarded by everyone as a leisure-time activity, and to have always been only that, for the very reason that it's always been looked upon as such.

The most illiterate and untutored people have some notion, I think, that a certain amount of hard work goes into becoming a dancer, or a pianist, or a sculptor. But however unromantic and realistic and scientific this world of our time, all those time-worn romantic ideas about the writing of poetry still prevail among the uncultured masses. To them it still has much more to do with the "heart" than with the "intellect", and owes much more to divine inspiration and sentimental tears than to what is generally understood as "work". Even other writers—the fic-tion writers who contribute to the big-circulation magazines and who despite their intellectual and cultural lacks, are a lot better educated than the man of the streets, imagine that be-cause poems are so compact, they require not very much time and effort. And those public attitudes which a poet living in a world of poets and of cultivated people, does not feel, and which a person who is successful in some other profession can ignore, have a fatal effect psychologically upon someone in my position—especially since my only assets are completely tied up with my very much squelched creative and intellectual interests, utterly bankrupt as I am and always have been in the way of "looks" and feminine charm which are the chief means of any woman's being able to hold her own in the "ordinary world", even in the matter of getting jobs.

I feel that in my own fashion, in my own ideas, and in my particular vision of life, I have as much to contribute both to literature and to social progress as the next fellow, and a lot more than the majority of women writers. (Or at least that I did have—for now, at this stage of my life, even under the most favorable circumstances, I'd have a race with time to contend with, and a none too easy one now, with so many miscarried years behind me, and so few years ahead of me, and so much of my energy sapped by mis-directed stupid labors.) But I have had almost no opportunity—no, none—to do any kind of *sustained* work with writing, reading, or thinking. Even a 40 hour week job has been rarely just that for me,—never leaving me with at least my evenings and Sundays for work of my own choosing.

To people earning thirty or forty dollars a week, their free time is really free. But in my case, since for so long now I've had such low wages even when holding a job, (and thus have been unable to give out my laundry or eat out in restaurants) much of my "spare time" has had to go into washing and ironing and marketing and cooking (especially when my son has been with me) so that most of my "leisure" has amounted not so much to occasional hours as to occasional moments. And it's certainly not entirely nor even largely this ruthless economic system under capitalism which has all but buried me alive. I know from experience much better than any mere observer can know the extent of that ruthlessness, and the hopeless slavery to which it binds the masses. But in my own particular case (true only of course of individuals to whom the inner realities are the greatest) it's not being done out of my share of the world's material goods which has affected my life so disastrously.

I've already said, some pages back, that if I'd ever been able, during these past four years particularly (the most critical years for me in my intellectual development) to earn even the most meagre pittance from literary work, I'd consider myself the most fortunate of human beings and gladly put up with any physical hardships for the sake of that good fortune; and feeling that way so strongly, I very likely would have found some method of bringing it about (especially since I have wanted to do some work with prose too and since I am capable of tireless labors when it comes to activities of my own choosing) were it not that moving socially in literary circles is pretty much of a "sine qua non" for that sort of thing.

For my own personal frustrations therefore, it's not the economic system which I indict, but the attitude of the various literary cliques and of literary individuals generally toward the "stranger outside the gate"—not in their demands for outstanding literary achievement (no, they are lax there, and of necessity since after all not so many writers have more than mere talent) but for the high social barrier which they erect between themselves and the outsider—a barrier no less insurmountable than the very one they condemn between the economic classes.

In an accepted member of the literary world, any kind of temperamental peculiarity, and any lapse from what is general[ly] understood as practical responsibility are indulgently overlooked; and if that *person* has no private income and no profession apart from literature, it's more or less accepted that he should park on his friends, borrow money right and left, hold out for the sinecures in the way of jobs, let his wife or mistresses support him, and make use not only of his work but even more of his "contacts" in order to avail himself of the various respectable and dignified charities which exist for artists and writers with "pull"—meeting the practical problems of existence in these and similar ways not out of indolence, but quite justifiably in order to write.

But let a penniless outsider whose concern with literature is no less serious, but who has no social foothold in the literary circles, absent himself from a factory or a shop in order to sit under a tree and "invite his soul," or fail to hear his alarm clock because he sat up most of the night reading or writing, or let him turn down some obnoxious form of employment because its particular duties and routine would interfere disastrously with his mental needs, then that individual is looked upon as a freak, or a bum—as shiftless, lazy, or something of that sort; and if he can't pay his rent, well, of course, "it's his own fault"—"he doesn't want to work."

It *could* be mere coincidence (but I have reason to believe not) that all the particular poets and non-commercial prose writers without private incomes and with no other professions whom I have known, have not hesitated and have been able, merely on the basis of moving socially in literary circles, to avail themselves of all those special prerogatives which society at large would not grant them (poetry having so little importance there) and which those circles in which they move completely withhold from the outsider and grant only to their favored few, in no tangible way which one can exactly put one's finger on, but in that subtler more insidious fashion which springs from the same sources as "blue" blood or royal.

Heaven knows how things will turn out for me up here. If I were here under different circumstances, as a free-lance writer earning a few dollars that way, I shouldn't want to go back to New York at all—at least not for a long time; because I "belong" nowhere there and have no close friends, and because solitude is more bearable in the country than in the city—and with more time to myself, I shouldn't particularly mind the lack of modern conveniences (even with no male in the household) because the extra hours required for tending to fires and doing laundry without running water, wouldn't matter so much. But with things as they are, I have grave misgivings as to the outcome of my present situation; and think it was unpardonably inconsiderate of those people whom my son has been staying with, to let ten whole days go by without answering my letters or the telegram. It was apparent from those letters, that I had not received whatever word had been sent to me, while I was stranded in Norwich, in regard to the changed economic situation regarding his welfare and my responsibilities there, and that all my plans were based on my supposing that I had to provide him with the best home I could, immediately. But, as I said already, the situation is what it is now, and there is nothing I can do but make the best of it. The worst phase of things is one regarding my clothes and again resulting, like so much else, from the tangles created by that phoney farm job. Naturally, upon leaving New York (and going that way in the truck and with no money for taxi fare) I couldn't take all my belongings with me; and being forced to do something about them immediately (I applied for the job on Friday and had to leave on Saturday before dawn) I put my heavy coats in storage (and had previously put a winter jacket in the pawn shop)—planning to send for them from the farm where I'd have quite enough money for that (so I thought). But now I can't send for them, at least not at the moment,—especially with my present job changed for a part-time one at wages of 30 cents an hour; and it's already pretty cold here evenings (though the days are still warm). Such matters seem such trifles; and yet they can be such great problems!

That the people responsible for that false advertisement should be able to get away with a thing like that, seems almost incredible. And yet I understand (I have made inquiries) that the agrarian labor laws (so much laxer than the industrial ones) pretty much wink at such happenings—or at least are without power to prevent them.

If only I'd had a typewriter with me and a camera, what a story I could have done on those share-cropper colonies up north! It wasn't only that one particular farm to which I was sent, but several others in that same part of the state to which people were lured by offers of "free board" and then dumped into "living quarters" not fit even for beasts. The pictures themselves would have made a story; and yet when I tried to get one newspaper to send a reporter up there (certainly it ought to be exposed) the editors were so little interested that they didn't even reply to my note!

It's awkward talking about all these matters to which I have devoted this letter, in war-time;—especially in this case when I do not know how you feel about the war, and to what extent it may exclude from your mind at the moment any concern with so much else that has also to do with civilization.

That (the war)—concerns me too; and particularly the tragic ghastly farce of all that spilled blood for the sake of that to which I cannot bring the attitude of those who, whether in faith or cynicism as to the outcome, are able somehow to find an entire philosophy and a whole world outlook in only the shell of civilization which needs to be preserved certainly, but which has its kernel comprised of just such issues as those I've mentioned in this letter and also in my others to you.

I said somewhere in the previous pages—and repeat it here at the end because I have so much need to stress it—that to be conscious of your continued friendship would contribute a good deal to my peace of mind; as much as the outcome, in practical ways of the very difficult situation I'm faced with up here.

Hoping therefore, and very much, to receive a friendly word or two from you,

Sincerely,
Marcia Nardi

P.S. (to be read first)

The postscript comes at the beginning, because it's an apology for the great demands on your time of such a long letter (looking more like the manuscript of an article or short story than a letter), and for one written so sloppily and in such illegible hand writing.

But I am lost without a typewriter, have an awful time getting anything down on paper without one; and have a lot—so very much—to say to you.

Please therefore pardon this avalanche of my thoughts intermingled with an account of the events in my life since I left Norwich; and my presumption (and hope) that the former may interest you—even though the latter may make for dull and tiresome reading.

And if you will read all this in your leisure time so that you can read it carefully—I'll appreciate that very much.

Why I have not written to you sooner—that I have explained.

M.N.

I am almost afraid to get this letter off, because I know that if you cannot see and fully understand what I have said about the miserable position of a poet with no social foothold in the literary world—that in itself will be a great blow to me; and I shrink from taking a chance with the possibility of that blow.

1. The money she had asked to borrow from him in her letter of mid-August 1942 (see 19).

2. Grace Greenwood (b. Brooklyn, N.Y., 1905–), painter and WPA muralist.

. . . .

22. TLS-1 (T)

Oct. 6, 1942

Dear Marcia Nardi:

Though I have not yet quite finished reading your long letter there are one or two things I want to tell you without further delay. The blank paper enclosing the money order meant nothing, I was in a hurry and asked Mrs. Williams to take charge of sending you what you needed.

But on the day you left New York so hurriedly I had mailed you another money order for fifteen dollars intending to send you the additional ten dollars the following week. This first order, for the fifteen dollars, must have arrived after you left since you have not spoken of receiving it. I won't say it has been lost for I intend to try to have the post office trace it but I want you to know the facts.

Next, I have looked around to see what I could find for you to do and have discovered a lead in that same post office department. They are looking for censors of foreign mail, men and women with some scholastic training, capable of doing accurate paper work. One has to apply at the main office at 33d St. If you are interested I might be able to help you further. Certainly it would be more the sort of work most suitable to your general situation.

Please do not worry about the additional money order lying around somewhere waiting for someone to claim it or as it may be. If you can get hold of it through some friend take it and use it. If it has been destroyed or stolen I'll probably be refunded. It won't be lost. Forget it. Or rather get it if you are able. It's yours.

I'll finish your letter and then write you again in a week, after I have heard from you. I am very busy as you may well imagine but within my abilities and opportunities I am most anxious to help you. Certainly today with the demand there is for help of one sort or another there must be a place where you can earn a living.

Sincerely yours
W. C. Williams

. . . .

23. APCI-I (Y)

Woodstock, N.Y.
General Delivery
[Oct. 7, 1942]

Dear Dr. Williams:

The money order situation is this: Just before I left N.Y. I sent you a card (did you get it) saying that I wouldn't be at Grove St. to get any money order or check that might already be in the mails, and asking you to stop payment on such (because I thought I'd no longer need it).

Also I left my forwarding address for my mail generally at the local N.Y.P.O. (Station C)—and gave as that address: "Sherburne, N.Y. R.F.D. care of Howard Sisson."

But I stayed at Sherburne (where the farm was) for less than a day, for the reasons which you know about, and after that had no permanent address for about ten days; so that lots of my mail (as I've discovered since) went astray.

With your name on the envelope the money order should have been returned to you, so that I imagine it was taken and cashed by someone else. I therefore think you ought to trace it. (I'm curious as to who stole it.)

M.N.

P.S. I have just dropped a post-card to the post-master at Sherburne and at Station "C", N.Y. about the matter.

. . . .

24. TLS-1 (T)

[fall 1942]

Dear Miss Nardi—

I'm so sorry that you were upset by Dr. Williams' preface.[1] In reading it over I didn't feel that there was anything in it which did you discredit. Besides with a writer like him, where feeling and style are so knit together, I never like to change anything. I was pleased that he wrote for you because I think a new name is always stronger if it comes with some introduction from a man whose judgement is valued.

Your free copy of the book and a check for the balance owing you were sent to your former address. If they haven't been returned I presume they are still there waiting for you. You should—in all—receive two checks from me, the one I sent you quite a while ago and this second one.

Now don't you be upset about that preface. I'm sure nobody is going to misjudge you because of it.

Best wishes,

J. Laughlin

1. Williams's introduction to a group of seventeen of Nardi's poems published in *New Directions Number Seven*. Nardi had written Laughlin to say that she wished he had just published her poems without any additional personal information about her.

218 West 15th Street,
New York City
November 18th [1942]

Dear Mr. Laughlin,

I got my copy of New Directions. The mail-man left a notice about it at my former New York address asking me to call there for the package, which I did. But the check either was returned to you, or else left at 21 Grove Street and taken by someone else. If by chance, it *has* come back to you in the past day or two, then will you please send it out again to me here at 15th Street; and if [it] was taken and cashed by someone else will you please let me know about that as soon as you get the returned check from the bank with the signature of whoever endorsed it for me?

Right after I left New York at the end of the summer, a money order was sent to me at that address (21 Grove), which I never received and which the sender never had returned to him, so that if you didn't get the check back yet, it certainly looks as if somebody there at that house has been helping himself (or herself) to my mail.

While I was away, and at the time I learned about that money order having gone astray or being stolen, I wrote to the local postmaster at Christopher Street, telling him that I was no longer at 21 Grove Street and asking him to keep any mail for me until I could furnish a permanent forwarding address or else to return any that came to the sender. But apparently that request was neglected, because of the package-notice being there on the hall table; and the indications are that your check was left there too and then picked up by most likely the same person who made off with my money order.

I haven't any interest in seeing people who steal money (even my money) brought to justice or anything of the sort. But I'm curious as to who took it, if anyone did; and it's regrettable too that I didn't find your check there along with the package slip, because it would have come in very handy this particular week.

Anyway, please let me know about that check, when you find out about it.

Sincerely yours,

Marcia Nardi

. . . .

26. TLS-10 (B)

218 West 15th Street,

New York City

Thursday, November 19th

[1942]

I've decided to send the poems mentioned, in a separate envelope, which probably will arrive in the same mail as this letter.

Dear Dr. Williams,

I sent off to you so long ago now that post-card immediately and separately, because I thought it might help in the tracing of that lost money order. (By the way, Laughlin sent me a small check for a balance due on those poems, and that too—also addressed to 21 Grove Street—seems to have been lost or stolen.)

But out of a heartlessness and discouragement about things generally, I have lacked the will to reply to that part of your last letter about the possibility of the post office job. And I still lack the will for it, but am forcing myself to write to you because I appreciate so very deeply your interest in my poetry, and because, apart from that, I like you more than you know and therefore do not want to lose your friendship nor be misunderstood in my silence.

I don't want to again go into the million and one details connected with the continued misfortunes of my life outwardly, and of such a nature as to make it seem almost as if some sort of "jinx" had a hand in those matters. But it was to some extent a feeling I'd started to have about jinxes and sheer bad luck which paralyzed me up there in Woodstock to a point where all the effort which inevitably would have been connected with my trying to get that job you mentioned, required more outwardly aggressive activity and exertion than I was capable of at the time. So much *had* gone wrong! First, that first money order; then that farm job; then my being unable to use the second money order for any really constructive purposes for reasons mentioned in my letter from Woodstock; and then (what you don't know about, since it happened right after you wrote to me about the post office job) my son's "running away" from the place he was at, and his getting into a lot of trouble under circumstances which made it necessary for me to stay right where I was for the time being, so that I could be reached at any moment without difficulty by the public authorities who always concern themselves with such situations in the case of "minors".

All those ill-fated events concurred to create for me one of those psychological impasses whereby people are sometimes so chained to their past failures as to be robbed of all motive power.

But my greatest problem, the one that's always there at rock-bottom underneath everything else, is what I devoted the most space to in that very long letter I sent you from Woodstock (everything I said there about the business of writing poetry); and, combined with that, the increasingly wide gulf which exists for me between the external and the inward worlds—my sense of the very few years ahead of me and of my being now at the very end of my youth causing me to feel that gulf and to be terrified by it in more destructive ways than if I were ten years younger than I am (I am not in my *"early"* thirties, you know; I'm on the *other* side, the late side, now).[1]

All that squandering of one's time and energies which goes hand in hand with earning a living, *with* a good job or without one. One feels it less keenly (I myself felt it less keenly in the past) when one is young enough to hope that what can't be done today, may yet be done tomorrow. Or if I had some larger and more sustained achievements behind me, so that it were merely a matter of adding to past accomplishments and of keeping the ball rolling, as in the case of most writers (as in your own case, for instance) I could better reconcile myself to completely wasting 8 or 9 hours of every day and having only 3 or 4 at my disposal. But when in addition to being chained to the immediate Now (and a woman is of course more rooted in time than a man is) I find so much of what I want to do still in the form of a chrysalis, I succumb to such profound despair and am so gagged and bound by it, that instead of writing and reading a little, I do absolutely nothing—and sink into a state of spiritual and intellectual coma for days, even weeks, at a time.

That line of demarcation which people are always drawing between those who *work* and the loafers (I'm generally regarded as among the latter) doesn't of course exist. With jobs as with everything else in life, it's [a] case of Being or not Being, of finding life in chosen activities or death in forced ones, and what contributes to the one or the other is hardly ever the same for two individuals; and even in the case of one particular individual, varies according to the different stages of one's development. I had a most unpleasant experience yesterday in regard to that latter instance, upon going for an interview about a possible job as editor of a trade paper, in the ice cream field. I happened to have edited a trade paper quite efficiently some years ago and on the way to the interview yesterday in my usual penniless condition, all I could think of—and most eagerly—was the prospect of getting $40 a week, and the much needed clothes I could and would buy out of my first week's salary, if I got the job. But as soon as the publisher began discussing the details of the work with me, my heart sank. I had turned out reams of copy, like a thought machine, for that other trade journal in the past, in order to meet my son's boarding school bills then. But I found now that I couldn't—not any more. A glance at the editorials which were shown me, and that *I* would have to write, and at all those standardized wartime patriotic articles and pep talks and sales promotion ideas which would consume, to such false ends, all my creative energies and leave me mentally exhausted at the end of each day, revolted me so much and filled me with such nausea—that it was with a concealed sigh of relief that I heard the man inform me that he couldn't decide at once, that he had two other people to interview, and then would take a few days to consider the various applicants before making a definite choice.

[Nardi crossed out the paragraph which followed and wrote in the margin: "I have crossed this out for reasons explained later in this letter."][2]

So it is not with any eagerness, not with any enthusiasm, not with any hope of salvation in that direction, that I am now back in New York (I returned only recently) job-hunting again, and pretty much in the same situation which I described to you just before I left town in such desperation and with such unfortunate results. In all the time which has elapsed since my unhappy experience with H.B., I have not recovered from it in the slightest. My only hope for recovery was to have drowned myself completely in writing and reading. But I have been cut off from those and thrust up continually on the surface of my life, where I can find no life, by my continued economic difficulties which are so much more than that. Do you know that since last February or maybe it was early March (I can't remember the exact date of that last evening with Harvey) I have not spent an hour (with the exception of the night I met you for dinner) in the presence of anyone whose mind or personality could in any way have a stimulating and quickening effect upon my own; and in addition to that, the ascetic life I've been leading (it's so complicated and difficult and awkward to sleep with people only for reasons of sex) has taken its toll on my physical self in pretty terrible ways; and the one and only intimate relationship which I have with another person (that with my son) has grown worse and worse, leaving me now with absolutely no hope of ever reaching anything in that boy. He has never had any pronounced mental interests of any kind, as I've told you, had no interest in school beyond its purely social aspects, and now having become intoxicated with all the wartime offers of good money to boys of almost any age, he has left school altogether and taken a job with a printer who gives him $18 a week for running errands (women doing work on that level, get only ten or twelve a week); and this has gone so much to his head, and has given him so great a sense of superiority over me, that he has taken to hurling the vilest kind of insults at me in the language of the gutter. And not only that, but his sense of personal property is so strong, and his admiration of material possessions both in other people and in himself so very great beyond any other admiration, that my own difficult economic situation is much worse for me with his having that job than if he didn't have it. Last night for instance, after I returned from that trade paper job interview in the state of mind which I've mentioned, I asked Paul if he would use some of his earnings this week to keep things going here for a few days so that I would have a chance to look around for a job that would not be too unbearable as to the work itself and which also would pay more than the 30 cents an hour I've been getting. Whereupon he informed me in the most insolent tone that he had no intention of being a "sucker" for anyone; and later when I sat down at the typewriter to copy a poem written in pencil, he began shouting so loudly that everyone in the house could hear him, about his misfortune in having a mother who was such a "nut" as to spend her time on such "shit" (referring to the poem which I was trying to copy). And that's his attitude toward me, and the language in which he expresses it, at their very mildest!

And I cannot endure anything of that sort—certainly not. Nor would I expect any sympathy for myself if I did, because I do not have much patience for people who make martyrs of themselves for reasons only of social custom, and because I think that there's more of the ignoble than of the noble in the kind of long-suffering maternal devotion which writers like Maupassant get sentimental about in stories like "Une Vie." (But I am not entirely free of those blind maternal feelings—I disapprove of them, that's all.)

But just what to do about it is a question. And what to do about so much else, about everything, involves problems which I can't seem to cope with. And I can't cope with them (it's the chief reason for my helplessness) because the very thing which would bring about their solution would rob me of what I want most, of what I require most—that is, my time, my days, at least part of my time, part of my days—and thus render the solution in itself futile. My very working habits, my thinking processes, force upon me—(apart from those other important factors)—an inability to give forty or fifty hours a week to a job which completely disrupts the continuity of my consciousness.

Getting back into myself after such a disruption does not come easily to me—and the less easily the more of myself in mental ways I have to give to a job which forces upon me alien mental activities. And then when I do get back, I write slowly, and if I'm doing poetry (unless it's a first draft which I can generally dash off whole) I sometimes have to spend hours on just a few lines in order to get the exact words that I want—especially if it is an abstract idea for which absolutely precise words which allow of no substitution are more difficult to achieve than when one has before one, an objective model, such as a person's face or a landscape. And it's the same when I do prose, as I know from my experiences on two occasions when I wrote short stories which I have since discarded (though there are some others I'd like to do or at least try). I cannot just sit down to a typewriter and write freely, easily, covering page after page with words. I go at writing pretty much the same way as I used to at clay, a long time ago, when I had hoped to do something with sculpture. My mind lingers over words and sentences, my ear over sound, in the very same fashion that my fingers used to do over the clay; and if I were a novelist, it would take me—I am sure—and even working continually—several years to complete each novel because the language, the form of the book, of almost every sentence in it would concern me and occupy me much more than the plot or narrative in itself.

Despite all the roughness in my own poetry, despite my own technical inadequacies, and despite my having so much of the social reformer in me, and so much concern with morals and ethics, among those writers and poets who interest me it is the "pure artists" which I like best, so that while the ideas, the philosophy, of a poet like Rilke interest me very much as such, the poetry of such a poet does not mean as much to me as that of a poet like Mallarmé whose meanings one comes by, not so much by one's intellect [as] by one's aesthetic sensibilities. The complexions and contours of my own mind—at least in its creative needs both actively and receptively—are such therefore that even ordinarily, even, I mean, if the time element in my own personal life were not such an important factor with me now—I'd find it difficult to function (and *have* found it so, which is why I've written so little) with my entire days given over to the routine of any job which is *only* and *entirely* a financial necessity.

My crying need now is to crowd into one year or two as much intellectual and creative activity as is generally spread over many years, to thus say what I have to say about this world and this life through which I have passed without any happiness, and then call it a day! But how to do that—what a problem that is!

Maybe,—that would be best for me—I can somehow find a part-time job (I don't care much what the work might be) which would take up only five hours a day of my time at the most—and possibly only four, and which would pay about $15 a week for 25 or 30 hours. I could get by on that much now, with my son having quit school and gotten himself that job, as I couldn't do when I always had some financial responsibility towards him (for even when he did those farm chores for his room and board, I was supposed to supply his spending money and clothes and other such incidentals). And then, if I should find such a part-time job, I am going to make another attempt to get some books to review (I am [a] much better critic of other people's work than of my own, and my literary judgements are pretty sound). And if I succeed in that (and going on with my own poetry at the same time) I shall try to get into Yaddo for as long as one is permitted to stay there, and preferably as soon as the place opens next spring and summer—earning a few dollars from the reviews (if I should succeed in getting them to do) while I am there, and which would certainly be necessary since one always has other living expenses over and above room and board.

Yes, that is the plan I have now. I have just hit upon it during the course of writing this letter, and therefore will cross out one previous paragraph, as you will have noticed before you come to this. But the whole plan of course hinges upon whether or not I can find some such part-time job as I have mentioned—and so until I do there's no point and no use to my asking if you could and would help me with the rest of it (about the reviews and Yaddo for the coming summer). But I shall ask about that if and when I can find such a job.

The way I ignore the war—(I hope that doesn't shock you). But I have to, I *must*!

And now about those poems in New Directions, and your preface. As a piece of writing, as your writing, I like it very much; and also it was very kind and generous of you to lend your name to my work which is so deficient according to what I want to do in poetry, and don't, or can't. But it embarrassed me, that preface, because in my private struggles and problems I prefer to live anonymously, except in some few personal relationships, and because I had asked Laughlin to please just publish the poems in themselves without any comments on me personally.

I have become deeply interested in your prose (by the way), and having known only your poetry previously (I mentioned that when I saw you in New York) began to read the White Mule.[3] The Woodstock library has it. But I began it only a few days before I left (I had little time to spend in the library and a card cost two dollars), and therefore had to regretfully leave it behind me half-read, and will finish it now in New York, uptown at the central library's reading room if it is not available for circulation. But even in the projection of myself into another person's creative sensibilities—that too with me as with my own writing and ideas, is a gradual slow process which evolves for me rather than happens suddenly, so that I generally have to live quite intimately within myself with the work of another writer (that is, if the work interests me—I know right away when it doesn't) before I know fully and exactly how I think and feel about it. This would not be so perhaps if I had done much reading professionally. But since I have had little occasion for that kind of reading, and have turned to this or that book only to satisfy my own intellectual and spiritual needs, that's the way it is with me, so that I shall have to get more extensively and deeply at that phase of your writing and into it (which I shall probably do now that I have started the White Mule, liking it) before my feelings about your other work apart from poetry completely clarify themselves for me.

I received a copy of New Directions only two days ago, though I'd previously glanced at it in Brentano's last Saturday.

Therefore I haven't read your play yet, and have only skimmed over what you have to say about women's writing (as you know that subject is of great concern to me) in your article on Anaïs Nin.[4]

I sent several poems (a couple of old ones and three new ones) to one the editors of Partisan Review; and he sent them back to me with a note saying that he found no "art" in them, that I wrote too gracefully in standardized conventional forms, and "used no new words." I can well understand how he might not like my poetry. But it seems to me that the reasons he gave were not the right ones—not particularly good criticism. In one of the poems I used the common ordinary speech of an illiterate girl, making a poem of what she said—and my doing that was the art.[5] And in regard to new words—it's not new words which count (how many new words can one create?) but the use of common ones in new associations. But you can see the poems for yourself—the recent ones, which I am enclosing. And if and when you get a chance to read them (I know you are busy working on your own long poem Paterson from a note about it in N.D.) will you tell me what you think of them, which means that if you do not like them, you can feel quite free to say so because—as I think you know—I should never want you to be anything but completely honest with me in such matters.

Please forgive me for having caused you to waste both that money that you sent me, and your job inquiries on my behalf. My position is such that the slightest mishap affecting the practical affairs of my life have more fatal results than in the case of the average person. I was in the "mood", the state of mind, when I first accepted your kind offer to loan me some money for furthering my chances of getting and keeping a decent job, to go right ahead then and put through those plans I mentioned in my letter welcoming that loan. But after I dashed out of town so suddenly (I was in serious straits in the way of my over-due room-rent; and among other things, I was upset by your having said that I was quite mad not to have taken that other hotel job in the country)[6] and upon thus—and in such unexpected ways—going from the frying pan into the fire, I had knocked out of me, by despair, (and it has not returned since) any real "drive" at all toward getting on in the world materially.

I suppose that if someone were to knock at my door this moment and tell me of a job that involved work I'd really enjoy and would find worthwhile for its own sake, and which was right there waiting for me to step into, without my having to submit a complete case history of myself, the weariness which I feel in regard to the whole job problem would leave me; and that I would welcome most enthusiastically that opportunity to escape all this wretched poverty and lead a normal life. But that's not likely to happen (there are some jobs which I would enjoy for their own sake but they are beyond my reach) and in these past three months of being knocked around from pillar to post, I've completely lost (though I had some of it left in me when I wrote to you at the end of the summer about my financial plight) what it takes to get and hold the kind of job which is little more than a meaningless routine and which calls for the sacrifice of nearly all one's time and of one's very soul in return for nothing over and above some good clothes, three square meals a day, and a comfortable bed—which is never really comfortable anyway when one sleeps in it alone.

I think you can understand my state of mind in all that. And I hope—I hope so much, that you can and will.

Most sincerely,

Marcia Nardi

P.S. I feel a bit guilty at having included that paragraph about my son, because he is a "good boy" in the fashion of nice ordinary boys and nice ordinary people in general. He's inarticulate as most such ordinary people are, and therefore can't find any expression for his rages except that of the streets. And he has a right to his rages because it is really very sad for his sort of person to have a mother who has so little in common with the mothers of his boy friends. He has always felt so inferior among them because of me, so that it's natural that his crushed pride should turn for bolstering now to his job, to his ability to earn $18 a week with no experience, so little schooling, and at so young an age, and also that he should be utterly unable to understand, having no mental needs of his own, (I had a great many at 15 and 16, even at 13) how it is that if he can earn eighteen dollars so easily, I should not be earning at least twice as much just as easily. Yes, that is very sad and I feel the tragedy for him keenly. But there's my side of that tragedy too—which is that I had so much to give to a different kind of child, especially since I like children and find them a lot more interesting than most adults, and enjoyed more than any other form of employment forced upon me, a temporary summer-time job I once had working with a group of children in one of the city's slum sections.

P.S. (2)[7] If that money order was traced, and found to have been stolen, will you please let me know *where* it was cashed, and if the signature on it was in strange handwriting or an attempt to imitate mine? It *could* be mere coincidence, that Laughlin's check vanished in exactly the same way, that neither the money order nor the check (both addressed to 21 Grove Street) ever reached me, and that neither was returned to the sender, with the sender's name and address so clearly on the envelope of each. But it certainly does look as if someone has been helping himself or herself to my mail, and I'm curious as to just who, because I knew, in the way of casual friendship, several people who lived there in the house with me and completely trusted the negro superintendent. Those wretched bits of human refuse up on that farm (the ones who stayed there and slept in the chicken coops)—they would be capable of anything. But Laughlin's check couldn't have been forwarded there (for I'd long ago cancelled that forwarding address); [it] *must* have been delivered to 21 Grove Street, since the package notice about the book was right there lying on the hall table; so that it would seem as if the person taking my mail is someone at Grove Street and not at Sherburne.

1. A reference to Williams having said in his introduction to her poems in *New Directions Number Seven* that Nardi was in her "early thirties."

2. The crossed-out paragraph read: "But despite all that recoil, if I should be offered that job, I shall take it. Because I must. And if any other should come my way before I know definitely abut that one, I'll take it instead, again because I must. And if those post office jobs for censors should still be open by chance (if you did get any more information about them, may I please have it) I shall try in preference to be accepted there."

3. William Carlos Williams's *White Mule* (Norfolk, Conn.: New Directions, 1937) is a fictional depiction of his wife, Flossie's, family.

4. Williams's play *Trial Horse No. 1 (Many Loves)* appeared in *New Directions Number Seven*, 233–305, along with his introduction to Nardi's poems and the review of Anaïs Nin's book.

5. This poem ("People Are Decent, Nice . . .") and two others ("Dear Dorothy" and "In rocks, in trees") are those Nardi mentions in this letter as having been sent separately. They are listed as items G131 (a, b, and c) in Baldwin and Meyers, *The Manuscripts and Letters*. On the poem "Dear Dorothy," Nardi has added this note to Williams: "In his *Letters to a Young Poet* (just in case you've never read them) Rilke warns against irony (he *would*); and while I have greatly welcomed and liked tremendously everything he's had to say on the subjects of love and sex, I think he was frightfully romantic (scarcely less so than Dante and Cavalcanti and the rest of that circle) in his idealization of woman's love. I think he was right about woman's love being superior—but not realistically enough, only romantically so."

6. This letter from Williams is missing.

7. This postscript is similar in content to that which follows the long letter at the end of Book II of *Paterson*, 91–92.

. . . .

27. TLS-4 (B)

218 West 15th St., N.Y.C.
December 2nd [1942]

Dear Dr. Williams,

I've had no reason to expect an immediate reply to that recent letter of mine. There was no inquiry or request in it of immediate urgency; and I know that between your work and the affairs connected with your private life, you certainly have no time for idle letters.

But so much has happened to side-track what was most important to me in my contact with you; and I take that very much to heart and shall continue to, until I hear from you.

Also I have changed my mind in regard to what I said in that last letter about settling my economic problems first and then trying to get some kind of literary journalism to do in addition.

The job problem continues to be a nightmare for me. But just because it does, for that very reason, I continue to succumb to the deadliest kind of mental inertia; and lacking anything in my private life to stir the stagnant waters of mind at such times, I need badly the outward goads, the forced ones, for their own sake—as well as from the few dollars I might be able to pick up from occasional reviews if I could get them to do.

For over a year now (I mentioned that in some previous letter, I think) I have wanted to do a very long article on Gide (and timely too since it is tied up with his attitude toward world affairs),[1] and I should like too to turn much of what I wrote to you about in Woodstock (about the writing of poetry) into another article; and I've had in mind for a long time some articles on women in literature from angles pretty much my own. But I have let all this go because it is so difficult to do work of that nature (since it lacks that strong inner urgency of "pure" creative work) in a kind of void—cut off from the stimulating exchange of one's ideas with other people in the course of one's personal relationships and at the same time lacking the artificial props of an impersonal audience which writing with a view to publication supplies.

It is poetry which I care about primarily and, I think, only, since if I were a person without such very serious financial worries and with an intellectually richer social life, it is only in that direction that I would turn my creative energies. But there are times when even under the most favorable circumstances, one cannot write poetry; and it is important to keep one's intellect no less active at such times, and I would be better able to do so if something outside myself (such as reviewing books and then on the strength of those, doing something with those articles I've mentioned) forced me into reading and thinking about literature and all its problems, at those moments when I'm not inclined to do so because of the fatal combination of my economic maladjustments intermingled with my very bleak and barren personal life.

And so I am wondering if you know well enough any of the editors of those newspapers and magazines which give space to literary criticism, to help me get some books to review. When I write prose with a consciousness of style it is much better than in my letters where I write more carelessly; and I have ideas of my own about literature which in the particular aspects of it which they involve, quite hold their own with those of the professional critics. But if Cowley is back on the New Republic following his resignation from that Washington job, I couldn't possibly ask *him* for any books because of that note from him several years ago which I left with my poems when you first had them.[2] If it had been just an ordinary *polite* rejection slip it would be different. But after his telling me that I apparently belonged to the "S.S.A.—The Society for the Suppression of Authors", and informing me that, "in case I didn't know it", he too was [an] author, I wouldn't dare to ask him for any. And at strange places I'd probably be treated like a school girl, asked to submit "samples" and all that, which I can't very well do because although I have not infrequently jotted down some of my ideas about literature generally and of particular writers in fitfully kept note-books, these are intermingled with other comments on very private matters in my personal life.

I said in my last letter that my great need just now and overshadowing everything else was to pack into a year or two as much writing as is generally spread over [a] much longer period of time. But my doing that, if I should manage it, would amount only to putting into organized form much of what already exists in my mind in a chaotic disorderly kind of way. There isn't any uniform law, of course—there can't be, for the development of those forces which, in each individual mind—(sometimes consciously and under control and with deliberate cultivation; and, in other cases, way under the surface, almost subconsciously, and thriving like a weed even in neglect)—determine so uniquely for every person the nature and length of their own gestation period. But whatever the fashion of their development, there comes a time when they are done with passively taking shape, and when they must actively come forth and eject themselves however inconveniently and with no more concern for the external circumstances surrounding their urgency than an infant which gets born at just the wrong moment on a bus or in a taxi cab or in an air-raid shelter. And it is that way with me now in regard to poetry and other writing which I not only want to do but *must* do. I have absorbed so-called "experience", those experiences connected with outward activity, to the saturation point. I did need for myself at one time, in the testing of all those standardized values by which women are burdened to an even greater extent than men are, more contact with "real life" in all its aspects, than most men require who are deeply concerned with art and literature. But that need was more than adequately filled for me already four years ago; and the prolongation of experience to which one can no longer re-act except negatively, is just about the worst possible waste of life and living, and can serve no purpose other than an utterly destructive one in the case of those individuals to whom life is not so much a matter of happiness or unhappiness, of pleasure or pain, as one of self-development at any cost.

That is why I have fared so badly, during these past four years, in the business of earning a living, after having managed it much better and quite successfully at times in the previous seven or eight years and even longer (after all, I sent my son to a very good boarding school for a long time and to camp every summer until he was twelve, and it was I who earned all that money in no pleasant fashion).

It is why—not through indolence and not through shiftlessness which I am continually accused of by my son, my friends, and my various landlords, but only because it is writing that I want to *work* at now and must *work* at (I have not worked on it in the past—have merely breathed it out of me which is quite different)—I am more or less forced into considering the lilies of the field, and why I will be most grateful if you will put me in the way of getting some books to review, should you be able to.

If I do some of those, then any articles which I write will receive more careful reading and be taken more seriously than if I attempted to thrust the latter upon editors who are not inclined to take seriously the thoughts and opinion[s] of unknown people; and with work of that sort to show for myself, I shall be better able—in purely psychological ways (as important certainly as in practical ways, and for me more important) to hold my own with all those people who "work for a living" and who think that something like writing poetry or pursuing to its utmost limits and through all its subtle intricacies a purely abstract concept, is not work at all but just an idle pastime.

You know—but I cannot stress it too much—that in my entire life (not even as a young girl, for my family gave me no choice in what made for my spiritual and mental well-being) I have not had even one year, not even six months, to really devote, in any sustained and organized way and with fresh undrained energies, to work in a field of my own choosing. And I want that for myself before I die, even if I have to just about die to have it.

During the last three weeks I was in Woodstock, I made an arrangement with some people living about two miles out of the town, to assist them with their household tasks (the man had broken his leg) from 8:30 until noon every day in return for my meals and room and the rest of the time to myself. They were decidedly parsimonious people who measured just about every mouthful one ate and who, even though they owned 65 acres of woodland, eyed every log and even every bit of brush wood that one tossed into the stoves. But even so I was quite willing to put up with all that, and to endure the unmitigated isolation of living there without a house in sight and a two-mile walk to the nearest store, and with no pay except an unheated bedroom and the simplest kind of meals, for the sake of that opportunity to have so much time for reading and writing. They didn't live up to their end of the bargain, began piling all kinds of extra tasks on me that our original agreement didn't call for, and because they were communists of purely emotional convictions with absolutely no knowledge of economics or history and with that exalted idealization of the Proletariat so common among such people, they resented the nature of my reading, and because I happened to have some copies of Partisan Review, they suspected me of being a "Trotskyist"—and all that stupid business which I have had to contend with on other occasions with other such people. And then my son (after his "running away") finally arrived there, which wasn't part of the arrangement, so that it didn't work out. But if it had, I would have snatched even at that, at almost anything, in order to be free enough for some real work with writing.

May I please hear from you regarding what I have asked here in this letter about the reviews? And I'd be quite happy to hear from you anyway, due to my previously expressed regret at having thrust upon you so long and woeful a tale of my money problems in the past four years, and then having caused you to waste forty dollars (though accident mostly was responsible for that) of which I have not even started to pay you back, being in a position no different than if you had not tried to help me out—except that my attitude toward it is different now.

Sincerely,

Marcia Nardi

I am sending this poem[3] which I wrote a few days ago—for you to read, along with those other three, whenever you have the leisure for that. But of the other three, it is only the longer one ("In rocks, in trees") which I care about—the two shorter ones being quite slight and of no great consequence. I've made a few changes in that poem (in rocks, in trees) since I sent it, but it remains the same in its general outlines.

---

1. André Gide believed that artists had an obligation to involve themselves in world affairs.

2. Malcolm Cowley, literary editor of the *New Republic* from 1929 to 1944 and staff member of the Office of Facts and Figures, Washington, D.C., in 1942. The note from Malcolm Cowley cannot be found.

3. Nardi's poem "In a Frame . . . ," listed as item G131d in Baldwin and Meyers, *The Manuscripts and Letters*, 333.

218 West Fifteenth St.

Tuesday, December 8th [1942]

Dear Dr. Williams,

I find myself very much distressed today at not having heard from you—in a way I probably wouldn't be, if so much hadn't gone wrong in your attempts to help me straighten out my life in practical ways; and if, on top of that, my plans for myself since getting back to the city didn't continue to meet with failure.

What I said to you in that letter last week about the reviews: that I need desperately some tangible outward bond between myself and literature—I feel that way more strongly with each passing day. Yes, even more strongly now than last week!

My liking for that particular French poet—Tristan Corbière—has a lot to do with my having found in his work, thoughts and feelings and attitudes so much my own that it was almost as if I myself had written many of those poems. I mention this because if you know the mood which prevails in practically all those poems in Les Amours Jaunes, you will know exactly how I have felt for a long long time about everything. ". . . Et dans sa pauvre tête / Déménagée, encore il sentait que les vers / Hexametres faisaient les cent pas travers." That has been *my* misery not only continu- ally, but *continuously*, and "Non, petit, il faut commencer / Par etre grand-simple ficelle" and "Je sais rouler une amourette / En cigarette," et cetera are feelings which I have lived with all too in- timately and closely, and that "Epitaphe" is my own.[1]

The only difference is that I think poetry should transcend the purely subjective and accidental; and also that I quite agree with something you said in POETRY last summer[2] about superlative qualities of mind and spirit not being of the street; and with what Christ said in his attacks on the Pharisees in the Sermon on the Mount—"But thou, when thy prayest, enter into thy closet," et cetera. But it is impossible to replace one's relationship with the world by one's relationship with one's own solitude unless one is economically in a position to do so; because to concern one's self with art and literature as a nobody and in the midst of great poverty, and especially in a time of war, leaves one utterly defenseless against the attacks of those people who glorify *only* what Rimbaud called the "bons travaux abrutissants".[3]

Sometimes it is necessary to give unto Caesar the things that belong to Caesar, in order *to be able* to have and keep for God the things that belong to God. And the literary criticism primarily for money and for publication which I'd like and need to do, amounts to the former for me.

You said that night I met you for dinner, that you had come into New York to meet me entirely for reasons connected with my poems; and that meant a great deal to me not because I am not very much a woman in my relationships with men (which of course I am) but because I had never known any other man in my entire life—not one—who would have spent even two minutes with me out of any really genuine interest in anything connected with my mental life. Harvey, despite his having liked some of my work and despite his having wanted to send some of it to POETRY with his statement (an offer which I did not avail myself of) had no interest in either my poems nor my intellect that existed in its own right, uncolored and uninfluenced by that other interest which he had in me at that time. It is significant that he liked best and only my most subjective poems—those that had to do with sex and love. They made me more interesting to him not as a poet nor as a thinking human being, but only in purely physical ways, because he knew, as we all know, that sensibilities of mind and soul do not escape getting into one's veins and blood-stream. And I dare say (yes, I am quite sure of that) that if I wrote to him now and asked him (because he has a great many contacts with editors as the result of economic necessity) if he would help me get some reviewing to do, he would not be inclined to put himself out in any way to comply with that request, whereas at the time he felt a certain way about me he would have been quite glad to have done so.

But you already know how well aware I am of an intelligent woman's relationship to men with fine minds, being more often than not, no different basically from her relationship to mentally undeveloped men. And I mention it here again only by way of explanation and apology in continuing to bother you (when you have already done so much for me): this time in that matter of the book-reviews which I can not possibly obtain through the very few other people I have known with editorial connections; and which certainly I can not get merely by marching into a newspaper or magazine office and asking for them.

I imagine that your reward for being so kind and generous toward unknown writers must, at times, result in some very difficult situations for you. I hope that is not so in my case; because the only phase of writing which deeply concerns me is writing itself for its own sake. Ironically enough, the kind of life which women like Emily Dickinson have been pitied for, and which George Herbert found so irksome and unexciting when he was confined to that remote little parish in his last years, is the kind of life which I myself would find most desirable, and most conducive to thought and reading and writing. And if I could have that kind of life with its quietude and its seclusion, its private library filled with books of one's own choosing, its trees outside one's window, and its freedom from money troubles, I very likely would not know from one year to another whether such people as Malcolm Cowley and the Partisan Review editors, were living or dead—so little concern would I have with that aspect of the literary world. But as you said in one of your poems, "empty pockets make empty heads";[4] and empty-headed relatives and friends also make empty heads; so do those bons travaux abrutissants (I like that phrase!); and because I therefore go about with mine empty half the time, and have so great a need to keep it filled all the time, I hope you will forgive me for continuing to thrust my problems upon you in such long letters.

Sincerely,

Marcia Nardi

P.S. My over long letters are in themselves an indication of how desperately I need more outlets for self-expression in words, and my sufferings in the way of insomnia have been much more the result of my frustrations in writing than in my private emotional life, because I have a stronger feeling of physical well-being when I am reading or writing than at any other time. I feel well only then.

P.S. (2) If my letters seem frightfully ego-centric, it's not that I am unaware how your own life no doubt has its own cares and problems. It's merely that one can't help being ego-centric when one is fighting for one's breath; and writing, poetry and the whole world of literature and art are my breath.

1. Quotations from *Les Amours jaunes* by Tristan Corbière. "Et dans sa pauvre . . .": And in his poor head / With the door on the hinge, he still felt the queue / Of hexameters doing sentry duty askew (from "The Contumacious Poet"). "Non, petit . . .": No, little one, we must start / By being grown up, no easy task. "Je sais rouler . . .": I know how to roll a light affair / Like a cigarette (from "Guitar"). "Epitaphe": Except for lovers beginning or finished who want to begin with the end there are so many things that end with the beginning that the beginning begins to end by being the end the end of which will be that lovers and others will end by beginning to begin again with this beginning which will have ended by being only the end reverted which will begin by being equal to eternity which has neither end nor beginning and will end by being also finally equal to the rotation of the earth when you'll have ended by no more distinguishing when the end begins from when the beginning ends which is every end of every beginning equal to every final beginning of the infinite defined by the indefinite—This equals an epitaph which equals a preface and conversely (from "That").

2. In a review of *Poems* by Louis Zukofsky, Williams wrote, "Because a man lives obscurely does not mean that his work is good, but if he does good work in the arts—or perhaps I had better say, superlative work—it is more than likely he will remain in obscurity. There is a kind of monkhood in excellence, it does not become the street. I wonder, even, if superlative traits of the mind and spirit do not rightly detest popularity" (see "An Extraordinary Sensitivity," *Poetry* [September 1942]: 338–340).

3. Good mind-dulling work.

4. Nardi quotes from WCW's poem "Raleigh Was Right." See *The Collected Poems of William Carlos Williams*, vol. 2, 1939–1962 (New York: New Directions, 1988), 88.

. . . .

29. APCI-I (B)

218 West 15th St., N.Y.C.
[postmarked Dec. 11, 1942]

Dear Dr. Williams:

Are you vexed with me, disappointed in me in some way I don't know about? The ghastliest things have continued to happen in matters to do with jobs and money, that "vicious circle" of one thing leading to another—I haven't once been able to break it since I left N.Y. for that farm job! And the only way I *can* break it, is by such means as I've written to you about in these last letters of mine.

I don't want to sound sentimental or pathetic (of *that* I have a particular horror). But you *are* the only friend I've had in connection with what means most to me, and so my continuing not to hear from you deepens even more the sense of isolation I ordinarily feel. Once, my faith in myself was so badly shattered that my brain turned into a log for over two years, and I don't think that I could survive any such occurrence as that now. Also, in the past I wrote poetry blindly, and now I could write it seeing it, and all these things "and so much more" leave me quite miserable in not hearing from you and not knowing why.

M.N.

. . . .

30. TLS-I (T)

December 16, 1942

My dear Marcia Nardi:

I am trying to discover some means of assisting you to find work of the sort you might prefer though I cannot promise anything. I advise you to take anything that offers, there should be plenty of opportunities for you at such a time as this. You will hear from me one way or another as soon as anything offers.

Meanwhile please accept the enclosed money-order as due you on various scores.

You cannot hold it against anyone that they do not reply to your letters in detail. It is uncalled for for you to expect it. Others have difficulties as well as yourself, though of a different nature. Long accounts explaining this that or the other simply concern no one but yourself—that is, directly.

The important thing is for you to get proper work. After that it is up to you. I'll help you once more, after a proper canvass of the opportunities.

Sincerely yours
W. C. Williams

. . . .

31. ALS-1 (B)

218 West 15th St., N.Y.C.
December 23rd [1942]

Dear Dr. Williams—

I've been ill for the past four days, and at the same time going to a job which I got last Friday and which I can't afford to lose, even though it's very long hours and low wages. I therefore am tired to the point of exhaustion as I write this during lunch hour at my job; can hardly keep my eyes open; and can think none too clearly.

But I want to acknowledge your note, and to thank you for it; and to thank you also for that ten dollars which helped me to, at last, get my winter coat out of storage and to buy some much needed galoshes and warm gloves. And also I want to wish you a happy Christmas and New Year. But that's about all I can manage here with pen and paper, if I am to get this in the mail-box on my way home, which I am anxious to do.

Most sincerely,
Marcia Nardi

My handwriting is worse than ever when I'm tired, so that this scrawl, I'm afraid, is scarcely decipherable. (I fell asleep at 3.30 A.M. last night, and had to be up at 6.30 A.M.)

. . . .

32. TLS-1 (T)

Dec. 23, 1942

Dear Marcia Nardi:

This is to tell you, perhaps I have already told you, that I sent a money order for fifteen dollars to you just at the time that you were leaving for that country job which turned out to be such a fiasco. You never received it nor was it returned to me.

As soon as I knew what had occurred I entered a complaint at the local post office. They took it up with the New York Post Office. Today I saw a photostatic copy of the money order as sent by me but with your name forged to it by some stranger. Whoever it was he or she did not know how to spell your name but wrote "Nards" instead of "Nardi".

The matter is now in the hands of the Federal authorities. I mention this to you so that you will not be frightened if you are called on by one of the agents from the Post Office Department. The money is yours and must be paid to you. Every effort will be made to arrest and prosecute the forger.

Sincerely yours

W. C. Williams

. . . .

33. TLS-8 (B)

218 West 15th Street,

New York City

January 19th [1943]

Dear Dr. Williams,

I had been ill, as I said, when I sent you that brief note just before Christmas. And I have continued to be, in a way that I cannot describe in a word but which this letter in its entirety will convey.

What you said about other people having their cares and problems too—yes I knew and know that of course. It was merely (and remains so as I start this) that I suffer so acutely from the solitude which surrounds my life mentally, and at times am rendered almost witless by it, I'm afraid.

My great handicap in living (and therefore in writing) has been for a long long time, not my consuming job and financial problems, and not my educational limitations, and not even my emotional frustrations, but only and entirely my lack of any connecting links whatsoever between the operative and inner aspects of my existence—combined with my lack of any intellectual companionship at all from one year to another.

When I went after that book reviewing without success some years ago, it was entirely because I needed so badly some externalized bond between myself and the world of ideas to counteract the impoverishing effect upon my mind of having no such ties in my private social life. And of the various elements that entered into my great need for Harvey's friendship at just about this time last year, among the strongest was my feeling that knowing intimately a person with common interests would clarify my mind in regard to poetry in a way no amount of solitary poring over books could do. And later when you first wrote to me about my poetry, I found myself wishing so much that I had met you in a different fashion—that you happened to be, for instance, a next-door neighbor whom I would be bound to see from time to time, so that that accidental proximity in itself (without my even burdening you with any awareness of it) would put me in the way of learning a great deal about poetry from my personal contact with you; because I felt then and feel now and have felt for nearly six years that what my poetry suffers from most is my lack of any really clear objective critical faculty when looking at anything I write, as a result of my never having been able to freshen my eyes and clarify my vision in the way that most writers do (however subconsciously) during the course of their normal social contacts with other people's minds, or else by the very nature of their vocations and professions as in the case of established writers.

Not that I am any less "self-sufficient" (another meaningless word) than the next person. But *no* mind can thrive when continually locked in upon itself—especially when it has never experienced (as mine never has) any of those beneficial "influences" in its formative years which play such an important part in the development of people who come from educated families.

Anyway, my frustration in all that—especially my resulting inability to stand off (because I have only a void to stand off in) and look at my own poems objectively, and my not being able to write at all so often for that very reason—has had the unfortunate outcome in this past month or so, of plunging me into a world comprised of *nothing* but sex problems, for the easily understandable reason that when all those forces of life connected with one's mental and spiritual survival find themselves hopelessly blocked and dammed up, they must sooner or later all rush forth together in transmuted form to whatever open gate one's life may offer on the other purely physical side of existence.

And the particular jungles and panthers and marshlands which I have to face in my private sex world (when it gets completely cut off from my emotional life) are of such a nature (since I have no recourse to the bridles of conventional morality) that they can completely destroy me in the course of a single week—and in even less time—should I find myself cooped up with them alone without the escape of other outlets and concerns and sensibilities on other planes of existence. And what happened was that I did find myself cooped up with them in a corner (or rather a wilderness) completely segregated from all the other phases of living, so that my nervous system came in for just about the worst beating up it has ever received. And to make matters worse, I became easy prey—in that undermined condition—to a cold which turned into the grippe combined at first with a bad cough and then with swollen glands and finally with neuralgia and an ear-ache—all those ailments (coming together like the miseries of Job) having kept me continually in bed all this time—until three days ago when I got up for the first morning in weeks with some sense of physical well-being, but without knowing how to pick up the threads of my life because I have none really to pick up.

As you know—for I previously mentioned it—I sent some poems to Partisan Review while I was out of town, which were returned to me. I did that primarily because I was anxious to see if I could get any published on my own, especially since I knew (Laughlin having mentioned that) that it was entirely your influence which got those others into New Directions. So for the very same reason (to see if I could get any published on my own) I sent some also to Poetry magazine after I got back to town—those too being sent back to me with no comment except one of those formal rejection cards.

The matter of the publication, one way or another, meant very little to me. But what did matter greatly was my not being able to see my own writing—my being so in the dark about it. I mean that I had thought that one poem (I sent you a copy of that one) beginning "in a frame beauty . . ." was a perfectly good one.[1] And that it impressed the editors of Poetry as having absolutely no merit at all (which may be true—and which in itself is of no great consequence since no one's work is completely even) made me realize how lacking I am in any critical faculty regarding my own work. And that realization produced in me a kind of creative constipation which left me quite unable to continue working on a group of short lyrics which I had started a couple of days before receiving that rejection card from Poetry; and the impasse which I reached there, was the specific incident which led up to everything else which has happened to me in the past few weeks.

In some terrible way, all the events of my life in the past five or six years (I was not ready to do much living in the world of ideas before then) have on the one hand isolated me more and more from the only kind of people with whom I could possibly find some meeting ground; and on the other hand have encircled me more and more by those with whom I have least in common.

There are gains certainly in the way of broader human sympathies in having been thrust up as intimately as I have been against all kinds of people—taxi cab drivers, longshoremen, and men like that. There was a time a few years ago when I knew absolutely no one (they lived in the same rooming house with me and shared a community kitchen) *except* three semiunderworld characters—two girls on parole and a man now serving a jail sentence. But those gains have been cancelled by the great loss to me intellectually—by the great handicap to me that way and the crippling—of my never once having had in my private life the kind of relationship with anyone (whether in the way of family ties, or of love, or of friendship) which brought my mental faculties into play and which offered so much as a crumb of nourishment to my mind.

And that phase of things for me has reached in this past month or so a crisis beyond which I can't seem to budge an inch. And naturally it has affected my economic situation, has kept it still a very serious one, because life's too much of a piece for that to be avoided.

I finally had to give up that other make-shift job which I had when I last wrote to you, as a result of being continually ill. But there has been no great loss to me there certainly, because jobs like that can be gotten by the carload from the Journal American any day in the week, and one such job is as good as another. There's no doubt—I feel it too keenly for that feeling to be deceptive—that at the root of *all* my problems, whatever their nature, there always has been and remains that chief one of my having no outward ties of any kind which involve my mental life.

In everyone, I suppose, there's always one major need deeper than any other, which, when filled, lessens and mitigates all other problems even when not completely solving them; and which, when not filled, only aggravates those other problems and makes one's very attempts to solve them a matter of putting the cart before the horse. But for most women that major need is the emotional thing, just as for most men it's connected with worldly success of one kind or another. And in my own case, no matter how much I might love a man in those ordinary physical ways of being in love, and no matter how much I might be bound to him that way—without his intellect having an even greater reality for me, I simply am not contained there, and therefore can find no real motivating force for myself in those particular aspects of life from which women generally derive their sense of direction.

I do not mean to imply that I'm any different from other women in their thinking that love is indispensable for happiness. Certainly it is indispensable for that. But happiness as it's generally understood is not the greatest thing with me. It's a most desirable accessory to other things more important. But when it's lacking, those other more important things still remain. I therefore can bear with unhappiness. But what I cannot bear with is that continual contraction of my mind which I have experienced again and again as a result of the mental solitude in which I live, and which I have experienced much more fatally than ever before in this past month.

I have not read a book, not even a page, in the longest time. That book of yours which I started in Woodstock—it still remains unfinished; nor have I so much as glanced at anything else—not even at a magazine. I have done nothing but sit by—in the midst of the most wretched health—and watch my own brain rot away.

And on top of that, I have found myself seized lately by the most ignoble emotions—those of violent hatred and a rankling bitterness directed towards the two particular people (one of them Harvey of course) who could so easily have enabled me to escape from those terrible atrophying processes which my mind has undergone, and who failed to do so because they saw in my desperate loneliness *nothing* more than the most ordinary kind of emotional loneliness.

I do not continue to brood over that in the spirit of those priests or nuns or spinsters who have become embittered by having done so little living themselves in the way of physical love. Only one phase of my emotional life has crept into my letters to you, because the other side has been too divorced from my mental and spiritual existence by circumstances. But on that other side, I have done plenty of living. Not so happily, but still very, very much of it; and I have never had a bad conscience (my morality has to do with other things) at having a very strong sensual animal attached to me.

For that very reason, however, I feel the solitude in which my mind is imprisoned all the more keenly. It's as if my intellect had been completely lifted out of the context of my whole life and left suspended in some ghastly void quite disconnected from all my other experiences; and the mental sterility resulting from that is not at all the same kind of thing as that other kind of aridity which emotional loneliness alone can bring about. In the latter, it's only the well of the "heart", of the soul, which goes dry; and while one may have to wait for it to fill up again before having any so-called "inspiration" for writing, one can at least read in the meantime and do other kinds of writing which are good technical exercise and which keep one in trim for more productive moments. *That* sort of thing can happen to almost anyone and I suppose it does, because certainly the inner fountains don't keep gushing continuously day and night like the water spouts in a public park.

But *this* that has happened to me (not for the first time but more fatally this time) is quite a different matter; and it drives me now to make of you a request which I hesitate to make and at the same time must. Will you let me spend an hour or so with you some time very soon—anywhere and any time (I could arrange that for your convenience)? I don't want to talk about my troubles. I am too bored with those. But I should like to have with me one or two very short poems, or just some few lines of a poem (and if they happen to be very bad poems, so much the better for the purpose) and ask you about certain problems with poetry which they would illustrate. And the same thing in regard to a paragraph or two of prose of my own which could be easily read but which would also illustrate certain problems which writing has for me. And there are some other things in connection with writing that I should like to ask you about—and also one thing (not connected with writing at all) in regard to one particularly puzzling aspect of my health difficulties which, as a physician, you may be able to throw some light upon, and which I cannot so easily take up with some unknown doctor whose intelligence I know nothing about, since it *may* (though I do not know) have psychological roots.

Apart from those very specific things that I should like so much to talk to you about (those to do with writing being more important to me than the other) I have been almost obsessed with the feeling for at least two weeks now, that this deadness of my mental faculties which I cannot seem to dispel, would immediately vanish if I found myself for an hour or so in the presence of someone whose own mind had a great deal of reality for me—and whose personality too of course since one cannot possibly sever the two. And also I have been feeling—and in such a desperate way—that merely to match my own mental stature with another person's during the course of almost any kind of conversation, would enable me to get back some sense of my own personal identity in mental ways.

You may be so busy that you simply don't have the time for that. And as you said, other people have their cares and problems too. And also (I don't know anything about your writing habits) you may feel some need within yourself to stay so close to your own writing if and when you happen to be doing a lot of concentrated work on it, that any alien writing problems would be a great burden to you at such a time.

But if you can possibly see your way to granting that request I make of you, it would mean a million times more to me than anything you could possibly do for me in purely practical ways— regarding jobs, et cetera.

I do not underestimate the latter. But the state of mind to which I have devoted this letter is even more serious than my economic situation, and to a great extent the cause of it.

If I should hear from you that you can and will let me see you some time soon, the mere prospect of that, I think, would snatch me into life.

Sincerely,

Marcia Nardi

P.S. I did not yet get any visit from the Post Office authorities, but I cannot think about such matters at the moment. Anyone could steal a thousand dollars from me if I had it and receive not so much as the mildest reproach from me, if things were not so bad with me in those other ways.

P.S. (2). It may seem odd to you that I should have known for the most part the particular kind of people I've referred to in this letter. But the only other people I could have known (the set-up of my life being what it is) were all those would-be Village writers and artists who used to sit around Life Cafeteria at Sheridan Square and who belonged to the Writers Union and later were on the WPA projects; and the particular ones of those people whom I happened to meet had nothing more to them than the frothiest kind of intellectual pretensions with nothing real and genuine underneath, so that I had to choose as the lesser of two evils the most ordinary kind of individuals who at least were real on a lower level of experience and awareness.

Even in the case of Sydney,[2] and despite a very simple kind of emotional attachment I had to him at one time, he had nothing to offer my mind. As far as I could make out (though I may be mistaken) he had not very much intellect: only certain instincts and feelings about poetry, and even those were both limited and lax. And worst of all, he had a romantic sentimentally reverential attitude toward "Poets" (very much like that reverential attitude which uneducated Catholics have toward any picture of Christ), and ideas of an abstract nature simply didn't exist for him at all.

I don't mean that about Sydney in any unkind way. I mention it only as an example of how I've been cut off from any of those relationships with people that contribute something to one's mental life.

I'd give up the most wonderful lover in the world (if such a person figured in my life at the moment) for those other things which I need so badly. And *my* saying that means an awful lot, because when I fall for anyone in the ways of just sex and desire, I fall pretty hard.

---

1. See photocopy (33.1) of poem Nardi included with her letter to Williams. "In a Frame . . ." is listed as item G131d in Baldwin and Meyers, *The Manuscripts and Letters*, 333.

2. Christopher MacGowan suggests in his notes to *Paterson* that Nardi may be referring to the poet Sydney Salt (277–278). Nardi and Salt were neighbors on Charles Street in Greenwich Village in 1941, and MN mentions a "Sydney" in her letters to WCW on a few occasions. In addition, Wililams wrote an introduction to Salt's book of poems *Christopher Columbus and Other Poems* (Boston: Bruce Humphries, 1937), and Salt dedicated this book to "Jean Rivers."

33.1. (B) MN Poem

marwa Nardi)

Page I

POEM

(In a frame....)

In a frame beauty always,
Imprisoned motion -
In a Degas, a mirror,
Another's devotion:
Alice who could not get back,
Alice loved into seeing
A glass-walled self
On an adamant bed
More real than being:

Never moving across the bridge
Over ocean or lake or stream;
From side to side only...
Tied
To that face less its own
Than the stream's,
Like the paralysed running feet
In the tomb of an agonized dream:

Getting no farther from Feltro to Feltro,
To Akron from Antioch,
Than in the night-long pacing
Of a room
Stretched into miles,
Into centuries,

(Continued on page 2)

By the mirror-reflecting mirrors
On every wall.

What we would hold,
Us cannot hold···
Fixed in the statue
By us created;
Flowing rooted away
(Stay ,Eva! How the child-heart breaks
When Tom underseas in the Water-Babies!)
On the marble waves of the never-free
Unfailing inspiration:
The Perfect State, the lustless
Niobe,
The infant Savior's myrrh-sweet stable,
The fresh-scrubbed arm-pits which
To stir would ~~give~~ leave
with
Odor again of perspiration.

Thou still unravished bride,
Most fittingly
In shape of delicate urn you yearn
For the livid, impure,
And living earth
In Isabella's Pot of Basil!

But how the mirror's slaughtered

(continued from page 2)   — 3 —   (on a frame — — —)

Sing like living water
When
The hymns begin
Of praise
And adoration!

End

Note: I think (though I may be all wrong about that) that
it is quite legitimate to utilize even factual
inaccuracies in a poem if they serve the poem's purpose
— that a poem, for instance, like Keats' First Reading Chapman's
Homer is no better or worse for referring to Cortez's
discovery of the Pacific when Balboa discovered it. And so
whatever Dante meant by "Feltro to Feltro" has
nothing to do with my poem, nor has "Alice Through the
Looking Glass" anything to do with it except that the poem could
make good use of the image and symbol suggested
by that title in itself regardless of the actual story.

81 West 12th Street, N.Y.C.

February 4th [1943]

Dear Dr. Williams,

Forgive me please for my persistence in thrusting my problems upon you.

I am in *such* a bad way; and don't know how to avoid a complete smash-up, unless I can turn to some one person as a friend, and immediately, and without being forced to play either a pathetic role or a burdensome one.

I was reading that play of yours last night (Many Loves) and what you have Peter say in it about Hubert: "He waits only to be loosed by his writing," et cetera—the whole passage there—describes my own desperate need for writing much better than any words of mine could do.[1] Only I cannot recapture any confidence in the validity of my own thoughts and ideas unless and until I find myself, momentarily at least, in the presence of someone whose mind would restore my own to me.

God knows I want little enough from external sources, only two very simple things: (1) any secure regular income at all, no matter how small, so long as the earning of it leaves me with enough time and energy for work in which I have my heart; and (2) some one or two friendships with people whose personal values and realities are not completely alien to my own. And yet the lack of that little for such a long time leaves me now a very lost woman in most critical ways. Or rather, a very broken one (because I *see* all too clearly the necessary conditions for my survival). And you are the only person I know who could help me achieve those conditions—which is why I have taken the liberty of burdening you with this wretched existence of mine. One can turn to almost anyone in the case of purely physical disasters. And even in the matter of being in love (if it is the love of desire alone) chance and accident play a large part in determining the object of our passion, in that fashion which Proust analyzes so well. But on the other side of one's being, certainly no such replacements and substitutions and compromises are possible; so that while I cannot throw off this really desperate need which I have to see you and have a talk with you, I nevertheless can channel that need in no other direction because certain qualities belonging to your particular mind and understanding would be lacking in another person—and it is because of those that I have that need so strongly.

That time I so presumptuously called upon you nearly a year ago (when I was having all that trouble with my son) I asked—you remember—if I could count on your help (as a physician in that case) should I need to. And you so kindly said I might. But in the end, I didn't need to, because the very knowledge that I could and the sense of security with which that supplied me, were enough for me then to be able to see the situation through by myself. And it's seemingly small things like that which have always played a much more important part in my life than seemingly more important things. And it is that way at this moment.

Everything is wrong with me as I write this. My nerves are in bad shape. My health in general is still wretched. I have no job (which means no money again) because I awakened every morning this week without even the will to look for one; and there are other things too connected with a girl and a threatening homosexual situation which has never happened to me before. Quite a mess surely—enough to make any outsider flee from such a tangle of woes. And yet beneath them all, is what I wrote to you about a week ago last Sunday; and I know so well that if I could only talk to you for a short while, the particular kind of good which one derives from that sort of thing, would enable me to straighten out everything else.

That is what I wished most when I came back from Woodstock. But I did not have the courage to ask it outright, knowing that you might not have the time. I am aware of that now too, as I was when I wrote to you a week ago last Sunday. But I am in such dire straits within myself (therefore outwardly too) that you will pardon me perhaps for telling you again—and with even greater urgency in this repeated request—what a tremendous lot it would mean to me if I could see you for however short a time.

I very likely seem deplorably lacking in constraint to you, in self-discipline and self-control, and even in that reticence which is merely a part of good manners. But it's not really that. I'm merely desperate in my constant hankering to lead a peaceful, scholarly, *civilized* existence of some kind; to have, above all things, a life of my mind; and it's impossible, unless someone out of that world from which I myself have always been exiled, comes to my rescue.

Sincerely,
Marcia Nardi

1. WCW, "Trial Horse No. 1 (Many Loves)," in *New Directions Number Seven*, 303.

. . . .

35. TLS-2 (Y)

81 West 12th Street,
New York City
February 14th [1943]

Dear Dr. Williams,

For reasons which you can understand, I have been trying to create imaginatively all possible situations which would cause one person to turn a completely deaf ear to some really urgent life-or-death request of another person. But (apart from that ordinary callousness of human beings generally which of course doesn't figure here) I can think of only two such situations: that, where the demands made upon one are for those emotional things which no one can give at will; and the other, where someone else's life and plight and unhappiness do not ring true somehow and where they lack any great reality for one's self.

If it's the latter situation in the case of those last two letters I sent you—then I am left without any faith even in my own sincerity which is the very worst thing that can happen to anyone.

This need which I have to be able to turn to some person whose intelligence I respect in personal ways which are not emotional ways, as a friend, is so great, so consuming, and so inevitable, that I have no words for it despite all the words I have put into those letters of mine.

One particular thing which I have wanted so much to see you about (apart from writing) finally made it necessary for me to go to a doctor last week; and he gave me some prescriptions for phenobarb to be taken at night and benzedrine to be taken in the mornings. But it isn't phenobarb that I need nor benzedrine nor love nor sex. It's what I wrote you about in those last two letters; and if it was presumptuous of me to have asked if I could see you for an hour or so, then it would be no less presumptuous of me—if I slipped and broke a leg on a deserted country road—to ask the only passer-by who happened to cross my path, to help me get home.

The emotionalism with which I say that has nothing to do with my emotions. That is the terrible part of things for me— that I am forced to write as intensely, as passionately, as desperately about friendship—about my mental loneliness, as other people generally do only in regard to their emotional lives.

I know that I am a stranger to you, that I have no right to make any demands upon you whatsoever in any personal ways, and that your own life probably holds no single crevice in it for the private problems of people not in your personal life. But I have reason to believe that you would agree (if you knew fully the reason, as you do not) that I am really forced and therefore to be condoned, in asking now for the third time if I could see you for just the shortest amount of time possible.

I have substituted the general for the specific and particular in my letters to you. But as a writer you know how the generalization which makes for abstract truths, means far less than the specific and particular in any individual's daily living. And the specific details of my life in the past couple of months (the very things I could not mention in my letters) would make your seeing me for a short while just about the greatest favor you could extend to anyone.

And regardless of whether or not you believe that, I remain,

Most sincerely,
Marcia Nardi

February 17, 1943

My dear Marcia Nardi:

Though I have tried to find work for you I have not succeeded, under present circumstances my best advice would be
for you to apply to one of the Federal Employment Bureaus and
let them instruct you.

There's nothing more that I can do or say. This brings our
correspondence to a close as far as I am concerned.

Yours very truly

W. C. Williams

. . . .

37. Draft of ALS-3 (T)

81 West 12th Street, N.Y.C.

February 22nd [1943]

Dear Dr. Williams—

This is no continuation of the correspondence you wish
ended. It's merely my own "last word" in that correspondence.[1]

You know so well it was not in regard to my job situation that
I wrote you all those *last* letters. And for you to have dismissed
the real issues as presented by those letters, in that evasive note
of yours about your weariness with my *economic* problems, is
the sort of thing I don't know what to think about. Right along
you've remained completely silent about anything I wrote you
which had to do with writing and poetry, and carefully avoided
even the slightest reference to *those* matters in your few brief
notes.

That I needed the friendship of someone in the world of art
and literature so very badly as to have expressed myself on that
point at such length and with such intensity—surely there was
nothing so unpardonably out of the way in my doing that! And
the particular kind of friendship I sought from you there, was
not out of keeping with the particular kind of interest you had
taken in my work. My having asked you about the possible
book reviewing, and then my wanting so much to go over some

of my poems with you in person, and my hankering to be even for the shortest time in the presence of someone who had some intellectual reality for me—all these requests were in no way in excess of the most ordinary kind of helps that people extend to each other in a world where no one can stand completely alone.

The physician and the practical man in you may have found all my neurotic physical ailments and my economic maladjustments decidedly exasperating. (There were indications of that in almost all your notes.) But the writer and poet and psychologist in you could not but know how destructively the repressions of the inner self can take themselves out on the body and on the whole external framework of one's life. Maybe something I said or the way I said it, rubbed you the wrong way. But if so, it was not because I hadn't appreciated deeply whatever you did try to do for me;—only because of that particular kind of clumsiness which so often goes hand in hand with being too dead-in-earnest. Or possibly someone or other (since you know a few of the people who have crossed my path) mentioned me to you in such a way as to completely destroy for you whatever picture of me you had created for yourself from my poems and my first few letters. But you know how little any of us are contained in those impressions of ourselves which we give to one person indirectly, through the eyes of another person.

But whatever guesses I may make as to the specific reasons for your withdrawn friendliness can get me nowhere in any actual knowledge of the true situation, so that I cannot even evaluate my relationship with you—and the evaluation of all our experiences is so important in itself.

I said—apart from poetry matters—that seeing you might possibly help me to throw some light on a serious health problem I have had for some time, and while that was overshadowed by the greater stress I placed on my intellectual solitude, it nevertheless was of great importance to me too. There can be no point in my going into that now after your final note. But in case you supposed I was referring to merely some minor neurasthenic condition—no, it was not that. I happen to have been suffering for some time from a puzzling cardiac disturbance (at least the trouble has been seemingly localized there) which, though only mildly troublesome when it first began several years ago, has now become very alarming, and so very serious in the past couple of weeks that I have spent night after night in great physical distress. That the condition has been diagnosed and prescribed for in such different ways (and with no relief to me) by different physicians, and that it further complicates my economic problems at the moment, is why I wanted to consult you about it.

But (as I've said) that counted less with me than the other phase of things. And even in regard to your financial assistance, and your attempts to find me a suitable job, and the publication of those poems—much as I appreciated all that, I would have appreciated much more some slight personal contact with you for those reasons which you know so well despite your evasive dismissal of them.

Just because in my daily living (and in all my falls there upon the thorns of life) I am not tough-skinned and hard enough to keep from bleeding, it does not follow that I am some sentimental slobbering idiot in my thinking. I dare say I am even more ruthless and clean-knifed and unflinching than lots of people whose intellects you particularly respect, in my objective evaluations and perceptions. As a matter of fact, my "heart" has been so shattered, and my physical and emotional energies so drained, that I am left with nothing *but* my mental faculties. And to find those threatened with withering away from lack of the handful of soil I sought from you, is a pretty terrible thing for me.

Or have you so reversed your first high opinion of my intelligence and my creative sensibilities, as to think that there wouldn't have been much there for me to save anyway?

But I shall not bother you again in any way; and I should never have sent you those letters with all their tearful outpourings, if you had not given me reason to suppose that I might perhaps receive from you a little of that sympathetic understanding which no one is above needing at some moments in a life time— however much the need for it may be scorned as a sign of unpardonable weakness.

Sincerely yours,
Marcia Nardi

P.S. I am not unaware of the great gulf that exists for all of us between those impersonal sympathies offered to a stranger at a safe distance and on paper; and that recoil which we feel at the slightest personal contact with any outsider's naked soul which somehow seems so much more indecent to us, however sincere its need, than the ugliest physical nudity. But I hoped it might be different in this case; and my reticence in expressing that hope, made me so much less to the point and much more round-about in all my letters than I otherwise might have been.

1. This is Nardi's draft; no "sent" letter has been found.

. . . .

38. APCS-1 (Y)

[postmarked March 5, 1943]

Dear Dr. Williams

I have at last gotten a job congenial to my interests! But in order to get it, I *had* to give one or two first class "references;" and so I gave your name together with showing my work in New Directions; and I do hope that's all right, regardless of how you may feel about me personally; because having a job that I like (and one connected with books) for the first time in years means so much to me! I'm not getting much in the way of salary—only $15 a week to start. But just as soon as I possibly can, I shall pay you back the money you loaned me.

Sincerely,
Marcia Nardi

. . . .

39. T-4 (B)

[April ?] 1943

Dear Sir [1]

Despite my having said that I'd never write to you again, I do so now because I find, with the passing of time, that the outcome of my failure with you has been the complete damming up of all my creative capacities in a particularly disastrous manner such as I have never experienced before.

For a great many weeks now (whenever I've tried to write poetry) every thought I've had, even every feeling, has been struck off some surface crust of myself which began gathering when I first sensed that you were ignoring the real contents of my last letters to you, and which finally congealed into some impenetrable substance when you asked me to quit corresponding with you altogether without even an explanation.

That kind of blockage, exiling one's self from one's self—have you ever experienced it? I dare say you have, at moments; and if so, you can well understand what a serious psychological injury it amounts to when turned into a permanent day-to-day condition.

If that situation with you (your ignoring those particular letters and then your final note) had belonged to the inevitable lacrimae rerum (as did, for instance, my experience with H.) its result could not have been (as it *has* been) to destroy the validity for me myself *of* myself, because in that case nothing to do with my sense of personal identity would have been maimed—the cause of one's frustrations in such instances being not *in* one's self nor in the other person, but merely in the sorry scheme of things. But since your ignoring those letters was not "natural" in that sense (or rather since to regard it as unnatural I am forced, psychologically, to feel that what I wrote you about was sufficiently trivial and unimportant and absurd to merit your evasion) it could not but follow that that whole side of life connected with those letters should in consequence take on for my own self that same kind of unreality and inaccessibility which the inner lives of other people often have for us.

And there's more to it than that. There's this too. I let myself suppose at the time I was writing to you after the summer, and particularly at the time when I wished so much to see you again, that my desperate need of that personal contact with you was based entirely upon my being so terribly stranded among mindless people, and upon what you might give me intellectually and in the way of some constructive literary criticism; and certainly

I did not exaggerate the contrasting effect upon my whole mental life of all that which I wrote you about so repetitiously and at such great length. But what I did not take into account was that while the isolation in which I'd always lived intellectually was due in part to circumstances, it was due as much—just as much and perhaps even more—to my great dependence upon the "intangibles" in my relationships with people, and to my utter inability to extract the slightest sense of reality from either the mind or the personality of another person—except intangibly, via my emotions, my senses, and my instincts, so that the reason for my having wanted so much to see you again was basically, not the circumstances surrounding my outward existence, but that I liked you personally, and indefinably—with the source of that liking located elsewhere than in those regions of one's mind which concern themselves with merely the technical side of writing.

I am deeply aware of that now, because since the time of my last letter to you, I have met and have been seeing several people with literary interests—only to find that those interests in common mean nothing to me in themselves, except in the most superficial ways. I spent two occasions recently (on one occasion until 1:30 A.M.) talking about literature and about poetry in particular with a man whose own poetry is of a quality that I especially like. But all that talk went up in smoke for me—rendering even more acute my sense of emptiness within myself and greatly lengthening the miles (instead of shortening them) which have sprung up between me and the center of my own consciousness ever since I got that note from you. The reason for that *could* be that my sickly ingrown loneliness has lived too long underground to feel at home and at ease anywhere else. But I think it's something else, yes it is. It's because, under [it all], it's writing one wants to do, only the doing (however imperfectly) counts—and not any of the talk about it; and because if and when one can't do it, then living itself is again better than the talk. And it was on the side of living (my very personal liking, and in the face of my hardly knowing you at all, made it so) that I had wished so much to see you at the time I mentioned it. On that other side, I'd have gotten nothing anyway out of the talk I wanted to have with you at that time, even if you yourself had offered it.

All those letters I sent you are not to be confused therefore with the innumerable letters you doubtlessly have received over a period of years from people of all kinds; some of them just wanting to express themselves to almost anyone who would listen; others turning to you perhaps for encouragement in their secret and pathetic literary ambitions; others (of your own world) wanting prefaces to their books and other such favors; and a great many, I suppose, sending you what's called "fan" mail.

My letters are entirely different, I don't mean in what I wrote about, and certainly not in my actual relationship with you which was that to a complete stranger, but in that I *could* not have written them to you, nor have had the slightest desire to know you in any way whatsoever, if you had not taken on for me (on those two occasions when I saw you) the kind of reality which gave you your place in my consciousness, much more as a *person* I should probably like very much, as a *man* whom I should probably like very much, than as merely a good poet and a writer of importance.

There is no doubt in my mind at this moment that our true history and our only claim to any personal identity (otherwise the individual is nothing—absolutely nothing) have their roots entirely in those elements of our being which make the poorest showing in the laboratory and under the microscope, and which need the darkness of what is felt rather than rationally perceived to cast their light. And my awareness of this at all times (though never before quite as strong as now) has been the one thing, more than any other, which has paralyzed me all my life in my spasmodic and losing attempts to hold my own in the world of action and practicality, and which has forced me to always lead such a substandard existence both socially and materially; and which has always put up so great a barrier between me and those numerous people who have seen my need for a "good job" as my greatest one (and which has always rendered me so helpless in my purely biological motherhood).

It has occurred to me at moments that possibly you built up for yourself a picture of me and of my life based on those illusions based on your partial knowledge of the facts of my life [*sic*] helped to create for you and that later other facts supplied possibly by other people (with their own very different picture of me) destroyed *your* picture so that my last letters lost their interest for you as a result of being written at a time when I was no longer perhaps the same person to you—your first imaginary picture of me having been altered.

That could well be, since we all have a tendency to judge and *see* those people whom we do not know intimately in any personal way by what we know of them through others. But that sort of thing is a very stupid business, because the facts in our lives mean nothing except in relation to what lies beyond them, and because that latter is seen from a different perspective by each different person whom we meet, so that outwardly on the surface of our lives we have any number of different selves, and rarely achieve a wholly integrated identity either within ourselves or in the eyes of others, except through love or through our creative work.

It has occurred to me also that you may have been annoyed about a letter I sent to Laughlin (in case he turned it over to you) in which I took him to task for not having published merely those poems without any additional material about me personally (as I'd requested). But should that have been so—well, it had nothing to do with you personally nor with my relationship with you, but only with other entirely irrelevant matters.

There are people—especially among women—who can speak only to one person. And I am one of those women. I do not come easily to confidences (though it cannot but seem otherwise to you). I could not possibly convey to any one of those people who have crossed my path in these past few months, those particular phases of my life which I made the subject of my letters to you. I must let myself be entirely misunderstood and misjudged in all my economic and social maladjustments, if necessary, rather than ever attempt to communicate to anyone else what I wrote to you about. And so my having heaped these confidences upon you (however tiresome you may have found them and however far I may yet need to go in the attainment of *complete* self-honesty which is difficult for anyone) was enough in itself to have caused my failure with you to have so disastrous an effect upon me. And my economic situation has been involved, of course.

That particular job which I got at the time I gave your name as reference, could have served a constructive purpose in my life (despite the small wages) only under circumstances where I was doing a good deal of literary work in my spare time with deep faith in that work. Its only value for me was (at the time I took it) that I was free to make my own time schedule, working more hours one day and less another, staying out occasionally for an entire day or two (if I made the time up later) with all that flexibility in the way of routine which is so great a consideration in the case of a person who suffers as I do from that disrupted continuity of consciousness which the average job necessitates. But upon finding myself robbed of all self-confidence, of all access to my own feelings (and, so, not writing at all) I have been forced to cut a ludicrous figure in holding down such a job when everyone around me is getting some fabulously large salary from defense work, so that I have thus further complicated my relationship with society as represented by my family, my acquaintances, and all those other people whom one knows and meets on the surface of one's life where honesty is a matter only of whether or not one confesses to having cut down the cherry tree.

With enough effort I might have gotten into the Office of War Information during this past month—the sort of job which I wouldn't have found too much against the grain even if I were engaged in literary work; and which I certainly would be glad to have now when I can do no literary work at all and when a lot of money therefore is of greater importance to me as it always is when one is inwardly bankrupt. But that same self confidence which one needs to keep alive inwardly, is also required for getting jobs of that sort where qualities of intelligence and personality count so much.

Whatever your reasons were for that note of yours and for your indifferent evasion of my letters just previous to that note—the one thing that I still wish more than any other is that I could see you. It's tied up with even more than I've said here. And more importantly, it is the *one* impulse I have that breaks through that film, that crust, which has gathered there so fatally between my true self and that which can make only mechanical gestures of living. But even if you should grant it, I wouldn't want to see you unless with some little warmth of friendliness and friendship on your part. For you to consent to see me as you might consent to see one of your patients outside of office hours, in that entirely impersonal way—no, thanks; not that for me. Nor should I want to see you there at your office under any circumstances. That is not what I mean (because I have no specific matter to see you about now as I had when I first called upon you as a complete stranger, nor as I could have had, just before your last note when I wanted so badly to have you go over some one of my most faulty poems with me). I have been feeling (with that feeling increasingly stronger) that I shall never again be able to recapture any sense of my own personal identity (without which I cannot write, of course—but in itself far more important than the writing) until I can recapture some faith in the reality of my own thoughts and ideas and problems which were turned into dry sand by your attitude toward those letters and by that note of yours later. That is why I cannot throw off my desire to see you—not impersonally, but in the most personal ways, since I could never have written to you at all in a completely impersonal fashion.

La Vôtre

C.[2]

---

1. This salutation has been crossed out in the typescript. Several excerpts from this letter appear in Williams's *Paterson*, 45, 48, 64, 76. The original letter has not been found, although it exists in two typescript versions among WCW notes for *Paterson* at Buffalo. These typescripts are identified as items E5a and E19 in Baldwin and Meyers, *The Manuscripts and Letters*, 209, 217–218. For use here, I have chosen the version entitled "Interlude" (E5a), concluding that it is a transcription of Nardi's original letter, which was subsequently retyped as E19. As evidence for this conclusion, I note that E5a contains a reference to a person called simply "H."

(probably Harvey Breit), changed in E19 to read "Z." In E5a, the initial "B" is written in the margin next to the name "Laughlin" (which has been crossed out), and in E19 the initial "B" is used. The signature "La Vôtre C." (added in E5a by WCW) was crossed out in the E19 version and not used at all in the published version. For an analysis of the differences between E5a, E19, and the published version, see the notes to *Paterson*, 268, 270, 272, 274.

2. This signature was added by Williams.

. . . .

40. T-6 (B)

[late spring 1943]

My Dear Mr. P.[1]

My feelings about you now are those of anger and indignation; and they enable me to tell you a lot of things straight from the shoulder, without my usual tongue tied round-aboutness.

You might as well take all your own literature and everyone else's and toss it into one of those big garbage trucks of the Sanitation Department, so long as the people with the top-cream minds and the "finer" sensibilities use those minds and sensibilities not to make themselves more humane human beings than the average person, but merely as a means of ducking all responsibility toward a better understanding of their fellow men, except theoretically—which doesn't mean a God-damned thing.

My attitude toward woman's wretched position in society and my ideas about all the changes necessary there, were interesting to you, weren't they, in so far as they made for *literature*? That my particular emotional orientation, in wrenching myself free from patterned standardized feminine feelings, enabled me to do some passably good work with *poetry*—all that was fine, wasn't it—something for you to sit up and take notice of! And you saw in one of my first letters to you (the one you had wanted to make use of, then, in the Introduction to your *Paterson*), an indication that my thoughts were to be taken seriously, because that too could be turned by you into literature, as something disconnected from life.

But when my actual personal life crept in, stamped all over with the *very same* attitudes and sensibilities and pre-occupations that you found quite admirable as *literature*—that was an entirely different matter, wasn't it? No longer admirable, but, on the contrary, deplorable, annoying, stupid, or in some other way unpardonable; because those very ideas and feelings which make one a writer with some kind of new vision, are often the *very same ones* which, in living itself, make one clumsy, awkward, absurd, ungrateful, confidential where most people are reticent, and reticent where one should be confidential, and which cause one, all too often, to step on the toes of other people's sensitive egos as a result of one's stumbling earnestness or honesty carried too far. And that they *are* the very same ones—that's important, something to be remembered at all times, especially by writers like yourself who are so sheltered from life in the raw by the glass-walled conditions of their own safe lives.

Only my writing (*when* I write) is myself: only that is the real me in any essential way. Not because I bring to literature and to life two different inconsistent sets of values, as you do. No, *I* don't do that; and I feel that when anyone does do it, literature is turned into just so much intellectual excrement fit for the same stinking hole as any other kind.

But in writing (as in all forms of creative art) one derives one's unity of being and one's freedom to be one's self, from one's relationship to those particular externals (language, clay, paints, et cetera) over which one has complete control and the shaping of which lies entirely in one's own power; whereas in living, one's shaping of the externals involved there (of one's friendships, the structure of society, et cetera) is no longer entirely within one's own power but requires the cooperation and the understanding and the humanity of others in order to bring out what is best and most real in one's self.

That's why all that fine talk of yours about woman's needing to "sail free in her own element" as a *poet*, becomes nothing but empty rhetoric in the light of your behavior towards me. No woman will ever be able to do that, completely, until she is able *first* to "sail free in her own element"[2] in living itself—which means in her relationships with men even before she can do so in friendships with other women. The members of any under-privileged class distrust and hate the "outsider" who is *one of them*, and women therefore—women in general—will never[3] be content with their lot until the light seeps down to them, not from one of their own, but from the eyes of changed male attitudes toward them—so that, in the meantime, the problems and the awarenesses of a woman like myself are looked upon even more unsympathetically by other women than by men.

And that, my dear Dr. P., is another reason why I needed of you a very different kind of friendship from the one you offered me.

I still don't know of course the specific thing that caused the cooling of your friendliness toward me. But I do know that if you were going to bother with me *at all*, there were only two things for you to have considered: (1) that I was, as I still am, a woman dying of loneliness—yes, really dying of it in almost the same way that people die slowly of cancer or consumption or any other such disease (and with all my efficiency in the practical world continually undermined by that loneliness); and (2) that I needed desperately, and still do, some ways and means of leading a *writer's* life, either by securing some sort of writer's job (or any other job having to do with my cultural interests) or else through some kind of literary journalism such as the book reviews—because only in work and jobs of that kind, can I turn into assets what are liabilities for me in jobs of a different kind.

Those were the two problems of mine that you continually and almost deliberately placed in the background of your attempts to help me. And yet they were, and remain, much greater than whether or not I get my poetry published. I didn't need the *publication* of my poetry with your name lent to it, in order to go on writing poetry, half as much as I needed your friendship in other ways (the very ways you ignored) in order to write it. I couldn't, for that reason, have brought the kind of responsiveness and appreciation that you expected of me (not with any real honesty) to the kind of help from you which I needed so much less than the kind you withheld.

Your whole relationship with me amounted to pretty much the same thing as your trying to come to the aid of a patient suffering from pneumonia by handing her a box of aspirin or Grove's cold pills and a glass of hot lemonade. I couldn't tell you that outright. And how were you, a man of letters, to have realized it when the imagination so quick to assert itself most powerfully in the creation of a piece of literature, seems to have no power at all in enabling writers in your circumstances to fully understand the maladjustment and impotencies of a woman in my position?

When you wrote to me up in Woodstock about that possible censor job, it seemed a very simple matter to you, didn't it, for me to make all the necessary inquiries about the job, arrange for the necessary interviews, start work (if I was hired) with all the necessary living conditions for holding down such a job, and thus find my life all straightened out in its practical aspects, at least—as if by magic?

But it's never as simple as that to get on one's feet even in the most ordinary practical ways, for anyone on *my* side of the railway tracks—which isn't your side, nor the side of your great admirer, Miss Hawkins,[4] nor even the side of those well cared for people like H.B. and S.S.[5] who've spent most of their lives with some Clara or some Jeanne to look after them even when they themselves have been flat broke.

A completely down and out person with months of stripped bare hardship behind him needs all kinds of things to even get himself in shape for looking for a respectable, important white-collar job. And then he needs ample funds for eating and sleeping and keeping up appearances (especially the latter) while going around for [the] various interviews involved. And even if and when a job of that kind is obtained, he still needs the eating and the sleeping and the carfares and the keeping up of appearances and what not, waiting for his first pay check and even perhaps for the second pay check since the first one might have to go almost entirely for back rent or something else of that sort.

And all that takes a hell of a lot of money (especially for a woman)—a lot more than ten dollars or twenty five dollars. Or else it takes the kind of very close friends at whose apartment one is quite welcome to stay for a month or two, and whose typewriter one can use in getting off some of the required letters asking for interviews, and whose electric iron one can use in keeping one's clothes pressed, et cetera.—the kind of close friends that I don't have and never have had, for reasons which you know.

Naturally, I couldn't turn to *you*, a stranger, for any such practical help on so large a scale; and it was stupid of me to have minimized the extent of help I needed when I asked you for that first money-order that got stolen and later for the second twenty-five dollars—stupid because it was misleading. But the different kind of help I asked you for, *finally*, (and which you placed in the background) would have been an adequate substitute, because I could have carried out *those* plans which I mentioned to you in the late fall (the book reviews, supplemented by almost any kind of part-time job, and later some articles, and then maybe a month at Yaddo this summer) *without* what it takes to get on one's feet in other very different ways. And then, eventually, the very fact that my name had appeared here and there in the book review sections of a few publications (I'd prefer not to *use* poetry that way) would have enabled me [to] obtain certain kinds of jobs (such as an O.W.I. job for instance) without all that red tape which affects *only* obscure unknown people.

The anger and the indignation which I feel towards you now has served to pierce through the rough ice of that congealment which my creative faculties began to suffer from as a result of that last note from you. I find myself thinking and feeling in terms of poetry again. But over and against that is the fact that I'm even more lacking in anchorage of any kind than when I first got to know you. My loneliness is a million fathoms deeper, and my physical energies even more seriously sapped by it; and my economic situation is naturally worse, with living costs so terribly high now, and with my contact with your friend Miss Hawkins having come off so badly. She steered me on to an O.W.I. *possibility*. But it turned out to be only the vaguest kind of possibility, necessitating all kinds of self-promoting sales letters to several different department heads, and numerous interviews—with weeks, even months, elapsing before anything concrete would result, if at all. So later I sent her a note asking if by chance there were any war-time replacements at the Museum itself: and I suggested several possible ones for which I'd qualify—such as conducting some of the gallery talks, or preparing some of the educational copy on modern painting and sculpture for the general public, et cetera. But she didn't even reply to my note, though a number of weeks have passed now since I sent it. Perhaps that's because I failed to thank her for an admission card to the Museum which she sent me. But I was buried beneath the despair of my failure with you at the time I received it; and my son has continued to cause me no end of trouble (earning more money than I do, but squandering his own and then coming to me for extra funds and making all kinds of vicious threats if I withhold them):—things I certainly could not explain when I wrote to her later. But I did explain that it was something more pardonable than rudeness that kept me from thanking her sooner for the card.

However, she may have had another reason for paying no attention to that note of mine—perhaps the reason of having found out that your friendliness towards me had cooled—which would have made a difference to her, I suppose, since she is such a great "admirer" of yours. But I don't know. [That] I'm in the dark about, too; and when I went up to the "Times" last week, to try, on my own, to get some of their fiction reviews (the "Times" publishes so many of those), nothing came of that either. And it's *writing* that I want to do—not operating a machine or a lathe, because with literature more and more tied up with social problems and social progress (for me, in my way of thinking) any contribution I might be able to make to the welfare of humanity (in war-time or peace time) would have to be as a writer, and not as a factory worker.

When I was very young, ridiculously young (of school-girl age) for a critical role, with my mind not at all developed and all my ideas in a state of first-week embryonic formlessness, I was able to obtain book reviews from any number of magazines without any difficulty—and *all* of them books by writers of accepted importance (such as Cummings, Babette Deutsch, H.D.)[6] whereas now when my ideas have matured, and when I really have something to say, I can get no work of that sort at all. And why is that? It's because in all those intervening years, I have been forced, as a woman not content with woman's position in the world, to do a lot of pioneer *living* which writers of your sex and with your particular social background do not have thrust upon them, and which the members of my own sex frown upon (for reasons I've already referred to)—so that at the very moment when I wanted to return to writing from living (with my ideas clarified and enriched by living) there I was (and still am)—because of that living—completely in exile socially.

I glossed over and treated very lightly (in my first conversation with you) those literary activities of my early girlhood, because the work in itself was not much better than that which any talented college freshman or precocious prep-school senior contributes to her school paper. But, after all, that work, instead of appearing in a school paper where it belonged, was taken so seriously by editors of the acceptedly important literary publications of that time, that I was able to average as much as $15 a week, very easily, from it. And I go into that now and stress it here; because you can better imagine, in the light of that, just how I feel in realizing that on the basis of just a few superficials (such as possessing a lot of appealingly youthful sex-appeal and getting in with the right set) I was then able to maintain my personal identity as a writer in my relationship with the world, whereas now I am cut off from doing so because it was necessary for me in my living, to strip myself of those superficials.

You've never *had* to live, Dr. P.—not in any of the by-ways and dark underground passages where life so often has to be tested. The very circumstances of your birth and social background provided you with an escape from life in the raw; and you confuse that protection from life with an *inability* to live— and are thus able to regard literature as nothing more than a desperate last extremity resulting from that illusionary inability to live. (I've been looking at some of your autobiographical works, as this indicates.)

But living (unsafe living, I mean) isn't something one just sits back and decides about. It happens to one, in a small way, like the measles; or in a big way, like a leaking boat, or an earthquake. Or else it doesn't happen. And when it does, then one must bring, as I must, one's life to literature; and when it doesn't, then one brings to life (as you do) purely literary sympathies and understandings, the insights and humanity of words on paper *only*—and also, alas, the ego of the literary man which most likely played an important part in the change of your attitude toward me. That literary man's ego wanted to help me in such a way, I think, that my own achievements might serve as a flower in his button-hole, if that kind of help had been enough to make me bloom.

But I have no blossoms to bring to any man in the way of either love *or* friendship. That's one of the reasons why I didn't want that introduction to my poems. And I'm not wanting to be nasty or sarcastic in the last lines of this letter. On the contrary a feeling of profound sadness has replaced now the anger and the indignation with which I started to write all this. I wanted your friendship more than I ever wanted anything else (yes, *more*, and I've wanted other things badly). I wanted it desperately, not because I have a single thing with which to adorn any man's pride—but just because I haven't.

Yes, the anger which I imagined myself to feel on all the previous pages, was false. I am too unhappy and too lonely to be angry; and if some of the things to which I have called your attention here should cause any change of heart in you regarding me, that would be just about the only happy thing I can conceive of as occurring in my life right now.

La Vôtre

C.

P.S. That I'm back here at 21 Grove Street[7] causes me to add that that mystery as to who forged the "Kress" [*sic*] on that money order and also took one of Laughlin's[8] checks (though his was *not* cashed—and therefore replaced later) never did get cleared up. And the janitor who was here at the time, is now dead. I don't think it was he who took any of the money. But still I was rather glad that the post office didn't follow it through because just in case Bob did have anything to do with it, he would have gotten into serious trouble—which I shouldn't have welcomed, because he was one of those miserably underpaid Negroes and an awfully decent human being in lots of ways. But now I wish it *had* been followed through *after* he died (which was over two months ago) because the crooks may have been those low vile upstate farm people whose year-round exploitation of down and out farm help ought to be brought to light in some fashion, and because if they *did* steal the money order and were arrested for it, that in itself would have brought to the attention of the proper authorities all their other illegal activities as well. And yet that kind of justice doesn't interest me greatly. What's at the root of this or that crime or any anti-social act, both psychologically and environmentally, always interests me more. But as I make that last statement, I am reminded of how much I'd like to do a lot of things with *people* in some prose—some stories, maybe a novel. I can't tell you how much I want the living which I need in order to write. And I simply can't achieve them entirely alone. I don't even possess a typewriter now, nor have even a rented one—and I can't think properly except on a typewriter. I can do poetry (though only the first draft) in long-hand, and letters. But for any prose writing, other than letters, I can't do any work without a typewriter. But that of course is the least of my problems—the typewriter; at least the easiest to do something about.   C.

Dr. P.:

This is the simplest most outright letter I've ever written to you; and you ought to read it all the way through, and carefully, because it's about you, as a writer, and about the ideas regarding women that you expressed in your article on Anais Nin,[9] and because in regard to myself, it contains certain information which I did not think it necessary to give you before, and which I do think now you ought to have. And if my anger in the beginning makes you too angry to go on from there—well, that anger of mine isn't there in the last part, now as I attach this post-script. C.

And if you don't feel like reading it even for those reasons, will you then do so, *please*, merely out of fairness to me—much time and much thought and much unhappiness having gone into these pages.

1. This letter appears in *Paterson*. The first two paragraphs comprise one excerpt; the remaining portion of the letter is that which concludes Book II (see 82, 87–91). The original letter has not been found among WCW's papers, although MN's handwritten earlier draft of the letter (undated, from 21 Grove Street, New York City) is with her papers at the HRHRC (in the Williams Collection). I have chosen to use here Williams's typescript (in his notes for *Paterson* at Buffalo and identified as item E5b in the Baldwin-Meyers catalog), which has several characteristics of a transcription. The names of several people and places in the E5b document have been crossed out and other names substituted, evidence that WCW intended to disguise the identity of the actual people named in the original letter (see notes 4, 5, 7, 8, and 9 below). Further evidence that E5b is a transcription of the original letter is found in the details it contains about MN's life, which WCW would be unlikely to have known or to have invented (see note 6). For further information about these details and a full comparison of E5b with the published version, see *Paterson*, 275–278.

2. Nardi is quoting from Williams's review of *Winter of Artifice* by Anaïs Nin in *New Directions Number Seven*.

3. In MN's draft of this letter (at the HRHRC) this line reads: "women therefore . . . *will* [emphasis added] remain content with their lot." This changes the meaning of the sentence considerably, and, without the "sent" letter as evidence, we cannot know if Williams (or a transcriptionist) changed this to read "will *never remain* [emphasis added] content with their lot" (probably in error). It is conceivable, but unlikely, that Nardi herself made the change; her point being that women (in general) internalize the prevailing attitudes of men toward them, and therefore *will* remain content until those attitudes change.

4. As Christopher MacGowan points out in his notes to *Paterson*, Miss Frances Hawkins, of the Museum of Modern Art, wrote to WCW on 9 March 1943 in reply to WCW's letter to the museum asking about a possible job for MN. In the Buffalo transcription, the name "Hawkins" was typed in, then crossed out and "Fleming" substituted (277).

5. In *Paterson*, WCW changed these initials to read "S.T. and S.S." Har-

vey Breit (whose first wife's name was Clara) is "H.B." and Christopher MacGowan suggests that poet Sydney Salt may be "S.S."

6. Book reviews written by Nardi during her early years in New York City include *Heliodora* by H.D. for the *New Republic*, 28 January 1925; e.e. cummings's *41 Poems* for the *New York Herald Tribune Books*, 14 June 1925, 4; *Honey Out of the Rock* by Babette Deutsch for the *New Republic*, 30 December 1925, 170; and the work of Marjorie Meeker, Margaret Todd Ritter, Janet Lewis, Josephine Pinckney, and Mary Carolyn Davies in "Five Women Poets" for the *New Republic*, 4 July 1928.

7. In this typescript, Grove Street, MN's address at the time, has been crossed out and Pine Street written in.

8. The name Laughlin has been crossed out in the typescript and Brown written in.

9. The name of Anaïs Nin is typed in and then crossed out (and her initials retained) in WCW's draft.

. . . .

41. TLS-1 (SL)

Tuesday [1948]

Dear Horace:[1]

Glad to hear from you. The purpose of the long letter at the end[2] is partly ironic, partly "writing" to make it plain that even poetry is writing and nothing else—so that there's a logical continuity in the art, prose, verse: an identity.

Frankly I'm sick of the constant aping of the Stevens's dictum that I resort to the antipoetic as a heightening device. That's plain crap—and everyone copies it. Now Rodman. The truth is that there's an *identity* between prose and verse, not an antithesis. It all rests on the same time base, the same measure. Prose, as Pound has always pointed out, came after verse, not before it—. No use tho trying to break up an error of that sort when it begins to roll. Nobody will attempt to think, once a convenient peg to hang his critical opinion on without thinking is found.

But specifically, as you see, the long letter is definitely germane to the rest of the text. It is psychologically related to the text—just as the notes following the *Waste Land* are related to the text of the poem. The difference being that in this case the "note" is subtly relevant to the matter and not merely a load for the mule's back. That it is *not* the same stuff as the poem but comes from below 14th St. is precisely the key. It does not belong in the poem itself any more than a note on—Dante would.

Also, in Book IV, the poem does definitely break out to the world at large—the sea, the river to the sea. This begins it.

And if you'll notice, dogs run all through the poem and will continue to do so from first to last. And there is no dog without a tail. Here the tail has tried to wag the dog. Does it? (God help me, it may yet, but I hope not!)

I'm going with Floss to Atlantic City for a short time to try to get on my feet.

My best to you,
Bill

1. Horace Gregory. From Thirlwall, *The Selected Letters.*

2. Williams is referring to Nardi's letter (see 40) at the end of Book II of *Paterson*, which was published in 1948.

Later Correspondence

1949
1956

Woodstock, NY

March 30, 1949

Dear Dr. Williams,[1]

Last summer I chanced upon a copy of Paterson II in the Woodstock bookshop, and opening it at random found myself reading the familiar lines of a letter of mine to you. The shop didn't encourage browsing except in the case of good customers, so that I couldn't read more than another fragment. Later I tried unsuccessfully to get both the first and second volumes at some out of town libraries (I've been away from the city for nearly two years) and I couldn't afford to purchase them because I have continued to live in great poverty, very much aggravated by serious illness and all the expenses connected with it.

In January it was necessary for me to go to New York for consultation with a specialist, and I had hoped to have an opportunity then to get hold of Paterson at the New York Public Library. But I was too sick to get around, and it was the same when I went back to see that doctor again. Will you therefore loan me the books—both of them, and just as soon as you possibly can? I wanted to write to you before this in an attempt to get them. But I was too ill to manage a letter—especially since I had certain psychological obstacles to overcome before getting in touch with you at all, and now it is not only in regard to Paterson that I am writing to you. There is something else too.

I was married several years ago (the bond is mostly shared economic problems, so much else having become hopelessly strangled for me) and we are living in a one room log house between Woodstock and Glenford.[2] We took the place—a roughly made cabin which rents for only $75 a year—in the early fall with the idea of making some improvements (J. has a special aptitude for things of that sort), raising our own vegetables, and in general of living in such a way as to need comparatively little cash to get along on and of thus having more freedom from financial worries than either of us had in the past. But at the very outset I became very ill, and all our plans were spoiled. The little money which we thought would see us through the next twelve months (J. wanted to work on a novel, and I had my own contemplated projects, though they cannot be put into two or three words) had been carefully budgeted—so much for food, so much for fuel, et cetera. We did allow a few dollars for emergencies, but only the smallest fraction of what we had to spend on doctors fees, X-rays and other tests, and medications of various kinds. Even before the greater expenses connected with the New York trips began, we had to spend in two months what we could have managed to live on for half a year. And then when the specialist had to be consulted, things were even worse. There were not only his fees and more tests and more medications, but also the cost of staying at hotels for several days at a stretch and the travelling costs, all of which took nearly every penny we had.

I am somewhat better now. At least I am up and about again, after months of continual confinement to bed and night after night of acute distress. But all the money is gone, and how to obtain the barest essentials is again a consuming problem. J. will have to take a job this summer. That's all there are here—seasonal jobs which aren't to be gotten until May or June; and in the meantime, I shrink from parting with our last ten dollars which will all have to go, in the next day or two, for food, another bottle of pancreatin and some more Lilly's liver extract (I have a disorder of the liver and gall bladder, and in addition am badly anemic—3 cc's of the extract injections having been required for some time now) and an overdue electric light bill.

I am writing this letter from the surface of my life—having made no attempt to get beneath it in my relation with anyone ever since that time, so long ago now, of that final note of dismissal from you. Even in my relationship with myself, I scarcely dare get beneath it, so that what lies there is dust and in darkness has become my own bluebeard's secret and terrible closet. But it was to open the door wide and to face whatever lay strangled there that I had hoped to use this past winter which turned out so differently from what I'd expected; and because it remains yet to be done, I find this continued lack of any economic security at all more of a hell than ever. And yet during this past week of prematurely early spring (the pussy willows were out ten days ago and the maple trees are already budding) I have been intoxicated with the joy of finding myself so close to the heart of nature after so many years of city brick and city rooming houses and tenements. The last place we lived in before leaving N.Y. was so infested with roaches and bedbugs that I had to use nearly all my time and energy scrubbing and cleaning and spraying without even get[ting] rid of them. In comparison the primitive conditions under which I live here (there's no plumbing and the pump is a five or six minute walk from the house) are nothing. And the grounds are beautiful, and several acres of land go with the house for which we pay so little rent, that if I had any literary hack work of any kind at all to do, I could get along nicely. And so I ask you again, as I asked you once, do you know of any for me? (Upon seeing so many of Harvey Breit's articles in the Times Book Review Magazine, I wondered if he had a staff job there, and if so whether he could get me books to review—if not the important ones at least the less important for shorter notices, but when I recalled how little friendship had been involved on his side and how, no longer young, I would have no existence at all for such a person, I couldn't communicate with him.)

If I had a couple of hundred dollars just now, it would mean so much to me—an inestimable amount. We could get our garden going (as things are we can't even buy fertilizer and seeds, cheap as they are), and J. could make some absolutely necessary repairs which have been held up through lack of materials costing only about fifteen dollars (this place is almost the same as our own, because it's part of the Hervey White[3] non-profit making estate; and according to the terms of the will it can't be sold so that we can have it indefinitely; and eventually—if we stay— would have to pay no rent at all, most of the places which have undergone renovation by the occupants being rent-free) and J. also could finish his book and try selling some short stories, having sold some in the past[4] and being unfitted for anything but unskilled labor in the way of jobs. (His whole approach to writing and to literature and art generally is alien to mine, the concrete world of externalities and events being his major concern and that of ideas and abstractions and inward occurrence interesting him not at all; and he doesn't understand poetry—except some very few "easy" poets or those who depart in no way from traditional form. But despite these limitations, his writing is creative and his own and it's the thing he can do best—he *is* a writer.)

In regard to my own writing, I cannot go into that here for the reason mentioned in the first part of the above paragraph. Writing to me is nothing that I can separate from myself as I can a chair or an easel or my clothes. It is too much interwoven with my whole being, too much just one thread in the fabric of my entire moral, emotional, and intellectual life.

Anyway, this communication has been directed by two things only; by my desire to see the two volumes of Paterson already published, and by my hope that in some way you might be able and willing to come to my rescue in this unceasing struggle with the worst kind of poverty.

Though nearer to Glenford than to Woodstock, we use the Woodstock post-office for mail because it has rural free delivery, whereas the Glenford post-office doesn't. My address therefore is R.F.D., Woodstock, New York, and I am known to the post office clerks and the postman only as Mrs. John Lang—having had no occasion to use my own name since we came here. And so if you send me the books or a letter, please address the package and envelope to Mrs. John Lang or to me in care of Mrs. John Lang.

I don't know how to end this except abruptly, not yet having learned how to be graceful in my social relationships.

Sincerely,

Marcia Nardi

P.S. Because you and I have no mutual friends and very few mutual acquaintances, it's not likely that anyone has asked or would ask you for my present address. But if such an inquiry were made of you, don't give my address—if you please—to anyone without consulting me first.

Some people around here who have only a moderate amount of talent and whose work is by no means known, have had Guggenheim scholarships. How does one get that sort of thing? Do you know? And would there be any chance of it in my case?

1. An incomplete draft version of this letter also exists in Marcia Nardi's archive.

2. No date of marriage has been established between Nardi and John Charles (Chuk) Lang (1914–1966), a writer and painter.

3. Hervey White (1866–1944) was a poet, novelist, and founder of the Maverick Colony, a community in Woodstock, New York, which attracted artists and social reformers.

4. In 1937, John Lang sold five stories to *Scribner's* magazine (New York: Charles Scribner's Sons). "The Cleansing" and "War" appeared in the February issue, pp. 38–42; "Return, and the Sea Gone" in the May issue, p. 25; "The Gift" in December, p. 37; and "Magnificence" in July, p. 32. These were his only published works.

. . . .

43. TLS-1 (T)

March 31, 1949

My dear Marcia Nardi:

I'll send the books to you at once. Both Laughlin and I tried in every way to get in touch with you when Paterson II was published, we enquired about the Village, we asked people, who we thought might know you, if you had been in communication with them (we even had a letter from one of your own family asking if *we* had seen you) but to no avail. Therefore we could do nothing.

The rumor even went around that you were dead. How do you like that?

I'll do what I can to come to your rescue—as I did my best to do before this but without much success I'll acknowledge. But I can't just hand you two hundred dollars in an offhand way, much as I'd like to. We might as well face that at once.

What I plan to do is to get in touch with Laughlin, telling him how he may reach you. That I must do. Perhaps with his assistance we can make some satisfactory arrangement by which some money can be advanced. I'll do my best. That's all I can promise.

Meanwhile, if the situation is as bad as you say, please accept the enclosed money order for twenty dollars as a token of my good will and appreciation for your assistance to me in the past. You've had plenty to contend with and I must say I admire your courage and persistence. No use going further into detail.

May your health also continue to improve.

Sincerely yours
W. C. Williams

. . . .

44. TLS-1 (ND)

March 31, 1949

Dear Jim:

Here's this—at last! Please put her letter and my reply[1] in your safe. Read her letter which appears to me to be perfectly sincere—after all she's always been a decent person with me— and if you can do anything to help her I'd greatly appreciate it.

At the very least I'd like to know what you think and if you can suggest any course of action, one way or the other, I'd like your advice.

My own viewpoint is this: the woman gave me verbal permission (tho' it would be hard to prove it) to use anything I pleased of her letters in *Paterson*. That I can swear to with a clean conscience. Second, it was necessary in my composition to exhibit an attitude of mind which she represented for me. I wanted her to know about this but after trying in every way to find her without success I was forced to go ahead with my plan. Third, I removed every trace of evidence which might in any way serve to identify her as the person who wrote the letter or letters. This I succeeded in doing. No one has mentioned her name.[2]

I hesitated a long time, you remember, and then went ahead.

I mention all this to tell you where I stand. Naturally I must count on you to corroborate my testimony if my word is brought into question.[3]

Let's get this out of the way before proceeding with Paterson III.

Cheerio! Tomorrow's the first of April.

Best

Bill

1. MN's letter of 30 March (42) and WCW's of 31 March 1949 (43).

2. How did Nardi come to be identified as the writer of the letters? Interested readers could have followed the clues found in the long *Paterson* letter (40), that is, Nardi's references to WCW's review of the Anaïs Nin book which appeared in *New Directions Number Seven* immediately following the group of Nardi's poems which WCW had introduced, and Nardi's comments about that introduction. WCW's introduction also described Nardi in such a way that anyone reading it (along with the *Paterson* letter and the Anaïs Nin review) might have guessed that Nardi was the author of the "Cress" letters.

3. In a postscript to a letter written a month later, Williams said: "Oh yes, as to the gal who wrote the letter—or upon whose letters I improvised toward the end of Pat III [Williams is referring to section three of Book II]—I ain't revealing identities even tho' you might guess. But many thanks for the evidence, if ever it should prove important to me, that her identity has been in no way revealed by my composition." Letter from William Carlos Williams to Fred Miller, 26 April 1949 (Special Collections Department, University of Delaware Library).

. . . .

45. TLS-1 (T)

New Directions,
Norfolk, Connecticut
April 2, 1949

Dear Miss Nardi:

I saw Bill Williams the other day, and he told me that he had heard from you again and given [*sic*] me your address. We are both certainly very glad to know where you are. The truth is we had thought or feared that you might be dead because we hadn't heard from you in such a long time.

At Bill's request, I shall be mailing a copy of Volume I of *Paterson*, and I also thought I would send along a few other poetry books which might amuse you.

Are you writing any poems these days? I shall be putting together a new volume of New Directions this summer, and if you have something which you think I might like, I wish you would let me look at it.

With best wishes,
James Laughlin
[signed] (by Barbara Asch)

. . . .

46. TLS-2 (T)

Wednesday [June 1949][1]

Dear Marcia:

These are the best you have ever written and, for they strike completely through my guard, they appear to me to be among the best poems of our day—so much better than what is being accepted as good that I feel ashamed for my sex, to say the least, which generally speaking monopolizes the scene. They are warm, defenseless and well made.

That last, the "well made" is, for me, the most important of all as it is unquestionably for you also. The metrical pattern is intrinsic, as it must be and especially for the female of our wits—for we are all male and female in varying degrees but a woman has her part in it strongest. I hope I don't sound "literary" when I speak this way. I mean that you have a rare trait of form which I, for one, have spent my life as a writer to make apparent. I think it is on the major track of our interests today. No need to go further into that now for it could run to an essay. I am sure from these poems that you have that absolute sense of meter and so have achieved what is active, essential and really new in our day.

You've got to have a book right away. When I think of the rotten drivel printed alongside of your beautifully put sentences

I want to puke—no less, but it's a tough road, as I don't need to tell you. But you've got to have a book. I hope you have enough things to make one. With the old stuff though you ought to have enough for a small book—and I'd like to see it small—to fit into the pocket.

It's all right to go into Laughlin's annual anthology—without introduction this time, for he pays well. [Make] it a big group (I'll drive him into the ground if he doesn't feature you) but the small book must follow.[2]

Critically, as to detail, you still have the common fault (due to timidity in the meter) of occasionally inverting a phrase. Don't do it. No matter *how* the line sounds, never invert a phrase. Work with the phrase, replace words of different syllables but satisfactory meaning but NEVER invert a phrase. It is basic if we are ever to discover anything about what is facing us in the making of the modern forms. Make your mind work at it and you may be the one to discover (for that's what it amounts to) the way out. But to toady to an old construction by inverting a phrase is plain suicide.

The rest is yours. You have a splendid vocabulary and about as fine a sense of values in the word as I know of. You use words beautifully and with great force.

But that doesn't solve the economic problem. As far as I am concerned I've never made anything at writing and I am about to be 66 years old. Floss figured I've made, apart from 3 prizes about 200 dollars a year over a twenty year span. It can't be done, not by a poet. I don't know the answer. But get a book together and perhaps you can get an advance or something to stand you by until you can find a way out.

I'm making a few marks on the script and will send it on with further comment in a day or two but knowing how you feel I'm sending this off at once.

Sincerely
Bill

1. Marcia Nardi has written at the top of the first page of her copy of the original letter: "I got this letter from Dr. Williams towards the end of

1949. I'd been completely out of touch with him for some time. But since there was no one of my friends and acquaintances who knew anything about poetry, I sent him, out of a clear sky—about twenty new poems—because I needed badly to look at my own work through someone else's eyes. And this is the letter which he sent me in connection with those poems." Nardi was mistaken about the date; this letter was written in early June 1949, shortly after their correspondence had resumed.

2. Apparently Williams sent these poems and Nardi's letter to James Laughlin (see 47).

. . . .

47. TLS-I (T)

June 14 [1949]

Dear Marcia:

I wrote Laughlin by the same mail which bore my letter to you strongly urging a book. I shall send him this last letter of yours to read as it stands. I think you yourself should write to him now suggesting or requesting the same thing. It is important to you as a writer that this be done and it is important to New Directions that Laughlin do it. I know you have a definite following, slight as your reputation may seem to you. I shall continue to press for your publication. I can realize also how badly you need the money; I think it is an investment which Laughlin should make at once—and I put it this way to avoid all other question than the merits of the work itself.

How much do you need to tide you over immediate cash demands? Would a hundred dollars be of any important use to you or is it completely inadequate? Please let me know.

Sincerely yours
W. C. Williams

. . . .

48. TLS-I (Y)

June 14 [1949]

Dear Jim:

I feel that I owe this woman something, both as myself and a fellow poet, and naturally I can't ask you to bear the responsibility; but I must continue to ask you to give her a book (a baby) with the added possibility that you will advance her whatever cash you think advisable under whatever pretext in order to help her in what seems her very real distress. I shall myself do what I can for her along the same lines acknowledging at the same time that I cannot do much. I think she comes legitimately under the aegis of New Directions—she's a good writer: even Parker Tyler [1] (while hating her as a woman) had to acknowledge that her writing had literary merit—of a sort, said he green with a sort of envy. [WCW goes on to discuss other issues, then closes by saying:]

Best luck in everything and please don't forget Marcia Nardi.

Yours

Bill

1. Parker Tyler (1907–1974), author, poet, and film critic.

. . . .

49. TLS-2 (Y)

Saturday, June 18th [1949]

Dear Bill,

Yes, a hundred dollars would be of great help in constructive ways—especially since supplemented by the psychological benefits which I already feel of being better able to preserve my identity as a writer at the very prospect of having my work published. (In the past, as you know, I was indifferent to publication. But I have grown to realize that there is no such thing as a ding an sich [1]—that there are only things in relation to other things, people in relation to other people, and that it is not enough to be a poet alone in isolation. Not only not enough, but almost impossible. One must be it in relation to the world, and it is easier to achieve such a relation through being published.)

This thought put in parenthesis has been most likely in my subconscious for a long time. But it clarified itself to my conscious mind only after my getting that letter from you about the poems I sent—that letter having had so stimulating an effect that ever since then my brain has been swarming with the germs of poems—so much so that last night in the midst of one of those horrible attacks to which I am subject I nevertheless managed to get down the rough drafts of three and am so impatient now to get them finished which I cannot do immediately because of physical exhaustion from the attack.

Unfortunately not all the poems in the group I sent Laughlin are of equal merit. A few need only very slight revisions already made on my own copies and on one I sent you. But there was one I should not have included at all, I'm afraid, because it was one of those poems cast from the very start into the wrong rhythmic mold (it has a rhetorical sound and I do not have Karl Shapiro's talent for that sort of thing), but which I refused to discard because of my liking for the theme. And what bothers me about this is that if Laughlin was more impressed by the badness of that poem and of the careless lines in a few others than by the best of the poems, he may have thought strange your enthusiastic note about my work. Anyway if he tells you not all the poems were something to be enthusiastic about, you can well believe him. But I suppose I myself shall be hearing from him any day, now that you have sent him my last note to you.

I appreciate so much—I cannot tell you how much—your interest in my much neglected work with poetry which—as Poe said of his poems "might have been under happier circumstances the vocation of my life". I did not appreciate it enough in the past. I was devoting or trying to devote my creative energies as much to living (perhaps even more so)—as to literature. I did not understand then as I understand now that in living we ourselves are the worked on raw materials of creative forces outside ourselves, that the only modicum of creative freedom which we are permitted—and even there so much is merely bestowed or loaned—is in literature or the field of art generally.

I hope you don't think that in so often using special delivery stamps I'm absurdly over-extravagant for a person in my financial position. I missed the outgoing mail both yesterday and the day before (we have only one a day R.F.D.) and unless I take this to Glenford and send it special, it won't go out until late Monday (this being a week-end with no mails at all on Sunday) reaching you perhaps not until Wednesday.

I also hope that my continual references to my poor health aren't as tiresome to you as such topics are to people generally. For reasons which I have not yet gotten to the root of, personal health problems are the one subject strictly verboten in conversation. But I can't avoid mentioning mine because they are so serious—though to what extent tied up with my economic situation and with possibly not adequate medical consultation, I do not know. For a while I made what seemed to be an almost miraculous recovery under the treatment prescribed by Dr. Gerson—Max Gerson. (Do you know of him—he is mentioned at great length in John Gunther's book "Death Be Not Proud".)[2] And then just as in the case of Johnny Gunther, I had a serious relapse, being thrown back now into almost the same condition I was in when I first went to Gerson. It was less puzzling, or rather puzzling in a different kind of way in the case of the Gunther boy who had cancer of the brain. In my case where there is a definite tie up between diet and diseases of the digestive tract it is indeed strange that after six or seven weeks of continual improvement while on the Gerson diet (I had started to feel very well and for a while the attacks vanished completely) I should suddenly stop responding so favorably to the very same regime from which I deviated in no way. I shall be going to see Gerson again as soon as possible—maybe some day during this coming week. But this time I am letting the fee go—having decided that I definitely cannot and will not give another penny to doctors as rich as Gerson (he is very wealthy) since I need to use every penny I can get for my daily living expenses in order to write.

Well, here's the post-man.

Sincerely,
Marcia

1. Thing-in-itself (German).

2. Gerson was the unorthodox doctor who attempted to arrest cancer and other illnesses with diet therapy. See John Gunther, *Death Be not Proud* (New York: Harper & Row, 1949), 88–89.

. . . .

50. TLS-2 (Y)

June 20, 1949

Dear Bill:

Please forgive my delay in answering you about Marcia Nardi, but I have been simply swamped with work, and haven't had the chance to study properly the little sheaf of poems which she sent in to me a few weeks ago. As you know, I am definitely sympathetic and favorable to her, and I feel sure that we can include some of her poems in the next *New Directions* anthology, and on that basis, I will include with this letter an advance check of $15.00 to her order. This isn't much but possibly it will help her out a little bit.

Now, as to doing a whole book of her poems, I would like to but I don't see how I can possibly finance it. At the present time, the book market is taking a terrible slump along with everything else and we are desperately pressed for cash for day to day needs. There is no question but what, in recent months, New Directions has got a little bit overextended. We did more books than we ought to have done and now we are paying for it.

You must not reproach me by making comparison between Roditi's poems[1] and those of Marcia Nardi. The fact of the matter is that Roditi paid for the entire production of his book himself and it didn't cost me a penny. Naturally, under those circumstances, I was very glad to help him out with the distribution because he is an old friend whom I like very much. Possibly things will pick up in the fall and then we can consider doing a little book for Marcia Nardi. [Laughlin went on to write of other matters without mentioning Nardi again.]

With best wishes,
Jas.

1. Edouard Roditi (1910–), writer, critic, and translator. His book *Poems 1928–1948* was published by New Directions in 1949.

. . . .

51. TLS-1 (T)

June 21 [1949]

Dear Marcia:

You've got to give me at least a week to work it out but you may count on it, one way or another (and it must come through writing) I'll see that you get at least a start on the hundred dollars which you are to get, now.

If you can produce a fairly long piece, something you specially [sic] like, say two or three pages—send it direct to me. I think I can sell it.

Sincerely
Bill

. . . .

52. TLS-1 (T)

June 24 [1949]

My dear Marcia:

Laughlin writes today, "I will include with this letter an advance check for $15.00 to her order. This isn't much but possibly it will help her out a little bit." "Now, as to doing a whole book of her poems, I would like to but I don't see how I could possibly finance it." "Possibly things will pick up a little bit in the fall and then we can consider doing a little book for Marcia Nardi." [1]

Meanwhile I shall do what I can to help you.

Sincerely
Bill

As a matter of fact, if the book is to appear in the fall, you will need all the time between now and then to get it in condition to print.

1. Nardi's poems did not appear in book form until 1956.

. . . .

53. ALS-2 (Y)

Woodstock

July 2nd, 1949

Dear Bill—

I got home from that New York trip much worse, and have been critically ill ever since, with everything made particularly difficult by the really strange differences of opinion among doctors regarding my condition.

There's more to the situation than this—other complications—worse ones. But it's a long story—the kind of thing that can't be generalized—for an understanding of which the details are necessary. And I'm not up to describing those here—having averaged no more than 2 hours sleep out of every 24 for at least two weeks now. But this is primarily about the "piece" of 2 or 3 pages for that magazine which might pay me $100 for it. None of my poems are long—the longest no more than 50 lines or so. I do however have several groups of from 3 to 6 poems, tied together by being variations on one theme, with one title and then sub-titles. Maybe one of these groups would do—though in a week or so (if only I can manage to get more sleep and to take *some* nourishment without distress) I may have a long poem in 2 parts all ready. I have the idea for it. But it's hard for me to force things. I need to let an idea do its own germinating—naturally, before getting it down on paper.

But whatever I decide to send you, I hope it's not too late. I couldn't communicate with you before this. I have been too ill, and now so much time has passed.

Marcia

P.S. I presume, since Laughlin *advanced* that $15, that he's using the poems I sent him in the Anthology. But just how much or how little he likes them, I still don't know. You said nothing about this (did he mention it?) and he has not once communicated with me—though it's two months now since I sent him those poems.

. . . .

54. TLS-1 (T)

Norfolk, Connecticut
July 5, 1949

Dear Miss Nardi:

Please forgive my delay in writing you about your poems. I have been so dreadfully busy that I haven't had the time to do more than glance at them. However, I liked what I read and I am sure that we will be able to use a group of them in the forthcoming number of *New Directions* anthology, which will appear just before Christmas.[1] With this in mind, I sent an advance check for $15.00 to Dr. Williams for transmission to you. Of course, this is not an exact payment for the anthology contribution. That will be figured out on a proportional royalty basis later on.

I am dictating this letter from Aspen, Colorado, where I am taking part in the Goethe Festival. As soon as I get back to New York in July, I will try to study your poems more closely and pick out those which we would like to use in the anthology, and return the others to you so that you can place them in other magazines.

I am terribly pleased to know that you are writing again, because I have always enjoyed your work, and I hope you will keep it up and have a success with it.

With best wishes,
James Laughlin
[signed] (by B. Asch)

1. Four of Nardi's poems ("City Sunday," "Pastoral Scene," "No Emily's and No Blake's," and "Being Left without a Poem") appeared in *New Directions Number Eleven*, 309–312.

July 16 [1949]

Really, Marcia, I may be unbalanced one way or the other by my prejudices but I have interrupted my reading of your poems to say as candidly as possible that I think you're Wanderful [*sic*] (I was going to say a wonder writer—but changed that). It's amazing how inconspicuously good you are. I'll go on now and read the rest.

Look, I take it for granted that you have copies of these poems for I want to send them at once to Italy—with the strongest possible urging that they be used, all of them—and paid for. They are beautiful and to hell with anyone who says they're not.

But shouldn't we try to get some money for them in this country? Someone should buy them here too. What are your objections to trying somewhere? You may hear from Norman Holmes Pearson[1] on the money question, if so take it up. He has the power to get you some cash if I can convince him of your worth and your need.

Best

Bill

The first poems are by far the best—the group to Rilke less successful. W

1. Norman Holmes Pearson (1909–1975), Yale professor, literary critic, and administrator of the Bryher Fund. See Williams's letter (61) to Pearson urging him to help Nardi with money from the Bryher Fund. Nardi was awarded the $250 Bryher Award in October 1949.

. . . .

Monday, July 25th [1949]

Dear Bill,

I wanted to write to you immediately upon receiving your last note because it was such a relief to me to learn that the poems you liked best were all my newest ones—those in the group to Rilke being much older. And also I wanted to say right away that far from having any objection to appearing in some of our American magazines, I'd like very much to do so (especially since it probably would help to make Laughlin interested in putting out a book for me). Only I'd want to get into the magazines that pay and that are discriminating in what they print—not into any of those countless little poetry magazines that print almost any old thing except for the contributions which they request from a few famous poets like you and Auden—these kindly granted contributions being the only thing that keeps such magazines from being all trash.

But I couldn't write sooner because I have gone through a really terrible ordeal in this past week—the economic situation, in leaving me with absolutely no freedom of movement, being more than I can cope with.

You know from some of the letters I wrote you in the past how I feel about the average man and woman relationship and this one is worse than the average—much, much worse. Apart from what goes against the grain with me in sex matters, Chuk is astoundingly immature. Though younger than I am, he's past his middle thirties and therefore no child. But he has that particular kind of hardness of heart which one finds so often in children and when burdened with any kind of responsibility he acts like a thirteen year old school boy who resents giving up any of his Saturday playtime to help with chores. And he has a decidedly old-fashioned attitude toward woman's place in the world—his mother whom he regards as the Perfect Wife having been one of those women who cooked and baked and scrubbed and mended from dawn until midnight throughout her entire adult life. And what I am less able to do anything about than about these things is his temper which when roused is almost maniacal, and his vile language which is even worse than what I heard continually when I lived in a New York tenement from drunken Irish janitors and longshoremen. There are women—I have met them who do not particularly recoil from this sort of thing in a man, who even invite it. But brawls, vulgarities, and cheap nastiness—all this contracts my mind to a point where I am robbed completely of myself—where my brain seems blasted. I shrivel up and die in such an atmosphere—and I have done so over and over again in this past year—without being able to escape because I have no place to go and never have more than a couple of dollars on hand, and it is his knowing that I am helpless in the situation and stuck here and dependent on whatever few dollars he gets hold of from occasional odd jobs that makes things worse than they would be if I had an income of my own. He would be a lot nicer if I had—knowing that I had a lot more freedom of movement than I have now. And so the money situation keeps getting more and more urgent with me all the time.

Am sending this off in a rush from Glenford because I have barely time to get home before dark. And the scrawl—so messy—due to my having had such [a] terrible time of things last night.

Marcia

. . . .

57. TLS-6 (Y)

Thursday August
[early August 1949]

Dear Bill,

I regretted having rushed off to you that note of about ten days ago. I have no right to barge into your life like that with all my problems. Moreover to separate a person's worst qualities from his good ones (as I did in regard to Chuk) and to present them in that isolated fashion to another person is unfair.

So please disregard those parts of that note in which I gave you so distorted a picture of my husband or rather so incomplete [a] one which amounts to about the same thing. The economic situation is another matter. He doesn't and can't earn enough money for two people to live on—at present (and this is the job season here) getting only temporary jobs—some of them a day's work, some a week's and all paying so badly that he averages no more than 12 or 15 dollars a week. And his experiences in the way of poverty (I can't account for it otherwise) have made him penurious to a pathological degree—certainly to a point where thrift becomes the maddest kind of extravagance—(I am not a good typist and the typewriter is an old one in poor condition—which is why my letters are so messy) forcing upon me hours of labor in order to save a dollar or even as little as a dime (and he did this even in New York when we had more money and when living costs were lower).

Whatever poems I manage to write I often have to do in the middle of the night. (It is often my only free time & the only time when I [am] spiritually free.) Then when I try to do more work on them during the course of the next few days, I am continually interrupted (I have no room of my own). One minute being asked to make a new shopping bag to replace a lost one, then to repair some old ragged pants fit to be thrown out, then having to hitch-hike to and from Kingston for groceries because we have no car and food there is cheaper than here. Then lunch to prepare and dishes to wash (with no running water and an old kerosene stove that's not much good), then getting the laundry ready for the wet wash and another couple of hours of cooking (because food that is both wholesome and cheap takes longer to fix) and then more dishes and pots and pans and extra laundry to be done here at home because there are things which get spoiled if put in wet wash. And this sort of thing day after day—without even the incentive of an attractive home to keep in order. And it was the same in New York before we came here. We had a shared job as superintendents of some tenement houses. And my part of it was to mop the stairs and hallways daily (and how dirty they were!) and then I had all our own housecleaning, cooking, dishwashing et cetera to do—the housekeeping there being especially difficult because the place was filled with roaches and had to be sprayed almost daily with everything taken off the shelves and rewashed and replaced.

And the situation was not greatly different when I lived with my son (I have not seen him now for several years, don't know where he is, and am very unhappy about it). And all the places where I've been burdened with so much drudgery have been so ugly. And in years I have not been free to spend a spare dollar if

I happened to have one on a book or theatre ticket or anything of that sort. If I should do so, Chuk would throw up to me that that dollar represented an hour and a quarter of unpleasant work on his part, and finally succeed in making me feel miserably conscience-stricken. And from *his* point of view—out of his own experience—he would be right, because although he has an interest of his own in literature and writing it doesn't seem to be related to him in the same intimate way that mine is to me. He always talks about wanting the leisure to work on a novel, but when he has the leisure (he's had at least half of every day to himself for months at a time) he uses it for everything but writing. The reason for this I've tried without success to analyze. But whatever it is, his interest in literature seems to be a kind of appendage to his life—connected with it but still external, separate; whereas in my case the interest *is* me—organically and chemically as much a part of my being as my blood or digestive system or the phosphorus and calcium in my body (apart from those other differences of male and female).

It occurs to me that there is this same difference in all people in their relation to the world of art and ideas—and in their relation to love also, and that this is connected somehow with all that still remains mysterious and undiscovered in the psychological aspects of disease—the latter having become of great interest to me because I feel often that my health would improve if I were not always so damnably lonely.

I don't mean to imply any superiority of one sort of person to the other. And that I don't *see* in Chuk any urgent drives of any kind doesn't mean they don't exist (sometimes people seem to be frittering away their time when it's just a period of gestation for them). But I simply cannot stand any longer the kind of existence I've been leading year after year. What you have mistaken for courage in me has been at times the resignation of despair. At other times just waiting for a stroke of luck that might change things. And also when we are young we live in the future—or rather into it (at least we *can* if we have to), whereas later as we grow older we need a sense [of] a past achievement—we need the past achievement to add to—being no longer at an age for beginnings. And if and when I think of how slight my own past achievement is, I become paralyzed and must make the greatest effort to keep myself from falling into the condition of Myra in the last part of your play.[1]

But for whatever years remain of my wasted life (I feel the waste all the more terribly since the sacrifices which I once made for my son were of no avail, and I shall never be able to forgive myself for my failure as a mother) I simply must have some little minimum of economic independence—I've got to be free to make writing—and not only writing but all phases of my intellectual life—the *chief* thing—fitting in other things the best I can instead of just the reverse, and free to define my own duties (as I see them) in my relationships with other people instead of having them defined for me as they are at present. This need would be urgent enough if I were physically a robust woman and a well-educated one (well-educated in the technical phases of poetry, I mean). But because I am not well physically and therefore have a limited amount of physical energy, the latter has to go into one thing or another. And because I am very much dependent on my moods, my feelings (on what is called "inspiration") I require more freedom in letting them have their way with me (in writing I mean) than someone who has the kind of training—the kind of knowledge—which enables him to cold-bloodedly sit down and write. And this never having around me or easily accessible certain books which I need either for practical reasons (such as a good dictionary—I don't even possess that) or, more importantly, because they have an important place in my thoughts, is insufferable.

But I did not intend to cover so much paper with all these tiresome details of so dull an existence as mine. (And in doing so the wonder of poetry—of the creative word—is again brought home to me—because there in two lines, in one line, you can say so much whereas in a million documentary lines such as these you say nothing.)

And now what I have been leading up to. Do you see any way for me to have things changed for the better? (And this means more of course than just being tided over a moment's emergency.) The man who you mentioned (Pearson) hasn't gotten in touch with me, and do you think I will still hear from him? And if I don't, why will that be? And how shall I go about trying to get some of my poems in magazines over here? I don't think that Partisan Review, Kenyon Review, Harper's, and other such periodicals would be apt to publish them if I myself sent them out because they go in for "names"—unless someone with a name sponsors them. So could you and would you send them for me? And if so should I send you some poems for that purpose? (By the way when you asked me about magazines here in connection with the ones I already sent you, did you mean that the same poems could be published both in Italy and here? I didn't quite understand.) And I want to ask you this too. If I should get a few poems published here and there and then got Laughlin to put out a book, would there be any chance of my getting a Guggenheim scholarship for work in Poetry?

I said in a recent letter to you that I've grown to realize that it's not enough to be a writer in private—that one must get published. But I feel that way due only to the circumstances surrounding my life, and I find all these practical details connected with writing a great burden. To strip one's life of all its superficialities—its "impedimenta"—all the baggage—and to live it out only in its essence, in its barest needs (or rather its deepest ones)—that is what I have always wanted and yet (what irony there!) mine has been more cluttered up with things and people not really belonging to it than that of anyone I know.

Anyway—things being as they are—will you please let me know about all I've asked regarding these practical matters. And please (I have wanted to say this before) do not think that I am a completely self-centered person, with little awareness of how matters connected with your own life must often make my demands on your time a great inconvenience. One of the things I can't bear about my situation is the way I'm forced to be preoccupied with such problems as those mentioned here and in other letters to you. Self-centeredness doesn't belong to my nature really (other lives interest me intensely)—but this too is part of the baggage with which I am weighted down. Also in any sidestepping from this kind of letter (if I were free for it) or from one about poetry, I would have to be on my guard lest I stray on dangerous or forbidden grounds, and this would make me self-conscious and artificial.

Sincerely
Marcia (Nardi)
The Sad Poetess of Pat.

Will your being Poetry Advisor to the Library of Congress make it necessary for [you] to live in Washington?[2] Or will you go on staying in Rutherford and keeping up your medical practice?

1. The character Myra appears in Williams's play *A Dream of Love*. The play opened off-Broadway at the Hudson Guild Playhouse in New York City in July 1949 (during a brutal heatwave) and closed after two weeks. Myra's condition at the end of the play was one of stoic acceptance.

2. Williams had been invited to become the poetry consultant for the Library of Congress for 1949–50 but was unable to serve because of his health (he suffered a heart attack in February 1948).

. . . .

58. TLS-1 (T)

Tuesday [early August 1949]

Dear Marcia:

Got home from a two weeks' rest in the country yesterday and found your letter awaiting me.[1] More of that in a moment.

Yesterday, by air mail, I sent the more recent of your poems to the editor of Botteghe Oscure in Italy.[2] I did not send the earlier group. I tell you this now to ask you to leave word at your post office that you are expecting a letter from Italy or Switzerland and that it will be directed to you and *not* c/o Lang. You see, I forgot to put in the c/o.

I strongly urged that the poems be accepted and further urgently requested that you be paid at once for them. So I have high hopes that you will get a generous check within two weeks at the latest.

Pearson left for Europe last week without replying to me upon the matter of the cash grant. I recommended you and Norman Macleod,[3] no one else. All I can do now is to wait and hope for the best; he should be back in September.

Keep writing as best you are able. If you can go on producing such poems as those more recent ones I'll push them as hard as I can at Tiger's Eye. They pay the highest rates in the game. Then, if we can get a group in there and another group in Botteghe Oscure, with a small book on the way with Laughlin you should definitely apply for a Guggenheim mentioning my name and the name of some other writer, like Marianne Moore, as backers (I'll talk to Marianne). It would be best though to get some recent work published in magazines first.

I don't quite know whether to send the older group of poems which I am holding to some such mag. as Poetry or not. Let me think about it a little longer.

The question of your personal life is something that distresses me, moves me and leads me, in itself, apart from your ability as a writer, to want to help you. But what am I to do? I'd like to give you money but somehow it doesn't seem the answer, quite apart from the fact that I have no money to give. But I feel morally obligated to stand behind you and to rescue you when crises occur. Perhaps before cold weather something can be worked out.

I have resigned as Poetry Consultant in Washington, otherwise I should have had to go there to live. They have made me one of the Fellows but I'm even going to resign that. I have no intention of working with Eliot on an American job.[4] I'll go on practicing medicine in Rutherford.

Best luck

Bill

1. Actually, Nardi's letter of 25 July 1949 had been forwarded to Williams c/o Charles Abbott, Linwood, Livingston Co., New York (postmarked envelope, SUNY Buffalo). According to Paul Mariani, Williams and his wife had been visiting the Abbotts at Gratwick Highlands in Linwood (Mariani, *William Carlos Williams: A New World Naked*, 590).

2. Marguerite Caetani, editor of the magazine *Botteghe Oscure*, which

was published in Rome from 1948 to 1960. Nardi's poem "In the Asylum" (*Botteghe Oscure* 4 [1949]: 324) was singled out for favorable mention in a review in the *Times Literary Supplement*, 17 February 1950. "And I Knew the Body a Sea" appeared in the 1950 edition of *Botteghe Oscure* (6 [1950]: 435–440), and two more poems ("Ah, But the Unloved Have Had Power" and "Love I Make It Because I Write It") were published in the 1956 edition (17 [1956]: 300–302).

3. Poet, novelist, editor, and teacher (1906–1985). In the mid-1940s, he was editorial director of both the *Maryland Quarterly* and the *Briarcliff Quarterly*.

4. T. S. Eliot had also been made a fellow of the Library of Congress. Williams thought Eliot had abandoned America and American poetry by living in England and writing poetry that turned to history and the classics for inspiration.

. . . .

59. TLS-1 (T)

Wednesday [August 1949]

Dear Marcia:

I feel as you do about those Rilke poems and did not send them to Poetry. They are not your best work. I'll wait for further instructions.

Don't be in any haste about Tiger's Eye as the editors are in Europe. If you can get your newer things to me by September 1st it will be time enough. If you will have enough work to make two groups mark one for Tiger's Eye and one for Poetry.

Could I send you a good dictionary, since you say you do not have one? If so, let me know directly and I'll find one for you.

Sincerely
Bill

. . . .

60. TLS-2 (Y)

August 24th [1949]

Dear Bill,

I received the check from Europe—$150![1] But it has taken me several days to grasp the reality of having gotten it (tomorrow one of our neighbors will identify me at her bank so that I [can] cash it there); and adjusting myself to the possibility that everything else—the book and Tiger's Eye and the aid from Pearson—may turn out as successfully as the placing of these poems in such a well-paying magazine, has put me in such a state of nervous excitement that several times I have had to call to mind a quotation I once used at the beginning of an old poem—"le Bonheur demande un apprentissage".[2]

Unfortunately I must accompany the good news of the check with the bad news of my having been ill again—and very ill—for three days—which held up my completion of the long poem in three parts for Tiger's Eye. But it's nearly done now, and I hope to have it off to you by September 1st along with the others for Poetry.

But in the meantime I want you to know about the check. And also I must ask you if you will please let me know right away if "Caetani" is the right spelling, and is the second part of the name "Bassiano"—and does the publisher of the magazine use both names or just the first part of her name? (She used her full name on the check and only the first part in signing the little note sent with the check—and the latter is in longhand so that the spelling isn't clear to me.) And will you verify this address "32 via Botteghe Oscure, Rome" which seems strange to me because I know absolutely no Italian so that I am puzzled at the magazine's name and the street address being exactly the same (and what does Botteghe Oscure mean?).

I need this information because I have to write to Miss Caetani (is "Miss" correct?—all these questions!) since she asked me to let her have some biographical material. And by the way I haven't the slightest idea what to send, because the only material really to the point would be that connected with my career as a writer, and I have none. If I knew definitely that I am to have poems in Tiger's Eye, Poetry and possibly some other American magazines this fall and winter and definitely that Laughlin will put out a book for me in the not too distant future, then I could mention all this. But I don't know *definitely*, though I hope so much that all these matters will work out as planned.

I have to write to Laughlin to find out why he doesn't let me know about the poems he has—which ones he is using in the Anthology (he sent me a note many weeks ago—I think in early July or late June—saying he hadn't had time to more than glance at my poems but that he liked what he read, and added "As soon as I get back I'll try to study your poems more closely and pick out those which we would like to use in the anthology, and return the others to you so that you can place them in other magazine[s]") and at the same time I may ask him if it would be all right for me to say in a biographical magazine note that I am to have a book published soon by New Directions. Or perhaps I shouldn't ask him. What do you think?

I suffer from so many timidities in such matters. I suppose it's idiotic. But it's so hard for me to overcome them—though I may be better able to do so after I get a few more things published—especially if you should like what I send you for Tiger's Eye. (What you think of these particular poems—the ones I'm now doing—is of very special importance to me for reasons which I'll explain after you see them.)

Do writers of all nationalities appear in Miss Caetani's magazine—or only those writing in English, or what?

Sincerely

Marcia

About the dictionary. How kind of you to offer to send me one! But I'll tell you about that in the letter which will accompany the poems.

1. The check was from Marguerite Caetani for Nardi's poem "In the Asylum."

2. "Happiness needs an apprenticeship."

. . . .

61. TLS-2 (Y)

August 31, 1949

Dear Norman:[1]

Marcia Nardi is not an old friend, I have known her only for about 6 or 7 years. She was literally blown into my office one night, soaked to the skin by a heavy rain and in frightened need, in desperate need. I helped her for a while but found it was too much for me and withdrew after the first year or so. But I was not so much moved by charity as by a deep and humble sense of her real worth as a writer.

I know little of her past other than that she is a college woman who did some hack work about New York ten years ago. Then, after an unfortunate marriage and a child (of whom it would be best to make no mention) she became pretty much of a bum. But not entirely. She merely sank to the bottom—and stayed there, unable to lift herself again.

All through this period she has tried to find something to cling to—womanlike, and has failed to do so. Now she is "married" again and living at Woodstock, N.Y. trying to live, the two of them, by doing odd jobs. She is small, frail, an avowed neurotic depending a good deal upon medical care which she wangles somehow out of a couple of surprisingly good nerve specialists.

But she has, I think, genius. She can write. At times I believe her (recent) poems to be as fine as anything I have ever read from the pen of a woman—not excepting Marianne Moore and H.D. She has an instinctive and not alone instinctive but rigidly intellectualized sense of metrical values—enough of that. Laughlin published a group of her early poems in New Directions some 5 or 6 years ago under a short introductory statement I wrote for them, somewhat to my regret. For some of my friends said I had been patronizing. See for yourself.

From then to the present day she disappeared completely. I heard she had died. Suddenly, this spring, she appeared again. She was married. She was ill. She was desperate and would I help her. I answered at once and said I would, to send me some recent poems. By return mail I received two of the best poems I had seen in years. Encouraged I wrote to Laughlin asking him to accept the group for New Directions: 1950.[2] He did so and sent her $15. I was disgusted but such is life.

We continued to correspond. Finally, under my urging she sent me a 3 pages poem, In The Asylum, that you will see shortly in *Botteghe Oscure*. You'll be surprised. Issue #IV of that magazine, BO, will be out in the fall. Princess de Bassiano, Marguerite Caetani (nee Biddle)[3] the editor of that swank magazine, agrees with me the poem is most excellent and we['ll] see what happens next. I am now coaching the woman, Marcia Nardi, trying to steady her a little; asking her to get a group ready for Poetry: Chicago, another group ready for Tiger's Eye. Thus with the early poems from ND, the group Laughlin is using in the new ND, the two poems to come out in Botteghe Oscure, the Poetry and the Tiger's Eye groups (if they are ever finished) we'll have enough for a small book by mid-winter. If you could help with a little money it would be as though we had put down the first story of a small pyramid. She desperately needs help even to eat and I think that she is extraordinarily gifted.

The extraordinary effect of her diction and her conversational prose style coming out of those rags is both shocking and delightful. And she is NOT an addict—so far as I know. Nor a drunk, a miserable, drowned rat all soft except for—a rat's will to survive and in her case to write, to nurse the genius that she feels almost drown inside her guts—somewhere.

Maybe we could meet, you and I, I mean, in the city somewhere sometime this fall. Glad you saw the play—and got to Europe.

Best

Bill

1. Norman Holmes Pearson. Included with this letter was a handwritten note from Williams (on a separate piece of paper) saying: "She wrote the letter at the end of P 2 (please destroy)," followed by the notation "[Wm C Wms]" and Pearson's scribbled initials (Norman Holmes Pearson Papers, Yale Collection of American Literature, Beinecke Rare Book and Manuscript Library, Yale University).

2. See *New Directions Number Eleven*, 309–312.

3. Marguerite (née Chapin, not Biddle) Caetani was born in New London, Connecticut in 1880 and died in 1963. She married Roffredo Caetani, prince of Bassiano, in 1911.

Saturday [August 1949]

Dear Marcia:

Well, that's fine. I'm glad the old gal came through so hand-somely. The name is, Marguerite Caetani and the address is, 32 Via Botteghe Oscure, Rome. She has taken the name of the street as the name of her magazine which is printed mainly in Italian but contains poems and prose in other languages, En-glish, French, German. Sometimes she offers translations of the foreign work for her Italian readers.

She should not, in fact cannot, be addressed as "Miss". Her official title is Princess Bassiano. I don't know her age, I think she must be in her fifties. She was a Biddle. I always address her simply as Marguerite Caetani.

I *think* Botteghe Oscure means dark grove or woods.[1] No one seems quite sure about it. It may mean small or obscure shop— which would be mildly ironical inasmuch as number 32 is the Palazzo Caetani where the lady lives. Or so I am told. I don't know her well.

Keep working and I'm sorry you are not well. For God's sake don't spend your money on doctors!

Sincerely

Bill

1. *Botteghe oscure* means "dark shop." The name of the street came from the dark arcades, filled with shops, which flanked it during the Middle Ages.

. . . .

63. APCI-I (T)

[postmarked] September 6, 1949

Poem rec'd.[1] It is excellent tho I agree the final page is not as fluid & so as good as the real body of the work—simple cutting might help. I'll be away until next Monday. I'll write again.

W

1. The letter and poem from Nardi referred to here are missing; the poem was probably "In the Asylum," published by *Botteghe Oscure* (November 1949): 324.

. . . .

64. TLS-2 (Y)

Thursday, September 22nd
[1949]

Dear Bill,

I'm sending the poems and some comments on them separately—this having to do with something else.

I've been ill again for a week now, hardly able to be up and about, and almost completely blotted out. And I'd like to tell you once [and] for all exactly what all this amounts to, so that you won't think I'm suffering from a hypochondriac's ailments and because you may be able to advise me.

The main difficulty is the great difference among doctors as to what's wrong. One group of doctors insists that the digestive disorder is functional rather than organic and that it has its roots in a neurosis of some kind. Another group insists just as emphatically that the digestive thing is entirely organic; and not only is there this disagreement in a general way but among the doctors of each group there are further differences of opinion—the nature of the organic impairment, for instance, having been differently diagnosed by each of the doctors who say it exists.

You would think that the X-ray pictures of last winter (and I had others taken previously in New York) would have helped to clarify matters. But each doctor saw in those pictures a confirmation of his own diagnosis and our local physician who does not handle such cases and who therefore can be more objective than the others told me that in certain instances X-rays mean little since they allow sometimes for a variety of "readings." And certainly almost anyone can cite cases where they were of no help. (Grant Wood, for instance, was treated for gallstones for a long time and then when he was almost on his deathbed it was discovered that he had cancer already in its secondary stage.)

In my own case I think that part of the trouble *is* "nervous." The frustrations connected with my private emotional life were bound sooner or later to take themselves out on my body with a vengeance, and this they certainly have done. I didn't need any doctor to make me aware of that. But at the same time I seem to have something alarmingly wrong with me in other ways. The slightest indiscretion in the way of food, cigarettes, or liquor brings on great physical distress. And even when I am extremely careful (I stopped smoking entirely for seven months and now take a cigarette very rarely and in a year I've had a little wine on only three occasions) I am seized by attacks so severe that they knock me out for days at a stretch. They consist of a bad pain in the upper right hand side of my back (though sometimes it's my entire back), a slight soreness on my right side and—what's much worse than the pain—a feeling of congestion in my chest and of great discomfort around my heart (the latter being the result of a "spastic" condition and gas). And of all the medications given to me (belladonna, atropine, hydrochloric acid, peppermint, et cetera) not one brings any relief. And the discomfort (it keeps getting worse all the time) lasts for hours—often all night and leaves me still exhausted even after I finally get seven or eight hours of sleep. And then as soon as I eat (or rather several hours later) it starts all over again.

I am not spending any more money on doctors these days. Even before you advised me not to, I'd already made up my mind against it. But there is a Kingston doctor (I first went to see him about two months ago after several days of really intolerable discomfort) to whom I explained my financial situation and who has been very considerate about it—trying to help me without any fee but having such a deep and all-absorbing interest in the so-called "psychosomatic" illnesses (as if everything in life weren't to a great extent psychosomatic!) that he doesn't even admit the slightest possibility of anything being wrong organically. He asked me many questions about my private life and immediately came to the conclusion that a sharp change in my way of living (more recreational outlets, changes of scenery, clothes, theatres, better surroundings and that sort of thing) would cause all the trouble to vanish (I think he's much mistaken—lack of *such* things could never make me *ill*. He thinks of me in terms of his own wife and *her* values). And yet a year ago another doctor was all for having me rushed off to the surgical ward! And then a month later Gerson pooh-poohed that idea—saying that my need was merely for better living habits (no smoking, drinking, and a special diet which I stuck to for seven months without getting better). Do you know that part in Proust's work where his grandmother is ill and all the great specialists come to see her each one diagnosing her condition and attempting to treat it according to the nature of his own specialized and prejudiced medical studies? Well, that is the situation here—exactly. I don't suppose there's any advice you can give me in regard to it (though if there is I certainly would welcome it). But anyway this matter of my health which I talk about so often is at least clearer to you now. And I'm glad to have explained it so as not to seem a victim of some imaginary ailment. I hate illness. I'm so impatient with it (in myself I mean, not in others)! And up until recent years my body was always at the mercy of my mind—always. And to have the situation reversed now—to have my mind so completely at the mercy of my body is an ordeal which I certainly would flee from if I only could. It involves a complete reorientation which I am not up to.

And now there's something else I want to mention—having meant to do so in my last letter and then having forgotten about it. I really should have returned to you out of the check I got from Marguerite Caetani the twenty dollars you gave me that night in Passaic.[1] At first I was going to do so. Then I decided that I'd better wait to see how other things worked out—Tiger's Eye, Poetry, Pearson, et cetera—so as to feel a little less insecure than I do now about this coming winter. Is that all right?

And one more thing. If I should hear from Pearson, is there any special thing I should be tactful about in answering any of the questions he may ask me. You referred to having given him at his request more information about me with discretion in regard to my private life. And I am stupid enough not to know what that means. Anyway I have a fashion, I'm afraid, of not infrequently saying the wrong things to people without any suspicion of their being the wrong things—so if there's anything it would be best not to mention, I'll appreciate your letting me know what it is. And I hope you won't think me an imbecile for making such an absurd request.

Though I'm sending the poems separately, I want to say here (because you said "if you want me to") that I appreciate more than I can express your great kindness in submitting them for me, and I've taken so long in getting them back to you because of so much illness again. I had to consider carefully your suggested changes and was in no condition to do so.

Sincerely

Marcia

P.S. I have another long poem which I must get to work on, and the way all this sickness holds up my work is one of its worst phases.

---

1. Reference to a third meeting between Nardi and Williams and a loan from him of $20. This meeting took place sometime during the summer of 1949, probably between 21 June and 2 July.

. . . .

65. TLS-1 (Y)

Tuesday, September 26th

[1949]

Dear Bill,

I can't remember whether in the new copy of "With a Poem Alone" I changed line 8 in Part 1. It was originally "still young enough to take upon your knee and fondle" and I felt it needed shortening and also that "still young enough" was superfluous in meaning. But I'm afraid that I forgot to make that revision. Yes, I'm almost sure that I did, and now I don't know what to do about it in case you have already sent the poem to *Tiger's Eye*.[1]

The last part of the first stanza should go this way:

"... or the child
you take upon your knee and fondle
Footloose ... your nostrils lowered
Over a roadside flower."

Since you have the original copy will you kindly compare the two versions, and if you agree that this change is an improvement, is it possible to send the change to Tiger's Eye (or if by chance you haven't sent the poem yet, maybe you could make the change for me by just running a pencil through "Still young enough to" and by inserting a "you" before the "take").

As I look at the poem, that line stands out for me in the boldest type with the unnecessary first few words spoiling the whole stanza and I imagine that it might stand out that way to the Tiger's Eye editors. Do you think so? And are poems rejected because of some one or two bad lines? If so, maybe that one line will cause it to be turned down.

Marcia

It's an amazing and annoying thing that no sooner do I get a poem out of the house and away from me, than I start seeing it more clearly than at any other time. Of the poems to appear in ND for instance there's one the ending of which I would like very much to revise but will have to leave it as it is because it may already be set up or possibly the dummy for the book is already done, so that the extra lines caused by the revision would disarrange everything and thus be a nuisance to Laughlin.

1. This poem was never published by *Tiger's Eye*. See photocopy (65.1) of original with Williams's and Nardi's comments on margins (the original is included with Nardi's letter to Williams in the Williams Collection of the Beinecke Rare Book Library at Yale University).

Page 1

ALONE WITH A POEM

1

The idea you innocently play with
Indifferent to what it may lead to
(Or, rather, not thinking about it at all)
Touching it, brushing against it -
The attractive stranger you dance with at a party
And at your liesure..for an hour's pastime..
May see again. Or the child
Still young enough to take upon your knee and fondle
Blood footloose as the nostrils lowered
Over a roadside flower -

How these gold virginal moments
Like those recaptured Edens
When the body wakes from sleep before the mind does
Will fade into the distance,alltheir myth's brightness
Misted and shadowy
When the child, a year older, shows
How a rose can turn lodestone
Or into your sun and air
Grows the attractive stranger -

When your idea
Thrusting upon you an unmade poem makes
The one rape that of Mary .

11

Alone with a poem
Its breath still homeless
And for its marrow no bones
And when like Adam
You are asked to provide them
Groping for your own

Your thought running from you
Just outside your window
At your call turning but running on
Because you have no face yet
Because it does not know you

Because you are the original Thurston
Waiting
For a world of his own making
In order to be born
The creator creating to be created
The womb within a womb

(a) Not as the prisoner of an island
Or ~~the~~ Beguinage's lonely ones
Only as the dying
Miles from the arms they lie in
With your poem alone
But towards those arms rowing
Not flowing from

Alone with a poem
Its bones not formed yet
Its pulse-beat awaiting a wrist
As if love came on Campion gallops to find you
And you raised up phantom lips for its kiss -

This loafing, this terror
This agony
This is the first of the forbidden pleasures
This is the chief of the eleven commandments'
Interdit's
And how you envy the committers
Of theft and adultery,
And all the sweaters
In mines and in factories
With their double
Sabbath day pay -
These how you envy!

What hold you then? What holds you?
Why not go? Why do you stay?
What binds you to this fire, half snow -
To this Gethsemane?
If you cannot answer
At least you know
That the Croesuses and Caesars
Have not so much to do
With the Sudras of all centuries.

(111)

I recall Anna saying that at Yaddo
Feuds arose sometimes
Between the artists and poets..

The latter boasting
More intellect -
Oh that pride of the beggared
And derelict!

But now you are one with the world -
A sound to make rounder
A vowel to measure
And yours too the sculptor's firm ground
And the painter's pleasure
Now you are one with the loved
And with the unloved who love
The congestion of cities
And one with the blind
~~And with those who are kind~~
~~And~~ Gentle to kittens -
~~With all who live tactilely~~-
Now you have something to touch
And with another touch or two
Your poem is finished..

~~Your poem~~..or is it?..
Going away like dew
Going away a stranger
Who bears on its beautiful limbs and face
Little resemblance to
The shape and the face of your daily behavior-
Oh what you have made
Is now the creator
Creating out of your name
Someone not you.

Should the word "interdit's" in the middle of page 2, be in italics? Foreign words usually are ~~italiced~~, are they not?

September 27, 1949

Dear Marcia:

About yourself, whatever the condition that is bothering you may arise from it certainly seems spastic in its outward characteristics. As you say, it seems confined to the upper abdomen. Well, the two outstanding organs that cause trouble there, trouble of that sort, are the biliary passages and the duodenum. Without having reviewed the findings in the case I wouldn't have the presumption to offer a diagnosis or even a suggestion toward one. I have used a tablet called Donnetal for relief of gastric spasms, it may be of some use to you in shortening an attack.

I suppose a diaphragmatic hernia has also been considered.

In my letter to Pearson I made no mention of your son. I thought it best not to do so. That's all I meant by speaking with discretion. He asked me about your history and I told him what I knew, all except that point. I thought that when he finally communicates with you, if you want to speak of that, you'll mention it yourself—though there should be no need of it as far as I can see.

I'll send the poems off today. In suggesting that you reverse the order of the stanzas I was looking at the poem as a whole. You know yourself that a poem is not a thought but a composition. The thought doesn't have to follow any logical order but can come in any way that the making of the poem orders. I thought that the poem, as a composition, was improved by the order I suggested; it made a stronger, more stirring end, a more forceful end by bringing the emotional or more emotional part in at the end— As you had [it] the thought is a mere tag, a weak compositional tail wagging at the end after the real poem has passed. You could even leave it out entirely without hurting what comes before.[1]

There's a promising looking new review, The Western Review, that also pays. Well, I'll send the poems off now and we'll see what we shall see.

You owe me nothing, forget it.

Sincerely yours
Bill

1. Nardi eventually did change the order of the stanzas when the poem (retitled "Alone with a Poem") was published in her book (*Poems*, 12).

· ·

67. TPCS-1 (T)

[September 28, 1949]

Fortunately I did not send the scripts away yesterday as I had planned to do. The change in the one for *Tiger's Eye*[1] will be made at once.

As[k] Laughlin please to let you have proofs of the work to appear in ND. Or, very briefly, ask him to make the change in the poem which you have now decided on. There'll be no trouble. Don't explain, just state briefly what you want.

Best
Bill

1. Williams is referring to Nardi's "Alone with a Poem," which has her note "For *Tiger's Eye*" on the margin (Y).

· ·

68. TLS-3 (Y)

Friday September 29th [1949]

Dear Bill,

Yesterday in the same mail with your letter, I heard from Mr. Pearson.

But first about that poem which disturbs me greatly now that you have so clearly pointed out its weakness as you see it.

You are right certainly—that the composition is the main thing, and also that the last part could have been left out entirely without spoiling the rest. And I wish now that for the time being (for Tiger's Eye, I mean) I'd submitted only the main body of the poem—later on looking at the whole thing again with freshened eyes, re-considering then your suggestion about the order, and restoring the other two parts to the poem in my book, if [*sic*] I finally got to see how right you were about the order.

I hope my not having followed your suggestion won't completely kill its chances with Tiger's Eye. And I hope also that it won't keep you from making other suggestions about my work, because none of your criticism is ever lost on me, even when it seems to be, since what I do not profit from at the moment of receiving it, I profit from later in the long run—which is the important thing.

You have been doing so much to assist me in practical ways that I cannot help but be extremely grateful for it. But apart from that, in a completely unadulterated way, quite disconnected from my material welfare, I greatly value your opinion of my writing, and not only of my writing but of myself (not being at all sure that Yeats was right in making so sharp a distinction between "perfection of the life" and "perfection of the art").[1] It therefore distresses me to realize that I must seem extremely stupid to you for not having been able to see the need for that reversed order and also blindly stubborn in that exasperating fashion of really stupid people. But it wasn't my stupidity—it's merely that as soon as I find myself thrust into a world of clocks and timetables (creatively, I mean, of course) my mind is not at its best; and I have to function in that world for the time being due to the practical importance to me of getting my poems published, if I can, right along as I write them so as to have a book out as soon as possible. But once I do get a fair number published, then I shall put every new poem aside for a month or two before sending it out (every new poem about which I am in doubt I mean) and then consider after such an interval has passed any suggestions that you give me for its improvement along with those of my own.

In regard to Pearson's communication,[2] he asked nothing about my private life. The only information he requests is that connected with my plans—because he needs that for the records. But here is the main part of his letter: "Could you give me some idea of your immediate objective—outside of writing well—so that when I bring up the matter before the Board of Directors I could present it in the form of a particular project? . . . Dr. Williams has spoken so highly of your achievement that I have no doubt whatsoever on that score and am much more interested in correctly phrasing a project that will look well on the record." The rest is about the Bryher Foundation, what it is, its limited funds at present, and its desire to put those funds to work as soon as possible. The letter in general is a very nice one—thanks to you.

I shall give the preparation of material for a book as my immediate objective (and I may say another thing or two about the work I'm doing at present and plan to do this winter—though I think that the book as a project ought to do for the records—do you think so?). And by the way in regard to the book, I have started going through all my work old and new, and there are some of the older poems I should like to consult you about—though not until a little later on after I have gotten some more new work done—this being my main concern at the moment especially since some of it will go into the book. How I wish I could have some day-to-day good health for a while! (that backache which I mentioned is so persistent. At the moment it seems to be boring a hole straight through me—and all this morning I was badly nauseated, this being something new). But with or without it, I hope to be doing a lot of work right along now, and so please do not withhold from me your further advice and criticism in regard to anything I send you, simply because of my having left the order unchanged in that poem which by now has probably reached Tiger's Eye.

I don't know what you thought of that new short poem (beginning "the stone body") for Poetry.[3] Since you made no mention of it, I presume you couldn't have liked it much. But if and when you have a chance to, will you let me know your opinion of that one? And if your kind offer to find me a dictionary still holds good and if it won't put you out too much, I'll be glad to have it—especially if it's an etymological one which all good dictionaries are, I guess.

It was my plan a couple of weeks ago to go to New York for a couple of days (I know someone there who would, I think, put me up for a night or two—hotels being more expensive than ever these days) partly for a change of scene and partly to visit the Fourth Avenue second hand book shops where I could very likely pick up a few much needed books at a fairly low price. But this awful health thing interfered and it interferes now, because I would feel uncomfortably guilty if one of these attacks caused me to make a disturbance in the middle of the night in someone else's apartment. So I don't know now just when I'll go in, and Kingston hasn't a single bookshop (apart from the lending libraries in stationery stores)! And the Woodstock bookshop only three miles from here isn't the sort of place to get dictionaries—being very much like Gotham Book Mart in New York except that its prices for everything—for both new and used books—are higher than those of Gotham.

Thank you for trying to throw whatever light you could on my health problem. But what I really meant when I asked if by chance you had anything to advise was whether—in your opinion—I ought to go on trying to get at the roots of what's wrong, or just put up with it, in the dark.

Saturday [30 September 1949]
(The afterthoughts on this page about that poem are more on my mind than things said about it previously—so I put the last of the letter first.)

I didn't give this to the mailman yesterday because I was to go to Kingston and planned to mail it there, then didn't go, and now today with it still unmailed I have taken another look at that poem and suddenly I see it more clearly, or seem to.

The trouble—the trouble for me—is that the last part (specifically the middle of the last page) is not good in itself and wherever I placed it still wouldn't be good. With the order reversed its inadequacies might be less conspicuous—would perhaps stand out less boldly in the reader's mind after he had gone on to read better lines, but still it wouldn't be right. And I made that last page *even worse* by my changes in the second copy (the changes you suggested were good but my own not so), and I have no words for my chagrin as I think of the Tiger's Eye editors reading that section that just dangles there so weakly in the way you described. If it were better done maybe even in its present position it wouldn't seem just a tag & would become, with more skillful handling, properly integrated with the whole poem. *That* I have yet to think about sometime in the future as I already said earlier in this letter—but the inferior quality of some of the writing there on the last page—whatever the order of the three parts might be—that I do see and could almost weep over.

If only the Tiger's Eye editors could be asked to consider for publication only the first two parts or only that one section ("alone with a poem") from which the whole thing gets its title! I'm sure in that case they would like and accept it—at least almost sure; and if that last page keeps it from being accepted I shall feel much worse about it than if the whole poem were no good.

Would you, will you, let me know (since I may have to wait a couple of weeks to hear from Tiger's Eye) what you think about the poem's chances for publication in its present form, and whether it would be out of place to do what I suggested in the previous paragraph; and whether if it is *not* the sort of thing one can do, the editors on their own accord might use the parts of the poem they like without turning down the whole thing in case they should happen to like the first two parts and not the last section?

But distressing as all that is to me, I hope to be working now on another fairly long poem already started, and maybe if it's good, it can be sent when finished to that new review you mentioned.

Again thank you for everything.

Marcia

I'm mailing my reply to Pearson's letter along with this.

1. Nardi is referring to Yeats's poem "The Choice," from *The Collected Poems of W. B. Yeats* (New York: Macmillan, 1938), 284.

> The intellect of man is forced to choose
> Perfection of the life, or of the work,
> And if it take the second must refuse
> A heavenly mansion, raging in the dark.
> When all that story's finished, what's the news?
> In luck or out the toil has left its mark:
> That old perplexity an empty purse,
> Or the day's vanity, the night's remorse.

2. Norman Holmes Pearson's letter to her (dated 27 September 1949) is with Nardi's papers at the Beinecke Library at Yale (Za Nardi, uncat.).

3. "They Said It Is All Clear Now," *Poetry* (March 1950): 331–332.

. . . .

69. TLS-1 (T)

9 Ridge Rd.

October 31, 1949

Dear Marcia:

I presume that you know that you have been awarded a grant of $250.00 by the foundation represented by Norman Pearson.[1] If you have not been notified, that is the case. I congratulate you. It isn't much but it's something.

Today I received the enclosed letter from Poetry with their acceptance of one of your poems.[2] You see what they say of the future, they are in financial trouble.

No word as yet from Tiger's Eye. You might yourself write them if you care to but maybe it would be best to wait a little longer.

Nothing new here. I work along as I am able mostly at Medicine but always with a fringe of prose or verse at the back of my head to keep my neck warm. I read a good book now and then and a few bad ones. I am in, almost in the middle of War & Peace. Pretty tough going.

My poor little (tough) mother died three weeks ago at the age almost of 93.[3] A sad figure.

Best luck

Bill

1. Pearson's letter to Nardi (dated 21 October 1949) announcing the Bryher Foundation award is with Nardi's papers at the Beinecke Library at Yale (Za Nardi, uncat.).

2. "They Said It Is All Clear Now," *Poetry* (March 1950): 331–332.

3. Paul Mariani points out that Williams's mother (Elena Hoheb Williams) was born in 1847, not 1856 as Williams had thought, making her almost 102 years old when she died (Mariani, *William Carlos Williams: A New World Naked*, 596).

Wednesday, November 3rd,
1949

Dear Bill,

So much time has passed now without my having heard from *Tiger's Eye* or *Poetry* or from you, that I'm wondering about those poems. Is it usual for manuscripts to be kept so long before a decision is made? (after all that trouble with my mail at the time your money order never reached me and Laughlin's check also, I'm a bit uneasy whenever I fail to get any letter that I'm expecting).

But I ought to be in good spirits as I start this, having received a check of $250 from the Bryher Foundation. And I would be—except that my getting it brings to a crisis a difficult situation which I must do something about immediately in order to use the money for the purpose for which it was given me.

The problem I'm faced with is one I've got to solve for myself, I know. But telling you about it, talking about it here, may help me solve it—(for days now it's been driving me almost crazy!).

The few days before I got the check from Botteghe Oscure, my husband lost a job with the township after having it only two weeks. We had expected it to last a couple of months at least. But with such jobs so tied up with local politics, the natives get first consideration and when funds ran low, Chuk was the first to be laid off. I therefore have had to meet *all* our household expenses including what we owed for rent, and I can't go on doing it if I want my work to benefit from the Bryher Award, as I certainly do.

Even if I could stretch my money so that it would support two people by lowering still farther our sub-standard way of living, I couldn't function either creatively or in purely bodily ways under such conditions. Were I more robust physically I could put up with the rugged primitiveness of them—and might even enjoy that phase of things, because I love the country and our grounds are beautiful—though the house itself is only a one-room shack that looks like a stage set for Tobacco Road. But even in that case the isolation forced upon me here in the late fall and winter months would still make this a most undesirable year-round residence. We are on a plateau on a wooded mountain-side with no neighbors at all now and with the road below us almost deserted from November to April. You don't see a pedestrian on this road for weeks at a time—sometimes not a single one all winter long, and in hours only one car or so passes; and on the main highway a couple of miles away there is so little traffic that hitch-hiking (the only way I can get anyplace without a phone and two or three dollar taxi fares continually) is very difficult and not without danger for a woman alone after October—a danger which I gave no thought to until about a week ago when a man who gave me a ride out of Kingston attempted to assault me—my narrow escape (a sort of miracle really) and the shock of the episode having affected me so badly that I feel more of a prisoner than ever.

My husband feels that if he should settle down to some real work on short stories for a couple of months, he'd very likely sell them since in the past he did sell a few and stopped doing so because he turned to painting for a while and then to writing an unsuccessful novel. But what I'm concerned with is having *now* in the immediate present living conditions under which I can do the most and best work with poetry. If I don't, I not only will misappropriate the funds given me by the Bryher Foundation for a definite project which I outlined to Mr. Pearson, but I'll also be headed for a complete nervous breakdown.

When I try to discuss the situation with my husband I'm up against the stone wall of his utter inability to look at any problem except in the light of how it will affect him economically—this blindness being due to nothing shrewd or mean or materialistic in his character (he's none of these things) but merely to an aversion amounting to horror which he has of the job world.

Due to that aversion, he does the most impractical things—thinking them the most practical. This place, for instance—which I was against taking but which he talked me into taking because the rent is only $75 a year in cash. It's not as cheap as he thinks. We had to furnish our own stoves for both heating and cooking. And the fuel for heating (since it's not well-insulated) is expensive, whether we pay for it in cash or with the labor of chopping the wood ourselves. And the absolutely essential repairs (fixing a leaky roof, replacing a rotten and broken down door, and turning an open summer kitchen into a winter one) have cost a lot; and Chuk has put hundreds of dollars worth of labor into building an extra room which is not yet finished—all of which would be very well if we owned this place and the land around it, but which is madness since it's a rented place and since—despite all that labor—it's not greatly improved—the use of only logs instead of bought materials and the lack of power tools having made the attempted improvements such slow going.

But he doesn't see the folly of it. He doesn't see that if he got a job (almost any job) for the next few months (he can't get one here, but he *could* elsewhere) our improved living conditions would give him much more time for writing, even with the job, than he has now when he spends whole days at a stretch cutting down trees, peeling logs, going to the well (the equivalent of a whole block away) for water, et cetera; and that he'd enjoy the summers here much more if (with the rent now paid anyway) we came back in April with a little money in our pockets and in a position where we could perhaps buy a second-hand Ford—a car making so much difference here.

If I had only my own needs to consider, I'd immediately try to find a room in Kingston and start as soon as possible to carry out my plans as mentioned for Mr. Pearson, and then later on after being inwardly fortified by actually doing what I planned to do (nothing fortifies one more than that) I could give some thought to the future which in practical ways would take [care] of itself, I think, if I did some good work and had behind me a sense of achievement.

But Chuk would regard this as a definite and irrevocable parting of our ways and as the worst kind of betrayal. And it *would* be the latter and so I can't consider only my own needs. I have to consider his too, not only from a sense of duty and obligation, but also out of affection—because there is love and love, and a love in which we are not wholly contained sometimes makes greater demands on us than one in which we are.

And so I'm as helpless in this situation as I was in that with my son. And here I am tied not only by bonds of obligation and affection, but also by those of fear. The fear that if I left, I'd find myself homeless not as a temporary measure, but as something permanent, for the rest of my life. It was depressing enough to have no home but some God-forsaken furnished hall bedroom when I was younger. It would be worse to live like that as an aging, ailing woman all alone in the world without even those fair-weather friends that sheer youth attracts. I've seen such women in such rooms in houses where I've lived—and always with a shudder of pity and horror. And so I recoil from the very thing I need most—my freedom.

I cannot write any more now because I have to mail it soon and see about getting home from Kingston.

I had another series of those attacks so bad (really agonizing) that I simply had to come in yesterday to see the Kingston doctor already referred to in another letter. He thinks now (and I feel this way myself—very strongly) that there may be some purely physical disorder of the biliary tract. But he points out (and he's quite right about that) that unless I make some change in my way of life, unless I get myself into more congenial surroundings, it's impossible to diagnose and treat the condition, and he considers Chuk's attitude toward things preposterous and outrageous.

I stayed overnight (had to—with no way of getting back before dark, the doctor's office hours being too late in the day for that) and slept badly—the pills that were given me having done little good—perhaps because my nerves are so disordered by my being unable to solve this whole problem of my relationship with Chuk.

That I have you to talk to about it in this letter, is something! I don't know what I'd do if I didn't have at least that. But it's so much *my* problem—so much one which I have to solve for myself, that God knows what you can say to help me with it. But will you please drop me a line anyway? Merely to hear from you would, I think, buck me up somewhat.

Sincerely
Marcia

9 Ridge Rd.
Rutherford, N.J.
December 19, 1949

Dear Marcia:

The poem was returned from *Tiger's Eye* a few days ago. I enclose it, with her letter.

Botteghe Oscure, Winter issue (I suppose) has not yet arrived. I know nothing of it but find myself as impatient as you are to know what is going on.

New Directions, 1949 or whatever it is, No 11, came today with your poems and mine. Looks like a good issue.

Many things have happened to keep me closely occupied. This is a season when practice takes almost all my time.

I hope you have a Merry Christmas and a Happy New Year. (I notice Laughlin makes mention of your forthcoming book,[1] which pleased me no end. I was afraid he'd duck it.)

Best luck
Bill

1. In the "notes on contributors" in *New Directions Number Eleven* Laughlin writes: "Marcia Nardi lives in the country not far from New York. A group of her poems were included in *New Directions 1942*. She hopes to have a book of verse ready for publication soon."

. . . .

February 10 [1950]

Dear Rayaprol:[1]

The letter at the end of Book II is a real letter or a combination of two actual letters written to me several years ago by a woman whom I had attempt[ed] to help as best I could—without being Christ and giving her everything I had. I am still trying to help her when possible. No good. Its position in the book gives it whatever significance it has by being the "woman's" reply to the man, Paterson. You might call her Mrs. Paterson. It is the woman striking back at the man, at all men. But there is also in my use of the letter a recognition of the writer of the letter as a writer. It is in many ways good writing. That is the final reason for including it. I hesitated a long time over whether or not to leave it out. Finally it went in. Some think it is the best thing in the book, that it makes me look second rate. Wouldn't that be a good thing if it were true? And perhaps it *is* true: all the more reason for having printed it. I have nothing to sell.

This is a hurried note. I'll write later of the poems. I wrote to Laughlin, who is at the moment at Aspen, skiing, giving him your address and asking him to introduce you, directly or through me, to his friends the Cosgriffs in Denver. I don't know what will happen, he may do it directly or through me. We'll have to wait.

Your description of the woman with the eyes is very interesting. Don't mistake her for a tiger and shoot her.

Best luck

Bill

1. Srinivas Rayaprol was an Anglo-Indian engineering student studying in the States at this time whose first love was poetry, according to Thirlwall, *The Selected Letters*, 281. Rayaprol had apparently written to Williams to ask about the significance of Nardi's letter in Book II of *Paterson*.

. . . .

73. TLS-2 (Y)

Woodstock

Tuesday July 11th [1950]

Dear Bill,

At last I am able to write to you primarily to find out about the enclosed poems—what you think of them (the most finished of my recent writing—so much of which—too much—remains in rough draft).

I have wanted over and over again in all these months to write to you about other matters—merely to write to you, but to have done so would have been to thrust upon you too great a need on my part for one thing and another—for so much in every way.

I have been very ill—all winter long—reduced for days at a time, for weeks at a time, to nothing but a suffering carcass from which all mind and spirit seemed to have fled forever. The doctors here all advised me to go to New York for tests of various kinds because the hospitals in Kingston have no gastroenterologic department and because it was felt that my condition could be diagnosed only by the physicians connected with such a department. But the expense was too great (it is in illness that the greatest gulf exists between the rich and the poor). I did go for a while—and had more x-rays made—a great many which threw little light on what's wrong. But I had hoped to be able to stay at the apartment of a friend (the only friend I have in New York) and certain changes in that person's mode of living made it impossible and I couldn't find a room—nothing at all reasonable in price with the housing situation still so bad, so that I had to go to [a] hotel—and every day was costing so much money that I had to go home without having the other tests. And not only that. I had been very ill while in New York—so sick that it was hard for me to even travel around the city. And I continue to be—though now I do manage to have a few well days due to the help I get from the medicines now given me.

God knows I need desperately some really sound advice in regard to this health problem and I know no one of course better able to give it to me than you. And yet it is not in regard to that that I shall be waiting anxiously for your reply to this one letter in all these months. It is in regard to the poems that I shall be— am now already—impatient to hear what you have to say.

The long poem (or rather, the five poems on one theme)[1] I want to send right away to Marguerite Caetani if you think it good enough. She wrote and asked me to let her have something for the fall issue of her magazine and to get it to her by August, and I need the money so badly—the medicines cost so much, and when I do not have them my physical distress is so great I cannot write at all.

I find that I cannot go [on] with this. All the fame surrounding you[2] these days frightens me; and besides I should have to finish quickly since the neighbors who drove me to the post-office in town are going to leave soon. So I will just send the poems—and another letter in a day or two.

Marcia

1. Nardi's poem "And I Knew the Body a Sea" appeared in *Botteghe Oscure* 6 (1950): 435–440.
2. The National Book Awards committee awarded Williams its first annual Gold Medal for Poetry in early 1950.

. . . .

74. TLS-I (T)

Friday [14 July 1950]

Dear Marcia:

I'm leaving here day after tomorrow for a month. I've wondered what you were up to. I don't and of course can't understand what your illness may be. Too much for me. Sounds like a duodenal ulcer that is contracting and giving you pain. Why in hell, then, don't they do a stomach resection and have it over with?

What about Medical Clinic at New York Hosp E 68the [*sic*] St? That's where I'd go if I were broke. I'll help you after Sept. 15th if I can.

I don't like the diminutive mood you occasionally fall into. The first 4 or 5 of these poems strike me as worthwhile. By all means send them to Marguerite Caetani. Send 'em all if you want to but the more serious ones are the best. I think she'll take some and pay promptly.

If Laughlin doesn't want to do your book perhaps Ciardi of Twain [*sic*] Editions[1] might be interested.

Don't let me [*sic*] "fame" frighten you.

Best
Bill

1. John Ciardi (1916–1986), poet, educator, editor, critic, translator. At this time, Ciardi was a teacher at Harvard and an editor for Twayne Editions.

RFD Woodstock, NY

September 19th [1950]

Dear Bill,[1]

I'm afraid this letter is going to be a disappointment to you because it's not motivated by anything to do with my literary work which is the phase of my existence that interests you most. I'm writing to you this time out of the same desperate loneliness that prompted my one-sided correspondence with you eight or nine years ago and out of the need for someone to talk to.

My illness, my domestic ties, and the uneventfulness of my outward life in recent years enabled me to turn my back on those old emotional problems that made me want to know you more intimately than you permitted and which left me inwardly frozen for a long time after I got that final note of dismissal from you then.

But this summer, especially the last part of this summer, Chuk and I got drawn into the social life of this community, so that I began to meet other men again and to find myself faced with the very same emotional situation that has arisen for me again and again throughout my entire life and that has almost destroyed me at times as it threatens to do now once more.

When I first met Chuk I had been leading an ascetic existence for so long that my purely biological self asserted itself pretty strongly for a while. It was bound to—it couldn't have been otherwise. But after a while I couldn't stand the void that always existed for me *afterwards*. I couldn't stand being left high and dry spiritually and intellectually. As a result my senses began to retreat (not deliberately—it simply happened—without my really wanting it to) until finally all the sex got so locked up in me that it would no longer come free even when my body demanded it (and this was and is, I am sure, one of the reasons for my failing health, because it certainly worsened—as nervous tension is bound to do, whatever organic ailment I may also have). Then when we began seeing a great deal of our neighbors this summer, one particular man, a composer and a very nice person,[2] played some of his music for me on several occasions—

all of them occasions when his wife was not at home and my husband did not know I was there—until finally the situation became—well you know of course just what it turned into. But no, you don't and can't because much as I wanted to give myself up to it and needed to and still need to, I didn't and can't—at least not completely because the cost for me, in the way I feel about such matters, would be too great. In the first place, it would involve no end of difficult maneuvering and an endless amount of deception and underhandedness, the sort of thing that goes very much against the grain with me. Also my feelings about this man X have their roots entirely in desire, more starkly so than any other such feelings I've ever had (or perhaps it's just that I know myself better now). And—what is even more important—he has nothing to offer me intellectually (and my own reality for him is little more, I think, than a purely physical one). He lives entirely in the world of music, and very narrowly in that world—in a world, I mean, of only musical ideas and abstractions—ideas and abstractions in any broader sense having little or no existence for him, whereas for me they are the very breath of my intellectual life, so that the whole thing with X, if I accepted it, as my body is urging me to do, would be like turning from some tiresome and too familiar highway into a side road leading nowhere and culminating after a block or two in nothing but a dead end.

. At the same time the hunger which he has aroused in me after such a long time of all this locked up sex (I have suffered from it for two years now) is something I can't throw off. It has been torturing me so terribly for the past week that for the first time in five years I have taken to smoking and drinking again—and that of course is very bad, my health being what it is.

I can imagine you thinking in your down-to-earth matter-of-fact fashion "What a silly stupid woman! What the hell—if that's all it is, why doesn't she get into bed with the man and have done with it!" And if it *were* as simple as all that, it's exactly what I would do. But it isn't—things aren't like that with me. I never could be casual with anyone. The more I had of him the more I would want, and I would find myself involved in a very serious affair. And the more I became bound to him physically, the more I would grope for and miss the things he just doesn't have to give me in other ways—until there would arise for [me] the very same abyss of spiritual desolation which I experience with my husband.

I may have given you a wrong impression of my husband in a couple of the letters I wrote you last year about another angle of my domestic problems. He has a great many very fine qualities (most people like him a lot) and he has worked hard—too hard—to make some kind of home out of this place—and at the sacrifice of his other interests which is unfortunate and makes me feel bad because he has talents which shouldn't be neglected the way they have been (incidentally he has been working on another novel—now two-thirds finished—which I think might interest Laughlin to whom I am going to send a section of it).[3] But his mind is of a kind that simply offers no stimulation to mine. It's concerned too exclusively with the external and purely factual, and he brings to love nothing but a completely healthy sex animal wholly divorced from all other phases of his being (to do otherwise is, to him, neurotic and sick) and in living his values are all completely utilitarian. And apart from that, I simply am not cut out for marriage as it exists for most couples unless they have money enough for big houses with lots of rooms and for domestic help and the other things that make for freedom and independence. This continual being together and sharing of *everything*—of a common living room, common bedtime, and common mealtime, with jointly chosen pictures on the wall and even friends and books that belong to *both*—the use always of "ours" and "our" and "we" and "us" and, in this case, not even having a work-room of my own—it's enough to drive me mad, and my writing has suffered greatly from the situation.

It was, basically, my inability to cope with this we-ness in everything that broke up another such union in my life years ago when I was very young, and even before that—as little more than a child—I had such a precocious fear of it that a composition which I wrote on the subject shocked my teacher and resulted in my mother being called to the school.

But this time I am trapped. I have nothing to take its place—nothing to exchange it for but the shabby miserable kind of existence which I was leading when I first met you. If I had had anything else, anything better, I never would have gotten myself into this prison. If you for instance had offered me any kind of personal contact with you—any kind at all—I never would have gotten into it. You are the only man I've ever met who could have offered me the sort of relationship in which I could be completely contained, and if you had, God how much it would have meant to me during these past eight or nine years! You will never know how much.

If I were talking about the usual love affair or any love affair at all, it would be absurd of me to say this with such certainty, because I would have to assume in that case—and it would be absurd for me to assume it—that you could have been in love with me. But it was your friendship that I wanted—and one existing on a plane where it could not be set in a cubbyhole and tagged and labeled as "platonic" or otherwise, since I would not have made any demands one way or the other—except in my being conscious of the polarity and needing to keep it alive for myself by seeing you once in awhile. I would have been in my attitude toward you and my feelings about you like those simple primitive creatures (those lower forms of life that are really superior) that having no specialized sense organs and no actual eyes, can see with their skins. That is what I mean by being completely contained in a relationship with a man. And for other reasons too I could not have made any demands on you outside the bounds of friendship. I know—or rather so it seems—and I don't see how it could have been otherwise—that as a doctor and a doctor so very different from the average doctor, you must have had (and now that you are so much in the public eye it must be even more that way) any number of lonely women throw themselves into your [arms?] and I would have had a horror of being confused with those women—a horror born of pride.

I would have made fewer demands on you than on any man I've ever known. And yet, that is the bitterest part of it all for me—you of whom I would have made the fewest [demands?] are the one I have wanted most to know and at root [from?] my fears of the male animal in a man, the one I have perhaps desired most.[4]

I suppose that these last few paragraphs are embarrassing to you, and I am sorry for that. But I am driven by too great a loneliness for silence, and I find myself growing old without ever having once known—not once for even a single year out of all the years—the kind of contact with a man that I have wanted and for which I have again and again from my childhood on made the most reckless sacrifices in the way of social and economic security and bodily comfort. And I could never find—and cannot now—any compensation in writing. I have already expressed to you, in the past, my feeling that there is something anomalous and adventitious in my literary interests. Real writers, true artists, need to create in order to live. Like the character in one of your plays they wait only to be loosed by their writing.[5] Whereas in my case I have to be loosed *by* life *for* writing. A place like Woodstock is, for that reason, no good for me. It's a nice enough place—for those purposes very pleasant—to come to for a couple of months in the summer and even for week-ends year-round. But as a permanent place of residence—as a place to live in month after month as I have done for three years now is no good and it has had, and has increasingly so now—an atrophying effect upon my creative powers. There is a graciousness to life here (if you give yourself over to the social life of the community) which in contrast to the harsh environments I have known, has a certain charm to it. But the people—at least the ones I've met—have only superficially cultivated minds—minds with practically no depth or scope to them and are so lacking in independent judgement that the *NY Times* book review section on Sundays serves just about the same purpose here as the Social Register does, or Dunn and Bradstreet, in other exclusive communities, with the result that Henry Morton Robinson,[6] author of *The Cardinal*, and a man named Gilligan[7] who gets huge checks from the *Saturday Evening Post* and you and Eliot and Auden are all grouped together indiscriminately as the Great Writers. And whether one is famous or not and regardless of whether one's work is good or bad, the Great Thing is to Write or Paint. Are you a writer or a painter or a musician? That's the question put invariably to any stranger coming to live here (and with a take-it-for-grantedness that he *must* be something of the sort), and should he not be any of these things—and especially if he has no private income and is forced to work as a butcher or baker or a shoe salesman—then he is as much looked down upon as those excluded from the little clan of the Verduring's in Proust. And I cannot thrive in an environment so cut off from ordinary life and ordinary people—especially since the artists and writers here are themselves such ordinary ones of very limited and minor talents and none of them intellectuals in the best sense of the word.

But all this about Woodstock is beside the point, for certainly I would feel less keenly its stifling effect if I were less lonely in my private life—and maybe in that case I could and would find some way of not spending the whole year here. Ah, if only I could have kept buried all that consuming emotional hunger that has come to the surface again. But I really did not keep it buried, for I know now for certain that it has been an important factor in my illness and is at the moment. During those days when I was going clandestinely to X's house, almost overnight I got miraculously better. I had to continue being careful of what I ate, but during the course of nearly two weeks I had to take a frasentine tablet only twice (I had previously had to take at least three a day for months) and the attacks on those two occasions were very mild and of short duration. But as soon as I found myself in the frustrating predicament which I have gone into detail about, they got very bad again. And now I will tell you something else (I might as well since I am being so outspoken about everything). When I was in New York last winter for some more X-rays and so very ill (the time I referred to in my last letter) and staying at the Colborne in the Village, as I sat there in my room looking at the telephone I felt strongly and with such conviction (and the conviction was not of my mind but of my blood) that if I knew you well enough to pick up that phone and call you up and ask if you would come to see me at the hotel, and if you did, I would immediately feel much better. I could not throw off the conviction, and it was because I couldn't and because at the same time it was all so futile (not for the reasons I gave) that I came home feeling worse than ever without even finishing the tests.

There are some practical matters I have wanted to write you about for advice and very slight assistance—waiting until after the 15th since your reply to my last letter indicated that you would be pretty much pre-occupied until then. They are connected with some grants of about three or four hundred dollars each given each year to three or four artists in any field living in Woodstock—need and merit being ostensibly the basis on which the recipients of the grants are chosen but "pull" counting as much or more—so I am told. However, I shall have to leave a detailed account of this until some other time because it has no place here.

I must however inform you that Marguerite Caetani accepted my group of poems "And I Knew The Body a Sea" (I sent only those) and paid me most generously for them. You will hardly believe it, but the check was for $200. I don't know what I should have done without it, but that was in the first week of August and there were so many expenses to meet, rent included, that with the cost of living so high still, I have only a little of it left. But even my economic problems, serious as they continue to be—fade away and become nothing along side my loneliness.

I was going to send you a few of the poems I wrote just before I got plunged into this emotional turmoil. But I can't at the moment. Poetry, literature generally, is too far from me. I hate words when they are a substitute for living. I get no pleasure from putting together the words and sentences that form this letter. They are for me like the fence through which prisoners are forced to communicate with the outside world during visiting hours, better than nothing, but at the same time—as a symbol of imprisonment—something to be hated. And despite them, even in using them, I feel dumb—inarticulate, and like those in your *Paterson* who do not know the language and who die incommunicado.[8] Perhaps I am all body. Perhaps everything else about me is a fraud. I feel, right now, that it is. And yet in our reaching out to things and people from the prison of ourselves, our emotions, if they find all the other exits blocked—those provided by friendship and travelling and books and family ties and so much else—will crowd to the only exit permitted them—that of sex. Or is that mere rationalization? I myself cannot answer that question. I know only that during the entire period of writing this long letter (I have not written it at one sitting—I began it three days ago) I have not been free for a single moment from a feeling of terrible inanition in all my bones and throughout my entire being.

I have already expressed my regret for whatever embarrassment I may cause you by this letter. I don't want to make it any worse by expecting a reply. And anyway, I don't see what you could reply except out of politeness, in some forced way. For that reason I am registering this and requesting that the signed receipt be sent me, so that I can be sure of your having received the letter.

Marcia

1. This letter was transcribed from a photostatic copy found among Nardi's papers. The original letter (once in the possession of the Williams family) has been misplaced.

2. Willam Ames and his wife, Alison, were neighbors of Nardi and her husband at the Maverick colony in Woodstock. Nardi left her husband for William Ames in the fall of 1950; in April 1951, Ames abandoned her. Nardi and John Lang remained friends, and she occasionally visited him in Woodstock.

3. John Lang's novel was never published.

4. On the photostatic copy, this paragraph has several blurred areas, rendering some of the words (those in brackets) almost illegible.

5. Hubert in "Trial Horse No. 1 (Many Loves)," of whom another character says: "He waits only to be loosed by his writing. That aside he is a prisoner, dim-witted, furious, raging at his prison . . . There is only one door. Writing! Stop him and he'll destroy you" (*New Directions Number Seven*, 303).

6. Henry Morton Robinson (1898–1961), educator, poet, editor, and author of the best-selling novel *The Cardinal* (New York: Simon and Schuster, 1950). Robinson was a long-time resident of the Maverick colony.

7. Edmund Gilligan (1898–1973) contributed stories to *Collier's* and the *Saturday Evening Post* in the 1950s.

8. *Paterson*, 9.

. . . .

76. TLS-1 (T)

September 22, 1950

Dear Marcia:

Your very moving letter rec'd. I do not reply out of politeness, as you put it, but out of a very deep respect for your extraordinary abilities and your tragic situation, tragic in that you cannot escape it.

Whatever the "grants for art" are that you speak of I do not know of them but if you will specify more particularly what you have in mind I'll do everything I can to help you get one. I'll try elsewhere also. For by this time you must realize that I have always been convinced of your distinction as a poet and that I have done what I could as a friend to assist you.

As artists we do our best work when we are most moved, not when we are unhappiest, tho' it comes sometimes to that. We need close friends, surely, to whom to "confess" at times with a sure feeling that we shall be given unfailing sympathy and unquestioning support in our emotional agonies. I am that sort of friend to you. But the battle itself we must undergo entirely alone.

The Princess has proved herself really a "princess". I am happy to hear that she has bought more of your work and shall look forward to seeing it in the next issue of *Botteghe Oscure* with the greatest interest.

a fine title, by the way,   Sincerely
"and I knew the body a sea."   Bill

Wednesday, October 11th
[1950]

Dear Bill,

For the first time in weeks I am or seem to be in possession of my wits again (your sympathetic note meant a great [deal] to me when I got it and it means even more to me now) and I want very much now to get back to my writing (I did the rough draft of a new poem this morning). But I am again distracted by money problems and the first thing I have to do is to attend to matters connected with the grants I mentioned.

The enclosed letter sent to people in the community when the Foundation's[1] Benefit play was given (the money is given out just before Christmas—the day before) will explain the whole thing. But although the grants are supposed to be made quite impartially on the basis of both merit and need, "pull" and knowing the right people count even more in a local thing like this than when the geographical boundaries are less narrow; each of the trustees and members of a special consultation committee having his or her pet applicant (usually of course a friend), and I know none of the trustees except Mrs. Emmett Edwards[2] and with her I have little more than a nodding acquaintance.

I do however have a few friends and acquaintances who are trying to help me get the grant and one of them (Frank Mele[3] who directs the Music Festival here in the summer and who will be with the Pittsburg Philharmonic Orchestra this winter) suggested that I ask you to write a letter to the Foundation praising my work to the skies and putting it on so very thick (the praise) that in making the request of you I feel like a whore smearing on her powder and paint in order to drum up trade.

I myself have already sent in the letter of application, and whatever else I could find that might make a good impression on those connected with the Foundation who, not being competent judges of merit themselves, are far less interested in seeing an applicant's work than in seeing and hearing the comments made about that work by people who count for something in the world of literature or painting or music.

I got hold of and sent in a copy of the NY *Times* in which there was a review of the last *New Directions* anthology with my name mentioned in it, sent also the clipping from that English review[4] which Marguerite Caetani sent me (I told you about that) and I tore out and sent a page from that article you wrote on Anais Nin's *Winter of Artifice* (the page on which you mentioned my work with poetry)—Frank thought I ought also to send the introduction you wrote to the fifteen poems in 1942 and the letter you sent me last year about my work then which you liked very much (I showed him that letter—I hope you don't mind—since I had to in order to get his assistance— he is a person of integrity who wouldn't want to put in a word for me—I like him for that—unless he could do so honestly). But I don't want to because I would find it much too embarrassing to "promote" myself in such an undignified way—or in any way at all. Doing that sort of thing paralyzes me creatively, and besides it would make a better impression I think if you wrote directly to the Foundation mentioning my work as [a] whole both past and current.

As far as I know I am the only person in the community with absolutely no regular income. Many of the other applicants are without much money and a few are poor according to ordinary standards—especially those for artists who are not expected to live by bread alone. But the very poorest next to myself has a regular income of one hundred and five dollars a month which though so very little would seem like a lot to me if I had it. That is the only reason I am applying. I would not do so otherwise partly because I do not like competitions of this kind and partly because so many of the things one has to do to get the money go against the grain with me. It was suggested for instance that I call on Henry Morton Robinson (he lives here on the Maverick and is the only really rich person on the Maverick with all his thousands of dollars pouring in every week or month from the Cardinal); bring him some of my work, and ask him if he would speak for me—his word meaning a tremendous lot in Woodstock. But I can't stand his work (if it can be called work in the sense that artists use that word) and I dislike him as a man. And I would not think of giving him the impression that his opinion of my writing means anything to me when it doesn't.

If you *do* write (it will of course help a great deal if you do), you might say, I suppose, (or anything you think better for a beginning) that these grants for art and my application for one have recently been brought to your attention—followed by all the rest about my work.

David Huffine[5] is the president of the Foundation and it was to him I addressed my application. But I think that Mrs. Edwards felt that this was a slighting of her importance on my part because her husband (I know him a little better because he *tried* to know me better, in ways you can imagine) made a special point of informing me that his wife was the secretary and of asking me: didn't I know it? And so that I won't offend either Mr. Huffine or Eleanor Edwards (you see how petty some of these people are) you had better address your letter to just the Woodstock Foundation, Woodstock, New York (Dear Sirs or Gentlemen or whatever one says in that case).

I should have written to you about this sooner; and am in a rush to get it to you. So—with one [of] my neighbors going to the post office in just a couple of minutes—I must close abruptly.

Marcia

1. The Woodstock (N.Y.) Foundation.

2. The painter Emmett Edwards and his wife, Eleanor, were residents of the Maverick colony.

3. Frank Mele, a neighbor of Nardi's at the Maverick colony, actually directed the Pittsburgh Symphony during the 1950–51 season.

4. "In the American section—given entirely to poets—Marcia Nardi contributes a powerful poem, 'In the Asylum'" (*Times Literary Supplement*, 17 February 1950, 110).

5. Huffine was a cartoonist and resident of the Maverick colony.

January 17, 1951

Dear Marcia:

It is not always possible for me to reply to your urgent letters[1] as you would like me to nor to secure money for you on short notice, much as I might want to at certain times. I'm glad you got the grant from Woodstock.[2]

I know of no one who has an apartment such as you describe for rent. In fact it is almost impossible to find anything of the sort these days unless it might be somewhere in New York City. Certainly the prices hereabouts are far beyond reason.

Sorry to hear you are suffering from a duodenal ulcer, you have probably had it all along though the diagnosis has been hard to make. I'm glad you finally got to the bottom of the thing; I presume they have not suggested surgery which is sometimes the answer.

Sincerely yours
Bill

1. The letters Williams refers to here are missing.
2. The Woodstock Foundation awarded Nardi $400 in November 1950.

. . . .

79. ALS-3 (Y)

August 6th [1951]

Dear Bill—

I suppose you have received by now my other note,[1] and also that your phone answering service told you I phoned twice.

I was prepared of course for the possibility of your being away altogether for the whole summer. But that you were there in Rutherford and had merely gone away for the weekend (so that if I had come in a few days earlier or later I might have seen you)—that was a bitter disappointment! And I wanted so much to see you that if I had known for certain you'd be able to, and would (upon your return) let me, I'd have remained until at least Tuesday or Wednesday—even longer. But since I was not sure about that, I returned last night—late—staying over in Kingston for the night and writing this now in Kingston before taking the local bus back to Woodstock.

I write it to make the same request—only not leaving it to chance now, but asking in advance if I may have a little talk with you at some specific time—at your convenience, of course, but quite soon. May I? It would mean so much to me (more than I can tell you) that I will take the bus in especially for that purpose, and would do so even if it were an entire day's journey instead of only a 3 hour trip.

My not having written to you for so long (after all you did and tried to do for me in regard to my work) and then suddenly out of a clear sky barging into your life like this, and at a time when you have been ill[2]—well, it's not really like that. It seems like that—it's bound to seem that way—only because one brief note received from a person whom one knows only at a distance, is like a single sentence or paragraph snatched from the context of a long book and lost to its relationship to the whole, and thus robbed of much of its meaning.

To make it otherwise—to *explain*—well that would require a long long letter—one of those long letters I at one time used to send you. And I am not up [to] it, nor have I the will for it. If I had, it would amount to a substitution of the letter for the personal contact; and if I had found that substitution possible, I'd not have sent that special delivery note in the first place, nor would I now be dashing off this one.

Hoping so much that I will hear from you shortly, and most sincerely,

Marcia

The address is Woodstock:
(*Arcade Cottage, Woodstock, New York*)

1. This letter is missing.
2. Williams suffered a stroke in March 1951.

August 8, 1951

My dear Marcia Nardi:

You had no reason to expect that I would run off to New York to meet you last Thursday even if I could. You assume much too much. Therefore you have no occasion to be disappointed. It would have been pleasant to talk to you if it had been possible but it was not possible under the circumstances. I count on you to accept the fact accordingly.

I hope some day to feel better and more free to go about as I used to do but I'm not sure that such a time will ever come again. I write, in fact now that I am not practicing medicine, I write more steadily than usual but I'm not at all satisfied with what I'm doing.

For one thing I'm doing no poems. I wrote one under duress which I forced myself to do to meet a dead-line but it was difficult going. I simply forced myself to put the words down. Another 3 stanza lyric I did also under contract to a medical house for an annual publication. That is all.[1]

What's going to happen in the future I cannot tell. At the moment I am depressed and do not wish to see anyone. My autobiography will be out in September, it was writing that that seemed to finish me. I don't know that it was worth it.[2]

I'm glad you're in better financial condition now than you were last year.

Sincerely yours
W. C. Williams

1. "The Desert Music," written during Williams's recuperation from a stroke and while he was trying to complete his autobiography. The poem was written at the request of the Phi Beta Kappa chapter at Harvard University and read by Williams at their commencement exercises on 18 June 1951. The second poem Williams mentions is "December," *The Collected Poems of William Carlos Williams*, vol. 2, ed. Christopher MacGowan (New York: New Directions, 1988), 236.

2. *The Autobiography of William Carlos Williams* was published by Random House in September 1951.

Woodstock, New York

October 23rd, 1951

Dear Mr. Laughlin,

I have not, in the past (as you know) taken any initiative to speak of in getting my work published or trying to. I have not done so because I did not feel that the work merited it, and because publication for its own sake has never meant anything to me.

Now however I have a fairly substantial amount of work which I think is not without some distinction, part of which I have gotten together for a book of about thirty or forty poems. Of those already published in the ND anthologies I have included only six. Ten were published elsewhere more recently. The others have not been submitted anywhere. But if the book were to appear, I could perhaps in advance of its coming out, get a few more of the poems into magazines, should you feel this to be necessary for practical reasons.

Anyway, now for the first time I wish to interest you in my work, and ask permission to send the manuscript for your consideration.

I don't want to thrust it upon you unless you are seriously interested in going through the manuscript which is so arranged that you will be able to tell—after reading just the first dozen pages or so—what you think of it (or at least get a good idea of what you think).

Will you be so kind as to let me know about this as soon as possible?

Sincerely,

Marcia Nardi

. . . .

82. TLS-1 (T)

9 Ridge Road

Rutherford, N.J.

October 25, 1951

Dear Marcia:

I have written Elizabeth Ames, the Director at Yaddo [1] a letter recommending you and sent her your letter. [2] I urged her to take you on if there is any opening. I think you will hear from her.

I am glad you are working. I'll keep the poems or perhaps, yes I'll do that, send them to Laughlin for inclusion in this year's ND anthology (if it is not too late).

As far as my general health is concerned, I'm getting along. I have setbacks from time to time but that is to be expected. Most of my trouble comes still from trying to take on more than I can do.

I wish you luck.

Sincerely
Bill

1. Elizabeth Ames was not related to William Ames, the composer Nardi met at the Maverick colony in Woodstock.

2. The letter he refers to here is missing.

. . . .

83. ALS-2 (Y)

RFD. Woodstock, N.Y.
[1 November 1951 postmark
on envelope]

Dear Bill—

I want to thank you for having acknowledged my letter so promptly, and for writing to Elizabeth Ames on my behalf.

I have just gotten the application blanks from Mrs. Ames with a note from her enclosed.

On the application (according to the directions) I must list the names and addresses of my sponsors who in turn must "make detailed and informative statements" regarding me and my work. And Mrs. Ames in her note says: "Be sure the sponsors you list write us full and informative letters of recommendation."

Whether the letter you already wrote to Mrs. Ames was the sort requested, I do not know of course. If it was, I need trouble you for no other. But if it wasn't (if it was just a line or two) will you be so kind as to send another little note to them regarding your opinion of my poetry, et cetera?

I have written to Norman Holmes Pearson asking if he also will sponsor me, and I am making the same request of Laughlin (since I am supposed to have more than one sponsor, though just how many, I don't know).

I am waiting to hear from Laughlin about the manuscript for my book—whether he wants me to send it to him or not; and if I *do* get into Yaddo for the winter I feel strongly that the work I do there will quite justify all the confidence you have had in me, as a poet.

I'm so glad your health is better now and I do hope it stays that way.

I'm looking forward to the reading of your Autobiography as soon as I can get it at the library here. It's been out, each time I've looked for it on the shelves, and when returned goes out again so quickly that I've not had a chance to read it yet (especially since I don't get to the library as often as I'd like to—being so far from it and having no car).

Thank you again and may I please hear from you about that requested letter of recommendation—whether the one you already sent is adequate or if you are sending another one too?

Sincerely,

Marcia

I suppose you do take on too much and shouldn't. And yet how I envy you in a way for being so prolific!

. . . .

84. TLS-4 (Y)

Woodstock

November 15th [1951]

Dear Bill,

Again I hesitate to write to you—knowing how your own work and problems are already too great a tax upon your physical energies.

But since you have taken so much interest in my poetry and were so anxious to see me have a volume out, you seem the logical person for me to communicate with in the problem which this now presents to me in my pained bewilderment over the letter I have just gotten from James Laughlin.

Without even letting me send him the manuscript for the book—without even having had a look at it—he says this:

"I am terribly sorry to report that it won't be possible for us to give consideration to your book of poetry for publication here . . . We are a small firm and can only do so many books a year, and our quota is pretty well taken up for the next few years."

I know that it's indeed true about ND being a small firm and all that. But I also know that Laughlin is the first to promote a new poet, hitherto unpublished to any great extent, if he thinks that he or she has anything really important to contribute to American literature in general. And also there's the fact that New Directions is continually expanding and that he *was* interested in my book (at least to some extent) at a time when the firm was even smaller than at the present time.

What bothers me most is that he wrote me in this fashion without even seeing my manuscript. As a matter of fact, he has seen none of my work done in the past two years—and for all he knows, it may well be quite on a par (or even better) with the volumes of poetry he has put out hitherto.

I recall your telling me that Twayne might be interested in doing my book. But I don't know just how I should approach them, and it is in regard to this that I write to ask your advice.

Should I just send the manuscript in cold, or should I mention what you think of my work, et cetera?

Or (is this asking too much?) would you send Ciardi a note saying that you think the manuscript worth his consideration?

Of course you have not seen it either. But many of the poems I selected for the book are among those you have considered my best; others have been revised; some that formed a group (such as "In the Asylum" which appeared in *Botteghe Oscure*) have been expanded with more sections added—these new ones being even better, I think, than those forming the original group.

I did have great confidence (as I already told you in one of those recent letters) in the manuscript as a whole (which is unusual for me since, as you know, I have been inclined to underrate, if anything, whatever talent I possess). But that confidence has been greatly diminished, I'm afraid, by this communication from Laughlin.

It is also embarrassing for me—the situation with Laughlin, because in a letter I just got from Norman Pearson he writes "I hope that you can actively bring your poems together into a volume so that Laughlin can see them."

I think I told you that needing more than one sponsor for Yaddo (and also I was afraid I had completely lost *your* friendship) I wrote to Pearson, and he has done some very kind things for me. He got in touch with Malcolm Cowley who not only wrote to Mrs. Ames, but also contacted the National Institute of Arts and Sciences on my behalf.

I understand from Malcolm Cowley that you are a member of it, and since Miss Geffen of the Welfare Fund for Writers and Artists may have gotten in touch with you for information about me as a poet and since I have just received from her a check for a hundred dollars which I needed desperately, I want to thank you for whatever part you have played in my receiving this help.

The tragic events in my private life during this past year (which I cannot tell you about because the whole story is not only very complicated but also most extraordinary) were indeed more crushing than anything I've ever before experienced, believe me. There were times last spring when to have taken my own life would have been nothing to me—even though I had always had, prior to that time, a particularly great horror of death.

I not only could not write a line, but I could not even read. I would take books out from the library (among them the stories in your book *Make Light of It*) only to return them, both overdue and unread—and it took me close to six months before my mind could dwell on what had happened and accept the reality of it without bringing me as near as [a] sane person can get to insanity without actually going under.

I already told you something of this sort in my previous letter and I mention it again, because it is why I tried so hard to see you that week-end when I seemed so over-presumptuous in taking it for granted that you would have seen me had you been at home.

Now at last I have gotten my wits together at least (the heart-ache is of course something else) and it looks as if things may work out fairly well—things to do with the practical phases of living I mean.

I got a second letter from Yaddo (from the secretary of Mrs. Ames who has gone away for a couple of weeks or so) indicating that there may be openings in January, so that if the Admissions Committee (it meets about December 15) okays my being invited there, I can possibly spend January, February and March there (and maybe April too since the spring season does not commence until May). In the meantime I have found a room in Woodstock village, have the hundred dollars, and have sent out some letters to Francis Brown of the *Times*, Margaret Marshall of the *Nation* and Robert Hatch of the *New Republic* to ask for some possible book-reviewing since a hundred dollars won't last any too long with the cost of everything so frightfully high.

But my greatest concern is getting my book of poems published, because—in these practical ways—so much hinges around that. I had been hoping to inform the Admissions Committee of Yaddo before its December meeting that I am to have a book of verse out soon—but now of course I cannot. And also if the book came out and got any favorable comment from the book reviewers, I could apply—as you agreed for a Guggenheim with a fairly good chance of getting one.

For whatever advice you may give me in regard to this (the book), and for anything you can and would do to help me get it published, I shall be most grateful.

Also are there, to your knowledge, any new or recent literary magazines which pay at all well for verse and which would be inclined to consider some of my work for publication if I sent some out?

Are you writing poetry again? You said in a previous letter that [you] were not at that [time] able to—could only do prose, and were very much upset about it.

I have not yet read the fourth section of *Paterson* (I've been able to spend nothing at all on books recently—and when I did have a little money in the summer—well, as I told you, I was lost to everything) and your Autobiography is still in such demand that I never find it on the shelves—though now that I live in the village and so near the library I have a better chance of finding it in.

Have you by the way seen Laughlin recently, and if so did he by chance say anything to you about my manuscript other than what he wrote me, as quoted on the first page of this letter?

Of course I have known right along that he was none too keen really about my work and published it only, I think, to please you. And so I really should not find his letter such a disappointment.

Sincerely,

Marcia

It's possible that the last poems I had in ND were unfavorably commented upon. But if so, that is because Laughlin (or Villa) selected (with one exception) the poorest of the poems I submitted! I was amazed at this at the time (I think I mentioned it to you).

(over)

P.S. There is something which, I think, I ought to tell you. It's this—that if I seem and have seemed during my entire correspondence with you to be a completely self-centered person, it's largely due to the very special horror I've had of placing myself—in anything I might say—among that great flock of women "fans" that a literary man if well known so often attracts to himself and—I imagine—quite annoyingly so. I cannot speak at all—cannot get a word out—to people I do not know when it comes to *their* work, *their* activities lest I be confused with all those individuals who love knowing painters and writers and all artists with a "reputation". There are so many such individuals in Woodstock, and they are all so superficial, so silly, so shallow, so false and in general so awful! This is one of the reasons I've always lived so completely, in my private life, outside the literary world.

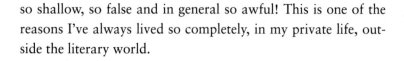

85. TLS-1 (T)

9 Ridge Road, Rutherford, N.J.
November 17, 1951

Dear Marcia:

You'll have to just cross Laughlin off your list. He'll be of no use to you and the sooner you forget him the better. No use kicking against the pricks. He has a bad reputation.[1]

Twaine [*sic*] is your present lead. Write *briefly* to Ciardi, using my name, telling him that you have a book, that you have been published in *New Directions* Anthology and *Botteghe Oscure* and that I am convinced that you are ready for a wider audience.

See what he says. If after you have approached him you want me to follow up the first advance with a letter I'll do so.

I'm glad you have a room for the moment and that the prospects for Yaddo seem bright. I hope the authorities there come through. Pearson appears to have gone out of his way to keep the ball rolling. That's good.

Best luck
Bill

1. Nardi was unaware that Williams had broken with James Laughlin and New Directions and moved (with former New Directions editor David McDowell) to Random House in 1950.

86. TLS-1 (Y)

Woodstock
December 4th [1951]

Dear Bill,

Upon my return from New York, I found a note from John Ciardi. Here is what he writes:

"I'd like very much to see the ms. I frankly don't know what I'll be able to do at this time, but I am interested and as hopeful as the dismal publishing weather allows me to be. Please forgive my haste. Sincerely. . . ."

I am sending the poems to him right away (his address is 84 South Street, Medford, Mass.). And at the same time I'd like to take advantage of your offer to write to him too as soon as I got a reply to my first communication. I think that the letter from you might help to get the book out despite the bad publishing weather. Anyway it would do a lot of good, I'm sure.

You'll be interested to know, I think, that I'm doing some book reviewing now—the book on Yeats as self-critic for the *Nation*, and the selections from Henri Michaux (put out by ND) for the *New Republic*, and the *Times* will be sending me books too, I think.

I'm afraid that I'll be doing a tremendous lot of work for little more than pennies (at the start, anyway). In connection with the book of Yeats, for instance, I'm reading all of Yeats' own comments on his creative processes and awarenesses as found in his various essays, letters and other autobiographical material; and the particular angle from which I'm commenting on Michaux requires a lot [of] extra reading too.

But the reading is tied up with a lot of ideas I need to clarify for myself anyway in connection with my own work; and I'm using the reviews to pave the way for a number of essays and articles I may eventually write on matters I've been keeping notes on for some time.

I'll let you know when the reviews come out because I'd like very much to know what you think of my prose—especially since at the moment I have a feeling of stage fright about it.

In the meantime thank you for the letter to Ciardi if you should send it.

Sincerely

Marcia

That Yaddo Admissions committee meeting will soon take place—in just about ten days, I think. And how anxious I am about it! I hope so much (too much) that they pass a favorable vote on my application.

. . . .

87. ALS-2 (Y)

[3 January 1952]

Dear Bill—

I feel very much ashamed and embarrassed now at having complained about the literary world's cold-shouldering of my talents—the talents which I do not possess.

I guess I am just a very ordinary woman gravitating in all my instincts towards a home and husband, and in my frustration there turning to work for which I do [not] have the ability.

I send you in proof of this the review I just got back from *The Nation* together with the comment on it.[1]

If it were just the review I would say I merely have no talent for prose—only for poetry. But no one thinks much of my poetry either.

Please, I beg you, do me [a favor, tell me?] as bluntly as possible what you think: Has my life been just one long self-deception where writing is concerned? It has been, hasn't it?

I wish I had realized it sooner, I can't say any more. I'm in such a dreadful position—no money, homeless, lonely and with no talent except in a kitchen and in the bed of a man whom I love and have lost. I feel like shooting myself, but I lack even the courage for that.

Let me have a *completely honest* reply,—please.

Marcia

1. Nardi's unpublished review of *W. B. Yeats, Self Critic* by Thomas Parkinson (Berkeley: University of California Press, 1951) is included among a collection of Nardi's correspondence at the Beinecke Rare Book and Manuscript Library, Yale University (designated Za Nardi, uncat.), along with a letter from Margaret Marshall (dated 2 January 1952) saying in part: "Judging from what you say the book is pretty special and my feeling is that it would have to be done in a brief notice if at all. Then too, I

don't find the review very convincing or the writing, since I think it best to be frank at the outset."

. . . .

88. TLS-I (T)

January 4, 1952

My dear Marcia:

I am keenly disappointed that you did not get the appointment to Yaddo, I had thought they'd give it to you. There must have been a large number of applicants, otherwise I'm sure you would have been successful. There's nothing more I can say.

There is another, similar colony, the MacDowell colony,[1] to which you might apply but it may be that that is only open to musicians. I don't know anything about it. Then there are various resident communities for artists in California. But again, I don't know how to advise you. Perhaps someone at Woodstock will know more about those things than I do.

As to making money out of writing, it's something I've never known how to do. I never attempted it. I have worked all my life, worked hard. Only now, approaching 70 have I been able to relax a little.

Margaret Marshall is a hard boiled editor, she is strictly held down by the requirements of her job. Even if she wanted to help you she couldn't do it beyond the limits of her space allotment. How can I look at what you do and give you an abstract, final judgment on your writing? It's impossible. I like what you have shown me but the commercial field is a hopeless one. I know several young people, men and women, who are starving to death as far as writing goes in New York. It's always so. One of them, Harold Norse,[2] has taken a job as a seaman. He had to eat.

Why don't you try Marguerite Caetani again? Meanwhile, as far as I can see, there's nothing to do but get a job at anything that will feed you. Quit writing for a year. Think it over. After a year you can do what you please, no one forces anybody to write. Put all your energy into earning a living by plain ordinary work.

Sincerely, yours
Bill

1. A Peterborough, New Hampshire, retreat for artists, writers, sculptors, and musicians; started in 1907 by composer Edward MacDowell. Nardi eventually stayed at the colony many times.

2. Harold Norse (1916–) is a poet, translator, and educator.

. . . .

89. TLS-2 (Y)

Woodstock
January 9th, 1952

Dear Bill,

You are quite right in what you say in that letter of a few days ago.

Certainly no one forces me to write and certainly you cannot (nor anyone else) give me any absolute final judgment in regard to my writing. The answer to all that lies within myself—which is just where I found it only a few hours after writing to you so despondently. That evening I found myself finishing a new poem started not long ago and commencing another one, and deeply involved with poetry once more and feeling that it is a very important thing in my life (and I suppose that's all one can know).

As to reviewing—I realized too why I failed in that. It's because in the first place I do not think much of professional criticism in general (it was forced, with me—I had no basic urge in that direction) and also because I cannot use language well unless I have definite ideas of my own to express. (The book I did for *The Nation* required a good reportorial job more than anything else—and that sort of thing is not in my line.)

And about taking a plain ordinary job—God knows I have spent the greater part of my life (and don't forget I'm [not] so young now, being well into my forties) enslaved by just such jobs—factory work, housework (I even scrubbed somebody's floors for a period), restaurant work,—and that I had another person to support for years.

I believe thoroughly (it's part of my attitude towards literature) that the artist should participate in the activities of the ordinary world—that he owes it to society to do so and that it is good for him. But I've done my duty there, believe me. I've served a long apprenticeship in the way of common ordinary labor—which is just why I have grown to feel so keenly now the need of an interlude for creative work alone.

There are ordinary jobs not as bad as the ones I've been forced to take, it's true. But one can't always get them. You know how hard I tried over ten years ago (at the time you tried to help me get one) and how little came of it. I have the intelligence (and it doesn't even take much) for any number of not-so-bad jobs. I could do proofreading certainly and the mechanics of editorial work (lay-out and making up a small magazine— even a trade paper) or work in a library. But it isn't intelligence that's asked for in the job world. It's the training and the record of past experience. Proofreaders have to be union members and librarians must have gone to a special school for such work, et cetera. And with a woman—(in other jobs)—"appearance" counts a lot—and I am simply not one of these smart chic females. And I cannot do anything that's physically exhausting— not any more, because I am not up to it in bodily ways. Whenever I get over-fatigued the ulcer flares up and makes me very ill for several days.

So even getting plain ordinary work is not always easy—as you see.

But what I'm hoping is that Mr. Pearson may be able to help me find something in a college library or bookshop (in any town or city—*that* doesn't matter). I've asked him to and I think he will try. And if I should get something of the sort I'll nevertheless re-apply for Yaddo for next winter and investigate the MacDowell Colony which you mentioned—only this time I shall try to present recommendations regarding my work only and say nothing of my personal plight which is apparently an indiscreet thing to do.

In the meantime my situation continues to be a desperate one—worse than you know (for reasons I have not been able to convey in other letters and which I cannot go into here). As soon as I get the rest of the money from Miss Geffen (I told you [I] think that I am to get another hundred dollars) I must go immediately to New York and take almost any job while waiting for something to come of Mr. Pearson's inquiries at universities, and book stores connected with them. But as you know, a hundred dollars is nothing just now. One *has* to go to a hotel temporarily—there's nothing else available without a long search (I investigated when I was last in New York)—which means eating in restaurants which costs so much. And my country clothes (slacks and old shoes et cetera) won't do for job hunting—so that I have to buy a couple of things to wear.

I shouldn't have counted so much on Yaddo. But if you only knew how much I yearn for a quiet undisturbed period to work on poetry and read and think and really live intellectually and creatively, as I've never been able to do!

Do you know these lines from Corbière? "... Et dans sa pauvre tête / Déménagée, encor il sentait que les vers / Hexamètres faisaient les cent pas de travers."[1] It was like that with me in regard to getting into Yaddo. But maybe I'll get good news from Ciardi. If I do, if he likes my poetry and puts it out, I shall—upon its publication, apply for a Guggenheim.

Anyway thank you for having done what you could about it (about Yaddo) and please do not think I'm over-indulgent in feeling sorry for myself (I imagine that's what you think). My folly in having gotten tied up with my former husband (an utterly impossible man—as even my friends know) and in getting so deeply involved with William Ames when he was already married too—well, they are follies only because I have no money. They would be just a natural part of ordinary human experience if I had any. The poor can't afford even that.

Sincerely,

Marcia

1. "... And in his poor head emptied out / With the door on the hinge, he still felt the queue / Of hexameters doing sentry duty askew." From

Tristan Corbière's poem "The Contumacious Poet," in *Les Amours jaunes*, trans. Val Warner (Great Britain: Carcanet–W.&J. Mackay Limited, 1975), 33.

. . . .

90. TLS-4 (Y)

Woodstock, New York
January 31st, 1951
[actually 1952]

Dear Bill,

I sit down to this letter in the bitterest mood I have ever been in.

There *are* openings at Yaddo (at least there were)—several of them, from January on throughout the rest of the winter. And not a person who ever went there needed to go as much as I do. But the admissions committee apparently didn't think that as a writer I was important enough for admission to those sacred precincts reserved so it seems for either the famous or those with all the "pull".

That is the gist (or rather the implication) of the brief disdainful note I got a few days ago from Mrs. Ames with her best wishes that I would be able to find *other ways* of going on with my work.

And I have no other ways. And I am desperate and don't know what to do.

I counted so much on being invited there *if* there should be openings (which I had reason to believe there would be). One shouldn't of course put all one's eggs in one basket. But I *had* to. That—an invitation to Yaddo—offered the only possible means open to me of having for once in my life "an undisturbed period for creative work." (I quote from the folder.) And I had all kinds of constructive plans regarding my work, which four months there (from January to May) would enable me to carry out, so that when I left the place I would have for the first time in my life some really solid ground under my feet.

And I had been working very hard towards those ends. For my review on the new book on Yeats which I already turned in, I read (in addition to the book to be reviewed) all Yeats's own comments on his creative processes as found in the autobiographies and also all the material on Yeats in that old issue of Southern Review devoted to him shortly after his death (I even made a special trip to New York to get some of that material not available in Woodstock).

And for the Henri Michaux review (which I can't even complete now because I am so distracted and have no place to stay and no money or anything) I read some of Breton and Soupault and Eluard so that I could place him in the surrealist movement. I even re-read Gerard de Nerval and Rimbaud's prose poems (and all in French which is not easy reading for me). And in addition to all this work, I wrote two new poems which though they *seem* simple and easy as so many of my poems seem, are very much worked on, and also I began revisions of several other half-written poems for a group of related lyrics.

I launched upon all this work under very bad working conditions, for my room was in a house which gave me none of the privacy and quiet one needs for such work (there was a radio in the next room tuned in on popular programs for hours at a time—it was horrible) and also because Woodstock itself is too intimately connected for me with all the heart-break I've been through in connection with my husband and with William Ames—the loss of the latter being the greatest loss I have ever known. He was, he remains, the world to me. There are times when I feel that I simply cannot go on living without him. (And he has a place here and my husband does—so that it is not good for me to be here where I continually see them both.)

But I accepted all this as make-shift, as something for the time being only, and was able to work in the midst of it all only because I regarded the situation as temporary.

Now, as I've said, I simply don't know what to do. I took my room (those were the arrangements) on a temporary basis and had to move out of it last week; and am parked for a few days at somebody else's house where I can stay only for a few days and where the set-up is such that I can do no work here. And I have no money. It's gone—the little I had. I am to get a little more from the Institute of Arts and Letters in a couple of weeks. But I have none at the moment, and even that money (when I do get it) won't last for more than about three weeks with living costs as they are—especially with rents so high beyond all reason. And so my work (at such a crucial point—since I had just gotten it going) has again been completely interrupted—with the moving from pillar to post, and all my manuscripts packed up, and the Michaux book and the notes for it and the poems I was working on, somewhere in a suitcase.

It's so unfair, and mean, and inhuman—my not having been invited to fill one of those openings at Yaddo. I know you won't agree with me (you'll probably find good excuses for it). But it *is*. The human situation counts. At least it *should* count, for it bears a much more important relation to the work of any artist than to that of the mechanical tasks which people do in the industrial world. And what a comment it is on the literary world that only after people are dead do their private lives in relation to their writing come in for any attention!

I have good reason to say this because Malcolm Cowley informed me that he unfortunately mentioned my "personal situation" to Mrs. Ames (it was at Pearson's request that he wrote to her) which he now feels was a great mistake perhaps and might have made a bad impression—the work alone, apparently, being the thing to be mentioned.

I did submit some of my work itself (poems which I felt were good ones). But, as I've already pointed out, my poems *seem* simple. They seem the kind of poetry which (so scorned by the literary world) gushes from the heart and is the result of a moment's inspiration and nothing more—whereas actually it is their very simplicity which I work on—since it is part of my conscious aim in the writing of poetry, to have them seem simple.

I know just what I'm about when I write poetry. I didn't once. But I do now and have, for a long time; and the more conscious I become of the craft involved, the more I use it to arrive at the most inconspicuous kind of literary achievement. Also, as you notice, I use very tight compact forms—at the same time very free ones without any conventional pattern in the way of form to lean on for external props while writing. And that combination—

very strict forms and at the same time no concern with traditional ones—makes my poems involve a lot of labor.

But because it doesn't seem that way and because also I am so much an "outsider" in my relation to the literary world, what chance do I have in competing with those people whose poetry is tied up with the "schools" and "isms" of the day in the way of style, and who in addition have [a] strong foothold socially in the literary world (that social foothold counts for so much!) and who possess all the grace and ease of manner that goes with it?

If you should pick up the telephone and call Mrs. Ames, and ask if my application can be re-considered—explaining of course the situation and stressing not only my plight but also (and mostly) my work and your opinion of it—something might yet be done to get me invited there at once. And I ask if you will please do this. You know Mrs. Ames. You were there. She has a high opinion of you personally, no doubt. And even if she didn't know you, your position in the literary world would give anything you might say to her great weight. I am sure of this. I also know that she is free too to do a great deal on her own without even consulting the Committee—since she has done so in the case of people I know of, who were there at Yaddo (and who incidentally did not have a great deal to offer in the way of creative talent).

I am in a more desperate situation than at any other time in my life. That I am so much older now, without the energies and other resources of sheer youth, make it more desperate as you can well understand. And I am much more the completely self-conscious writer with definite aims in view creatively, than in the past. And I have nothing *but* my work—not another damn thing, because when William Ames went out of my life last April all my chances for any possible happiness in my private emotional life went with him.

And if I cannot get to a place like Yaddo for a few months until I get my work going in those ways which I have in mind, where else can I turn? I possess none of [the] formal qualifications for the kind of jobs which some poets have—most of them teaching jobs; nor do I have the Name and contacts which sometimes make those jobs possible without the formal requirements in the way of college degrees, et cetera. And rents are so high everywhere—the most ordinary rooms—even dismal gloomy ones—cost fifteen, eighteen, twenty dollars a week, and many of them without kitchenettes so that one has to eat out in restaurants where the prices are exorbitantly high (if one has no home) as I have not. As a matter of fact, I lost William Ames almost entirely because of the housing situation. At the time he wanted in the worst way to live with me—we looked everywhere for a place to stay that would be within our means, and could not find one; and if we had been able to live together at that time it would have cemented our relationship. (In connection with this, I think of those lines from one of your plays where the man says: "No, I did not say I loved you. I said I wanted to marry you in order to love you"—and since that it is true [sic]—since our actions create our feelings no less than they are created by them,[1] Bill—this other Bill—would never have left me once we had actually had a home together. And if in that way there had been built up all those little habits of a daily life together by which people are bound more than by anything else—he stopped loving me and went his [way] elsewhere emotionally because, through our lack of a home together, those little bonds were not there to hold him. I also think at this moment of those lines of yours that "empty pockets make empty heads." They do indeed. My mind was so filled with ideas up until the day I got that note of complete rejection from Mrs. Ames (it was not a note that invited me to apply at some future time—no, it was one that dismissed me altogether as a proper applicant for a place like Yaddo). And now I haven't an idea of any kind in my mind. Everything has been scattered to the four winds.

My dreadful predicament is of immediate urgency; and whether or not you feel that you can telephone Mrs. Ames and see if something can still be done perhaps, will you please reply to this anyway as soon as possible? The whole thing has made me physically ill again on top of everything else.

Sincerely,

Marcia

1. In Williams's play *A Dream of Love* the character Myra quotes her husband's response to her question of why he wanted to marry her: "To love you, I suppose." *Many Loves and Other Plays* (Norfolk, Conn.: New Directions, 1961).

. . . .

91. TLS-2 (Y)

Woodstock, New York
March 17th, 1952

Dear Bill,

I am sending you the enclosed poems for a tremendously important reason. I cannot tell you what it is (it would be pointless) until I know what you think of them; and so will you please, *please* (if you can possibly spare the time) read them carefully and tell me if you share my feeling that they are worth more than a little as poems? And if you do not share it, of course be frank.

They have all (with the exception of the last) been written in recent months (I completed I SAW AND I KNEW just a few days ago), along with others (I do not send more than these lest I burden you with too many), and under circumstances more crippling than any I've ever experienced before.

I have been aiming at greater rhythmic plasticity—at more variety of rhythmic pattern—which is apparent (I hope so anyway) if you contrast that of "Pumpkins for Arms to Carry" with "How the Rich Move Softly," "I Saw and I Knew" and with the one with no title called "Poem" and also with the new section for "In the Asylum."

You began your first letter to me ten years [ago] "It is strange that you ask nothing of me regarding these poems" (or something to that effect). I wish I could go back to that period—not in the events of my life which were so wretched even then—but in its innocence. But alas "Il ne va plus les mains dans les poches tout nus."

My situation is more desperate than ever and I have been very ill again, the ulcer having flared up badly again and being accompanied this time by such bad insomnia that I have been taking continually increased doses of phenobarb every night (and even during the day) for about six weeks now.

But it is my poems that are most on my mind as I write this.

Sincerely

Marcia

I finally was able to get your Autobiography which I read with special interest for many reasons some of which you can guess and others I'll tell you about sometime—perhaps. (I liked particularly the chapter called "The Practice"—those marvelous passages about language—which tied up with the way you used that phrase "the language" in *Paterson*, giving it so many rich meanings which it never has when used ordinarily by people, even by writers.)

p.s. I'm afraid you will take me to task for not adhering to the word order of natural speech in the last part of "I Knew and I Saw," and again at the beginning of the 3rd stanza in "Poem." But while I agree with you thoroughly in regard to certain kinds of inversion and its being bad, I do so because it's so often the result of sloppy writing and of being at the mercy of rhymes that are too mechanical (this was true certainly of *my* inversions in many of my early poems). But the syntax in *these* poems, wherever it is not that of natural speech, is deliberately worked for and is thus creative and legitimately so—at least from my point of view. At present I have not completely clarified for myself my instinctive feelings in regard to this matter. If ever I do, I'll explain more adequately what I mean.

. . . .

92. TLS-1 (T)

9 Ridge Rd
Rutherford, N.J.
March 18, 1952

Dear Marcia:

If Thus You Can Erase My Life[1]—is a beautiful lyric. Not a flaw. It stands up with the best and shows that you still can do it, better than ever. Congratulations.

Ave Atque Vale[2] (trite) is also a good one. I attempted to add a refrain. Maybe you'll reject it.

The two first longer poems are also good though there are lines in them that could come out without doing them any harm—just omit.

The only poem I do not like is the last which, as you say, has not been realized.

Best luck. I hasten to return your scripts as you have asked me to.

> Sincerely
> Bill

1. See 92.1. Retitled "Late Love" in Nardi's collected poems (unpublished, MN archive).

2. Nardi did not retain a copy of this poem.

. . . .

92.1. MN Poem (MN Archive)

LATE LOVE

Now that the present shapes my past,
Now that the stem
I thought would bear no blossoms
Seems merely to have been
Itself the blossom
Waiting for its stem,

If thus, my love, you can
Erase my life re-writing it and bring
The sunlight to fifty years
That never knew the sun,

Oh what is history?

And Julius, Nero, Jesus—
Who are they
But ghosts not of the dead
But of the not-yet-born?

And could we not, then, by our acts
Snatch yet from Nero's hand the match
Make Julius milder,
And two thousand years date back
His birth tomorrow of Christ the Saviour,

If you can thus erase my life,
Re-writing it and bring
The sunlight now to fifty years
Already sunless run?

. . . .

93. ALS-1 (T)

Sept. 2/52

Dear Marcia Nardi—

Dr. Williams is critically ill[1]—and can under no circumstances write or give you any assistance.

With all good wishes.

Sincerely,
Florence Williams

1. Williams had had a stroke just weeks before this, while he and his wife vacationed with the Abbotts at Gratwick Highlands in Linwood, New York (Mariani, *William Carlos Williams: A New World Naked*, 648–649).

. . . .

94. TLS-3 (Y)

Woodstock, New York
January 2nd, 1956

Dear Bill,

I don't know how your health is now and I have no way of knowing (being no less an outsider to the literary world than in the past). And the worst of it is that I write this in the midst of such shattering circumstances that I cannot even manage a graceful and gracious prelude to this sudden communication after so long a time.

I can only plunge right in (with the hope that you will understand and overlook it) and say that I would be more grateful than I can tell you if you would be good enough to read the enclosed poems (if you are able to) and tell me what you think of them. I myself feel that they represent a considerable development beyond my earlier work which you were so enthusiastic about. But I may be deceiving myself; and it's terribly important that I shouldn't do that.

I am living in greater poverty than ever (and sick at the same time). But it isn't this that I care to concern you with, because the very source of it is my failure to have gained any recognition to speak of for my poetry. Had I been able to obtain that (to have gotten as much recognition as those numerous other women poets such as May Sarton, Jean Garrigue, Cecile Rich, et cetera) I too no doubt would have had bestowed upon me a couple of those very substantial Grants and Fellowships available these days to poets of standing. Also, even without a University degree, I probably could have gotten one of the numerous teaching jobs open to poets, on the strength of just my name, if I'd been able to build up a "name".

But year after year, I've received nothing but rejection slips from one editor after another.

I do, very occasionally, run into someone who likes my writing. Hiram Haydn of Random House likes it a great deal, I think. At least he said so and recently published something of mine in *American Scholar* (a poem which I have since then revised and improved).[1]

Also Thornton Wilder asked to look at my work a couple of years ago when I was at the MacDowell Colony and became so enthusiastic about it that he personally gave a reading of a group of my poems on the same occasion when he read aloud an act from one of his own plays in Peterborough. He later made copies of some of my poems to take away with him, and sent me a letter saying he'd spent part of an evening reading them aloud to Herbert Read[2] who was visiting him at the time.

But how good a critic of poetry, Wilder is—I don't know. Moreover, that merely private kind of praise gets me nowhere in the literary world—especially since his experience regarding my work was pretty much the same as yours. Just as Laughlin and the Tiger's Eye editor and other people thought you had a crazy, blind prejudice in favor of my poems, other editors took the same attitude towards Wilder's enthusiasm.

Marguerite Caetani is using two more of my poems in the coming Spring issue of Botteghe Oscure.[3] (At least, that's what she wrote me three months ago.) But that one acceptance, plus the one poem in American Scholar and another short one published elsewhere[4] in 1954, constitutes my entire success in all this long time. And the situation has grown to affect me so seriously in psychological ways that I suddenly find myself unable to write at all—my creative powers fatally congealed now from so much discouragement.

Perhaps I am not a good poet. Maybe I have had (as many people do) illusions as to my own talent. Or perhaps whatever talent I did have has been destroyed by all the frustrations in my private emotional life—the sort of thing which happens more often to a woman than to a man. If that is so, I have the courage to face it—to even burn whatever poems I have left. (I have already burned a number of them in moments of black despair.) But the *knowing* is important. It's the knowing for which I have such a desperate need; and there is absolutely no one whom I can turn to for an honest opinion and a sound one (one I can have real faith in) except you.

I enclose only 8 poems, so as not to make too great demands on your time—especially since the comments I've made for you on the manuscript itself will take extra time to read. But these eight are, I think, adequately representative of my recent work. Of those I destroyed in one of my blackest moments (because they had been rejected by 6 magazines) there were three possibly better than any of these. Nevertheless if these are nothing much, then either my work as a whole amounts to little or else I have been unable to fulfill whatever promise my earlier work may have had.

There is a tendency in all of us, I think, to always take with a grain of salt another person's protestations of seeking only the blunt truth, however unpleasant it may be. But in this case—regarding my poetry—you can take my word for it absolutely, that it is the blunt truth I seek from you and nothing less than that. I am deplorably wanting in physical courage. In the face of material privations and loneliness of a bodily kind or anything else that crushes the soul *via* the flesh, I completely crumple up and die over and over again the coward's million deaths. But my capacity for moral fortitude and the most ruthless self-honesty is much greater than that of most people. Moreover, there's something so very impersonal about artistic achievement (it's so tied up with the *Given*, whether merited or not) that my vanity is not at all involved there. In addition to this, I am too much the moralist, to accept the point of view expressed by Yeats in his reference to the choice between "perfection of the art or of the life". For me the two go hand in hand; and where a choice must be made (as sometimes it must) then I put first the latter—perfection of the life (spiritually, I mean, of course).

And so if you are able to read these poems and will be kind enough to do so, you need feel no embarrassment in being quite frank about them.

If they should strike you as good, not just moderately so but *really* good (that is, *important* poems) then the knowledge of it would perhaps release me into other poems, even under the wretched circumstances surrounding my life. If, on the contrary, they should seem to you nothing much, just the knowledge of that would bring to me benefits of another kind—especially since I am now faced with some serious spiritual problems for the solution of which I need badly to evaluate myself as a writer—which I can't do through my own eyes alone.

I have wondered many times how you were. As you may know, your wife wrote to tell me a few years ago how critically ill you were then (returning at the same time a letter I had sent you). Afterwards I sent her a note of anxious inquiry about you, and she replied that though you were making a recovery it would no doubt be a slow one.[5] Then later, noticing your name on the list of poets to give readings at the "Y" and seeing so much new work by you continually appearing, I assumed and hoped this was a sign that you had safely pulled through all that unfortunate illness. I trust this is so and that the New Year will be good to you.

> Sincerely and with
> warm regards,
> Marcia

I think it's wonderful how your poetry has gone from greater to greater development all the time—always saying something new and fresh and never repeating. I tie this up with the moral and human side of your work, and also with the spiritual side, because it is so rooted in love that transcends time as all major poetry has to be (at least for me and my evaluations of it). My poetry represents, alas, a much more narrow, time-bound world. But that is almost inevitable for a woman if she tries to write honestly, since men have never permitted her to emerge from those confines, in her actual living.

1. Hiram Haydn (1907–1973), author, educator, and, at this time, senior editor at Random House and an editor at the *American Scholar*, where Nardi's poem "News from Our Town" was published in 1955 (24, no. 3: 26).

2. Sir Herbert Read (1893–1968), British poet, essayist, and art critic.

3. Nardi's poems "Ah, But the Unloved Have Had Power" (formerly titled "I Saw and I Knew") and "Love I Make It Because I Write It" were published in *Botteghe Oscure* 17 (Spring 1956): 300–301.

4. "Was It the Honey Hearted Vowel?" appeared in *Poetry* (July 1954): 212–213.

5. Nardi did not retain this letter from Florence Williams.

. . . .

95. TLS-1 (Y)

> 9 Ridge Road
> Rutherford, New Jersey
> January 25, 1956

Dear Bill,

Do you happen to have a mailing address for Marcia Nardi now? I ask, because we will soon start assembling material for the next number of New Directions' annual, which will be an

American number, and I think back to her as one of the interesting, individual poets, to whom we'd give a hearing if she had some good new stuff.[1] [Laughlin went on to discuss other matters with WCW without further mention of Nardi.]

    With best to you all,

As ever,
Jim

1. Nardi's poems did not appear in *New Directions* again.

. . . .

96. TLS-2 (Y)

Jan. 26/56

Dear Jim,

    Glad to hear from you—about things. The new *New Directions Anthology* interests me, the new format is all to the good, I quite approve. When Jim Murray gives the word I hope the way will be cleared for the appearance of the *In The American Grain* in the new form.

    I'm glad to hear you—or see you speak again of Marcia Nardi. Her address is as it has been of recent years simply Woodstock, NY. I had a letter from her recently enclosing a number of poems among which were some of the best I have ever seen of hers. Indeed write to her, I hope you will see your way clear to publishing a generous collection of her work. [WCW continued this letter without further mention of Nardi.]

Sincerely yours,
Bill

. . . .

97. TLS-1 (ND)

February 21, 1956

Dear Miss Nardi:

    It's been some time now since I have seen any of your poetry and I was wondering whether you had any new ones that I haven't seen, which could be considered for *New Directions*.

Have you seen ND 15? I'll be glad to send one along, if you haven't. It was an international number, but 16 is to be all American.

I can't remember whether I ever told you that I had a most enthusiastic letter from Thornton Wilder about your work, not that I needed to be persuaded, having always found it most interesting.

Sincerely yours,
James Laughlin

. . . .

98. TLS-1 (Y)

Woodstock, New York
September 30, 1956

Dear Bill,

After you replied to my letter of nearly a year ago,[1] I was so destitute and so very ill from it, that even though I kept planning to thank you for that prompt reply, I simply couldn't.

But I send you now a copy (for yourself) of my little book which the Swallow Press has at last issued after endless delays. (I had to eliminate nearly half the poems in the manuscript which I originally prepared because all the volumes in Swallow's New Poetry Series have to conform in size, format, et cetera. But my next book,[2] for which I am getting a New York publisher, will be a much bigger one.)

I am about to apply for a Guggenheim Fellowship; and though I assume it will be all right if I include you among my "references" (on the basis of your having spoken so very highly of my work, in the past) I feel that I ought to ask your permission just the same.

In the past year or so my poetry has been receiving a great deal of favorable comment. (Randall Jarrell, by the way, likes it.)[3] But this in itself has done nothing to improve my financial situation which becomes increasingly worse. I hardly need to tell you, therefore, how much a Guggenheim would mean to me. So will you be so kind as to reply to this note as promptly as you can? I need to fill out and send in the Guggenheim application forms immediately.

Hoping that all is well with you,

Sincerely,

Marcia

You already know how incredibly gauche I am—so if this letter sounds awfully cold and curt, please forgive that. I often wonder how you are.

1. Nardi did not retain the Williams letter referred to here.

2. Marcia Nardi did not have another book of poems published.

3. Nardi wrote to Jarrell in March 1956 (a draft of this letter dated 6 March 1956 is part of the MN archive), enclosing some of her poems and signing the letter "Irene Mannix," hoping that, if he thought she had talent, Jarrell would recommend her for various financial grants and for admission to Yaddo and the MacDowell colony. In Jarrell's sympathetic reply, he commented favorably on some of her poems and offered to recommend her for a grant or fellowship; this undated letter, addressed to "Dear Miss Mannix," is part of Nardi's papers at the Beinecke Library, Yale (Za Nardi, uncat.).

. . . .

99. TLS-1 (T)

Oct. 5/56

Dear Marcia:

We've been away for a week. By all means use my name with the Guggenheim Foundation people, may it bring you luck. I'll give you as vigorous a recommendation as I am capable of.[1]

Not having time as yet to read the Sparrow book[2] as yet [*sic*] I can't say anything about it but it is good news that you have at last gotten yourself a New York publisher. You are one of the hardiest women and one of the most gifted and generous women I know, I am happy at your success.

Sincerely yours

Bill

1. Nardi was awarded a Guggenheim Fellowship on 30 April 1957.

2. Williams is referring to Nardi's book *Poems*, published by Alan Swallow. The copy Nardi sent to Williams is now in the Beinecke Library at Yale (cataloged Zab N166 956 P) and bears this inscription on the flyleaf: "To William Carlos Williams, whose confidence in my poetry bolstered up my own during many dark hours. Marcia Nardi."

Afterword

. . . .

Marcia Nardi carried one of William Carlos Williams's letters
(46) around with her in her purse for many years; in fact, the
original letter (now at the HRHRC) was folded and refolded so
often that it fell apart and the pieces had to be taped back
together. And while Nardi occasionally showed the letter to
people she knew in New York or at Yaddo or the MacDowell
Colony, she rarely told anyone of her primary connection to
Williams: that she was the woman poet whose letters appear in
Paterson. The letter—in which he lavishly praises her poems
and claims that she has achieved "what is active, essential and
really new in our day"—served as a kind of talisman, a re-
minder that someone whose intellect and sensitivity she respected admired her work.

She was pleased also by Williams's words of praise for her
personally (those expressed in his final letter to her), although
Nardi's "success" (as he referred to it) was short-lived. In the
years following the end of their correspondence, her haphazard
life improved very little. Her major problem continued to be a
lack of money, which brought with it a lack of mobility, of independence, of dignity. In the early 1970s, unable to find an
affordable room in New York City, she decided to return to
Massachusetts—nearly fifty years after she had departed for
Greenwich Village. Once there, Nardi lived another twenty
years (first in Marblehead and then in Cambridge) in what she
considered a state of exile. She missed New York, she missed her
friends, and she was now an old woman (her real age having
caught up with her) in the midst of a youth culture in a university town. She had exhausted the patience of her friends in New

York with her overwhelming needs and demands; now that she was isolated from them geographically also, her loneliness was complete.

Nardi found sporadic work as a book reviewer or copy editor during the years in Cambridge, but her meager income had to be supplemented by money from friends or grants from writers organizations such as PEN and the Author's League. Although she continued to write poetry (her last published poem appeared in the *New Yorker* in 1971, when she was seventy years old), she was not able to find a publisher for a second book of poems. She was no longer welcome at Yaddo or the MacDowell colony after she complained bitterly that many of the artists who were invited there could well afford to pay more to stay there (or to go somewhere else) and that preference should be given to those artists who could not. Her health—mental and physical—deteriorated, and she gained a reputation in Cambridge as an eccentric who called ambulances and police cars frequently to take her to hospital emergency rooms. In 1987, when she could no longer care for herself and because there was no one else to care for her, she was finally admitted to a nursing home. There, her condition was stabilized with the help of medication and regular meals. But visitors were rare, she had no interest in small talk with other patients, and she loathed the confinement of the nursing home. Given an opportunity, however, she could still speak with knowledge and passion about poetry and literature.

After I located her and began to visit her, Nardi spent many hours being interviewed about her life and reading her poems into a tape recorder for me. In 1990, not long before she died, I asked her what—if anything—had given her a modicum of satisfaction in a life that had offered very few satisfactions. She responded without hesitation that she was proudest of having maintained her sense of personal identity. That identity—a woman poet determined to experience life for herself and to find a poetic form in which to express what is uniquely a woman's experience—had been forged during long years of "pioneer living" (as she wrote in her long *Paterson* letter), when she fought to free herself from "patterned standardized feminine feelings." And Nardi understood the cost: that what might be assets to her in a literary sense (such as the "attitudes and sensibilities" she had formed about society and woman's "wretched position" there) were often liabilities when it came to living itself. The very same ideas and feelings which could endow a writer "with some kind of new vision" could often make one (in the eyes of the world) "clumsy, awkward, absurd, ungrateful, confidential where most people are reticent, and reticent where one should be confidential, and which cause one, all too often, to step on the toes of other people's sensitive egos as a result of one's stumbling earnestness or honesty carried too far." When that happened, such a person was no longer considered admirable but "deplorable, annoying, stupid, or in some other way unpardonable." Of course, having money would have made a difference in the way the world viewed her. Nardi once observed wryly to Williams that what the world saw as her "follies" were only follies because she had no money: "They would be just a natural part of ordinary experience if I had any. The poor can't afford even that."

In addition to being shunned by a disapproving family and society, Nardi was handicapped all her life by her difficult personality. Her utter sense of entitlement to the help of others—even as she criticized them for their lack of "awareness" or generosity—caused her to be abandoned over the years by lovers, relatives, and friends and assiduously avoided by acquaintances. She was impractical, even inept, in her day-to-day living and finally became, as she had described herself in *Paterson*, "a woman dying of loneliness . . . with all of my efficiency in the practical world continually undermined by that loneliness." Still, she had few regrets about the past. She did regret having become alienated from her son, Paul, and from other members of her family, and, sadly, only a month after she died, I located Paul Nardi. Nardi had not known if he was alive or dead, as the two had not met since 1968, when he visited her in New York City. Paul asked his mother then (as he had several times in the past) to tell him the name of his father, and she refused. When he told her that he would not come to see her again if she did not tell him his father's name, she ignored his ultimatum. He left and did not return.

In the end, all that mattered was poetry.

Works Cited

Baldwin, Neil, and Steven L. Meyers, comps. *The Manuscripts and Letters of William Carlos Williams in the Poetry Collection of the Lockwood Memorial Library, State University of New York at Buffalo: A Descriptive Catalogue.* Boston: G. K. Hall, 1978.

Graham, Theodora R. "Her Heigh Compleynte: The Cress Letters of William Carlos Williams' *Paterson.*" In *Ezra Pound and William Carlos Williams: The University of Pennsylvania Conference Papers.* Ed. Daniel Hoffman. Philadelphia: University of Pennsylvania Press, 1983. 164–193.

Mariani, Paul. *William Carlos Williams: The Poet and His Critics.* Chicago: American Library Association, 1975.

———. *William Carlos Williams: A New World Naked.* New York: McGraw-Hill, 1981.

Nardi, Marcia. *Poems.* Denver: Alan Swallow Press, 1956.

New Directions Number Eleven. Norfolk, Conn.: New Directions Publishing, 1949.

New Directions Number Seven. Norfolk, Conn.: New Directions Publishing, 1942.

Thirlwall, John C., ed. *The Selected Letters of William Carlos Williams.* New York: McDowell, Obolensky, 1957.

Williams, William Carlos. *Paterson.* Ed. Christopher MacGowan. New York: New Directions, 1992.

Witemeyer, Hugh, ed. *William Carlos Williams and James Laughlin: Selected Letters.* New York: W. W. Norton, 1989.

Index